THIRTEEN DISCOURSES ON THE
SERMON ON
THE MOUNT

THIRTEEN DISCOURSES ON THE
SERMON ON THE MOUNT

JOHN WESLEY

The John Wesley Collection
Andrew C. Thompson
Executive Editor

 seedbed

All Scripture quotations are taken from the Holy Bible,
King James Version, Cambridge, 1796.

Printed in the United States of America

Paperback ISBN: 978-1-62824-091-7
Mobi ISBN: 978-1-62824-092-4
ePub ISBN: 978-1-62824-093-1
uPDF ISBN: 978-1-62824-094-8

Library of Congress Control Number: 2014935051

Cover design by NikaBrik Design
Page design by PerfecType, Nashville

SEEDBED PUBLISHING
Franklin, Tennessee
seedbed.com
SOWING FOR A GREAT AWAKENING

CONTENTS

PUBLISHER'S FOREWORD

THE JOHN WESLEY COLLECTION

John Wesley's profound legacy and impact on world Christianity during and since his lifetime can be viewed through a number of lenses. The revival that arose under his leadership changed the social and political structure of eighteenth-century England as the poor and lost found hope in the gospel of Jesus Christ rather than in revolution against the crown. The influence of Wesley's Spirit-inspired teaching continued unabated as the Methodist movement spread scriptural holiness across the American continent and lands far beyond.

Wesley's influence as a publisher, if considered separately from all other of his extensive accomplishments, represents an astonishing record in its own right. Wesley lived in a time when Gutenberg's invention of movable type, which had immediately preceded Luther's reformation, had coalesced into specialized printing trades in London. Typefounders and printeries were becoming established and were offering exciting new pathways for the spread of the gospel through inexpensive printed text.

Perhaps more than any other figure of his day, Wesley embraced this new technology and issued sermons, tracts, commentaries, abridgments, biographies, and a host of other items that he considered relevant to the spiritual growth of maturing Christians.

Wesley was vitally driven by the reality of the inner witness of the Holy Spirit. His teaching on entire sanctification, or Christian perfection, is the capstone of his legacy. He worked tirelessly to abridge and republish seminal works by historical figures of previous generations, reaching as far back as the apostolic fathers of the first-century church. He constantly curated voices that communicated the work of the Holy Spirit in bringing believers into the fullness of salvation and lives of holy love.

These writings resourced the early Methodists in their quest to spread the gospel by providing the intellectual and spiritual moorings for the messengers of the movement. Seedbed believes these writings are as relevant to our context today as they were in the eighteenth and nineteenth centuries. Consequently, we consider it a sacred calling to join with those who are recapturing John Wesley's publishing vision for the twenty-first century.

With great joy we present The John Wesley Collection. In the years ahead Seedbed will reissue selections from this vast collection, which includes his fifty-volume Christian Library, some 150 sermons, countless items from his journals and letters, as well as innumerable tracts, hymns, poems, and other publications, most of which have been out of circulation for decades, if not centuries.

The John Wesley Collection is Seedbed's offering to the ongoing Wesleyan tradition, providing rare insight into the heartbeat of a movement whose greatest days are yet to come.

We encourage you to enter these texts with determination. Readers who persevere will soon find themselves accustomed to the winsome tenor and tempo of Wesley's voice and vernacular.

Seedbed's editors are constantly examining this extensive collection of more than 250 years of vital spiritual writing by the Wesleys and successive generations to find the most relevant and helpful messages that will speak to today's body of believers. We commend this old-new publishing work to you as one ready to be transformed by the latent power of these ancient truths. It is our prayer that these timeless words will add fuel to the fire of an awakening ready to ignite once again across the world.

Sola sancta caritas! Amen.

Andrew Miller
Seedbed Publishing

ACKNOWLEDGMENTS

Seedbed would like to thank George Lyons and Ryan Danker from the Wesley Center for Applied Theology at Northwest Nazarene University, Nampa, Idaho for their leadership in making these and other historical resources available to present and future generations of Wesleyan Christians. Their full digital collection of Wesleyan resources can be found at www.wesley.nnu.edu.

We also acknowledge the following individuals for their initial assistance in editing Wesley's discourses: Kimberly Horner, Discourse 1; William A. Buckholdt III, Discourse 2; Jennette Descalzo, Discourse 3; John Edwin Walker Jr., Discourse 4; Dekek and Beryl Johnson, Discourses 5 and 10; Vince Bos, Discourse 6; Jason Boldt, Discourse 7; Jean Fogerson, Discourse 8; Joel Nye, Discourse 9; Dian Williams, Discourse 11; Kristen Chamberlain, Discourse 12; and Debi Carter, Discourse 11.

And finally, we would like to thank Kristin Gelinas, Nick Perreault, Kristin Goble, Maren Kurek, Renee Chavez, Micah Smith, and Holly Jones for lending their various skills to this project.

INTRODUCTION

This is the religion we long to see established in the world, a religion of love and joy and peace, having its seat in the heart, in the inmost soul, but ever showing itself by its fruits.
—John Wesley
An Earnest Appeal to Men of Reason and Religion

In the cacophony of voices seeking to define Christianity in today's society, no more apt words have been penned than these from John Wesley. Our faith goes beyond rule-following externals and engages the deepest matters of the heart. We *feel* the love of God and joy in the Holy Ghost. But because we feel them in our hearts, we *produce*. Our witness has impact in the rough-and-tumble "dailyness" of work, business, politics, relationships, and community. "Heart" thus extends far beyond pious feelings or romantic notions of communion with God.

Few Christian leaders understood this dual problem as clearly as John Wesley. He battled in his day two common yet powerful misunderstandings of full, gospel salvation that afflict our times as well. We could call the first a kind of "do the best you can" morality, which is a version of "works righteousness" or legalism that we may decry, but to which we often succumb. It goes by the following: "If you believe in God and try to be a good person in all your dealings, then that is all you need to worry about." But, of course, in adopting this stance we usually measure ourselves against ourselves and come out looking pretty good to ourselves.

The other problem Wesley battled goes under the old-fashioned term "antinomianism," which may be summarized by a statement like, "Jesus paid it all. I'm required to do nothing but believe in him." This point of view so emphasizes God's grace that any hint that we might actually have to do something in order to be fully Christian gets shouted down as "works righteousness." It also tends to get people so focused on the condition for getting to heaven that they pay scant attention to discipleship in this world. The Christian life becomes a matter of coping rather than serving.

We can see that these problems are two sides of the same coin. Both are extremely common and both fall alarmingly short of the life God empowers and expects of us. This is precisely why meditating on these discourses on the Sermon on the Mount prove to be a salutary exercise.

First published in 1746 in a collection called *Sermons on Several Occasions* (*SOSO*), the discourses take care of the second of two major concerns Wesley was keen to address, those in response to the problems described above. The first twenty sermons in *SOSO* lay down fundamental evangelical themes: repentance, justifying faith, salvation by faith alone, the new birth, and the witness of the Spirit as our assurance of salvation. We know that we are saved by God's grace alone, without any actions on our part that merit God's love. We love God simply and only because God loves us and gave his Son as the atoning sacrifice for our sins. This divine activity alone makes our salvation possible. This is familiar territory.

The next thirteen discourses move us into what has become—in our day—largely unexamined territory, but no less essential. Wesley teaches us that, having experienced peace with God through Christ and having entered this new life, we undergo lifelong transformation. Since through grace we belong to Christ, we face and overcome any attitude, desire, or behavior that does not reflect Christ. Or, to say it more positively, we find that as we obey the Word of the Lord, God restores the divine image in us and we become fruit-bearing witnesses to the kingdom in every dimension of our lives. This part of the Christian life is by no means a second-tier option. It is, as Wesley said, "indispensably necessary to salvation" as much as justification by faith through grace alone!

Therefore, as you meditate through these expositions, keep in mind four critical markers laid down in the first discourse. Remember the *identity* of the Speaker. Jesus is, Wesley avers, "the [divine] Lord, our Governor, whose kingdom is from everlasting . . . the Great Lawgiver, who can well enforce all his laws." Jesus speaks with the authority of God. We do well to remember.

Second, listen to *what* the Lord teaches: "the *way* to heaven . . . the royal *way* which leads to the kingdom." Notice the term "way." Believers know well the first step, the means by which we enter the kingdom (see above), yet give insufficient notice to the daily sojourn, the holy living that bears witness to the kingdom. The way is not an easy one, for the gate is narrow and the road is hard that leads to life. Disciples radiate joy, but joy born of effort, habit, yes, even struggle.

Third, Wesley reminds us that these words are for all who are willing to learn from Jesus. It may seem obvious, but it needs to be said: this point implicates us today. The Sermon on the Mount is for *us*, for all who desire to walk with Christ.

Finally, Wesley considers the *how* of Jesus' teaching. Christ lays down the "whole plan of his religion," Wesley says, in a way not found anywhere else in scripture. The "eight particulars" of

xvi INTRODUCTION

the Beatitudes reveal the "sum of all true religion." The take-away? We are *happy* in this life because, by embodying Jesus' teachings summarized in Matthew 5–7, we are *holy* in this life.

Wesley's thirteen discourses divide into the following three sections.

The Sum of True Religion (Discourses 1–5)

John Wesley was convinced that the fount, foundation, and framework for Christian discipleship situates in the "affections" and "holy tempers." We need to reclaim these terms, and the Beatitudes illumine them. Simply put, affections are Spirit-prompted desires (appetites), and holy tempers are the Spirit-shaped attitudes and dispositions that emerge as we practice discipleship.

Practicing the Christian life therefore calls for self-reflection and awareness. It starts with poverty of spirit, which, Wesley says, is the "general foundation whereon the whole fabric of Christianity may be built." In this ground the affections can bear fruit. Poverty of spirit replaces arrogant self-sufficiency. Holy mourning (which is not mere sadness or moroseness) supplants thoughtless levity. Meekness takes the place of rage, impatience, and discontent. Exhibiting mercy reveals the love of God shed abroad in our hearts, a love that extends to all, including enemies. In these holy tempers we see the transforming power of Christ at work in believers.

The Necessity of Right Intention (Discourses 6–9)

In the second set of discourses, Wesley expounds on the requisite singularity of purpose needed to govern our actions. We do not rest and we do not settle for anything less, until Christ reigns supreme in our affections and makes himself known through our actions (no one can serve two masters). As students of Wesley know so well, his problem with people who practiced only the outward behaviors while remaining untouched in their hearts were no better off spiritually than open pagans. We need not fatalistically accept mixed motives as a given for the Christian life. God's grace continues to work until Christ rules alone.

Purity of intention flows from right affections, and so, in this second section, Wesley explains how affection and intention organically relate. "The eye is the intention: what the eye is to the body, the intention is to the soul. As one guides all the motions of the body, so does the other those of the soul." The "eye" fixed on God is full of light. The "eye" fixed on self-preoccupations is full of confusion and sin.

In this vein our prayers, Wesley says, "are the proper test of our desires." Hence, Christ teaches us to pray in a way that trains us to seek the kingdom supremely. Again, we see the need for reflection and self-awareness. How do we pray? What do we spend time and energy pursuing?

Hindrances to Faithful Discipleship (Discourses 10–13)

With the holy tempers described in the Beatitudes (Matt. 5) and with singleness of purpose guiding our actions (Matt. 6), Wesley turns to some common stumbling blocks to holiness of heart and life (Matt. 7). One of the most commonly committed errors and most fatal hindrances is that of judging others. We see the speck in another's eye and mistake it for the beam distorting our vision.

The reason we succumb so easily to these stumbling blocks? To come full circle, we lack poverty of spirit. Pride and self-will are the "parent sins" of a wide range of assumptions that lead us into the broad way of destruction. And by the way, ignorance is not an excuse. We are responsible to know enough of the Christian life so as not to be fooled by those proclaiming the easy and broad way. As Wesley said repeatedly, to use grace as a rationale for refusing to walk the narrow way of holiness is the highest folly. Our hearts become known by the fruit of our lives. The broad way is easy precisely because it is broad. The narrow way—universal holiness—is difficult, but filled with joyful life in Christ.

Keep Track of the Whole

All through his exposition of the Sermon on the Mount, John Wesley points to the organic wholeness of desires, dispositions, and actions in following Christ. Here we see "kingdom living" in its fullness, for we see Christ describing the character that he himself embodies and calls us to take up as well. This approach to discipleship is "the whole package," to borrow a phrase from the sports world. Remember the twin problems mentioned at the beginning of this introduction. Resist the temptation to reduce, to oversimplify. Read without haste. Read in the spirit of the affections described in these pages. And may our Lord bless you with the peaceful fruit of righteousness.

Stephen Rankin
Chaplain and Minister to the University
Southern Methodist University
Dallas, Texas

THIRTEEN DISCOURSES ON THE
SERMON ON THE MOUNT

THE INWARD KINGDOM OF HEAVEN

And seeing the multitudes, he went up into a mountain. And when he was set, his disciples came unto him: and he opened his mouth, and taught them, saying, Blessed are the poor in spirit: for theirs is the kingdom of heaven. Blessed are they that mourn: for they shall be comforted.

—Matthew 5:1–4

Introduction

1. Our Lord had now "gone about all Galilee" (Matt. 4:23), beginning at the time "when John was cast into prison" (Matt. 4:12), not only "teaching in their synagogues, and preaching the gospel of the kingdom," but likewise "healing all manner of sickness and all manner of disease among the people." It was a natural consequence of this, that "there followed him great multitudes from Galilee, and from Decapolis, and from

Jerusalem, and from Judea, and from the region beyond Jordan"
(Matt. 4:25). "And seeing the multitudes," whom no synagogue
could contain, even had there been any at hand, "he went up
into a mountain," where there was room for all that came unto
him, from every quarter. "And when he was set," as the manner
of the Jews was, "his disciples came unto him. And he opened
his mouth" (an expression denoting the beginning of a solemn
discourse), "and taught them, saying . . ."

2. Let us observe who it is that is here speaking, that we
may take heed how we hear. It is the Lord of heaven and earth,
the Creator of all; who, as such, has a right to dispose of all
his creatures; the Lord our Governor, whose kingdom is from
everlasting, and rules over all; the great Lawgiver, who can
well enforce all his laws, being "able to save and to destroy,"
yea, to punish with "everlasting destruction from his presence
and from the glory of his power." It is the eternal Wisdom of
the Father, who knows whereof we are made, and understands
our inmost frame; who knows how we stand related to God,
to one another, to every creature which God has made, and,
consequently, how to adapt every law he prescribes, to all the
circumstances wherein he has placed us.

It is he who is "loving unto every man, whose mercy is
over all his works"; the God of love, who, having emptied
himself of his eternal glory, is come forth from his Father to
declare his will to the children of men, and then goes again
to the Father; who is sent of God "to open the eyes of the
blind, and to give light to them that sit in darkness." It is
the great Prophet of the Lord, concerning whom God had
solemnly declared long ago, "Whosoever will not hearken
unto my words which he shall speak in my name, I will require
it of him" (Deut. 18:19); or, as the apostle expresses it, "Every
soul which will not hear that prophet, shall be destroyed from
among the people" (Acts 3:23).

3. And what is it which he is teaching? The Son of God, who came from heaven, is here showing us the way to heaven; to the place which he has prepared for us; the glory he had before the world began. He is teaching us the true way to life everlasting; the royal way which leads to the kingdom; and the only true way, for there is none besides; all other paths lead to destruction. From the character of the Speaker, we are well assured that he has declared the full and perfect will of God. He has uttered not one tittle too much—nothing more than he had received of the Father; nor too little—he has not shunned to declare the whole counsel of God; much less has he uttered anything wrong, anything contrary to the will of him that sent him. All his words are true and right concerning all things, and shall stand fast for ever and ever.

And we may easily remark, that in explaining and confirming these faithful and true sayings, he takes care to refute not only the mistakes of the scribes and Pharisees, which then were the false comments whereby the Jewish teachers of that age had perverted the word of God, but all the practical mistakes that are inconsistent with salvation, which should ever arise in the Christian Church; all the comments whereby the Christian teachers (so called) of any age or nation should pervert the word of God, and teach unwary souls to seek death in the error of their life.

4. And hence we are naturally led to observe, whom it is that he is here teaching. Not the apostles alone; if so, he had no need to have gone up into the mountain. A room in the house of Matthew, or any of his disciples, would have contained the Twelve. Nor does it in anywise appear that the disciples who came unto him were the Twelve only. Οἱ μαθηταὶ αὐτοῦ, without any force put upon the expression, may be understood of *all who desired to learn of him*. But to put this out of all question, to make it undeniably plain that where it is said, "He opened his

mouth and taught them," the word *them* includes all the multitudes who went up with him into the mountain, we need only observe the concluding verses of the seventh chapter: "And it came to pass, when Jesus had ended these sayings, οἱ ὄχλοι, *the multitudes*, were astonished at his doctrine," or teaching; "for he taught them," the multitudes, "as one having authority, and not as the scribes" (Matt. 7:28–29).

Nor was it only those multitudes who were with him on the mount, to whom he now taught the way of salvation; but all the children of men; the whole race of mankind; the children that were yet unborn; all the generations to come, even to the end of the world, who should ever hear the words of this life.

5. And this all men allow, with regard to some parts of the ensuing discourse. No man, for instance, denies that what is said of poverty of spirit relates to all mankind. But many have supposed, that other parts concerned only the apostles, or the first Christians, or the ministers of Christ; and were never designed for the generality of men, who, consequently, have nothing at all to do with them.

But may we not justly inquire, who told them this, that some parts of this discourse concerned only the apostles, or the Christians of the apostolic age, or the ministers of Christ? Bare assertions are not a sufficient proof to establish a point of so great importance. Has then our Lord himself taught us that some parts of his discourse do not concern all mankind? Without doubt, had it been so, he would have told us; he could not have omitted so necessary an information. But has he told us so? Where? In the discourse itself? No, here is not the least intimation of it. Has he said so elsewhere in any other of his discourses? Not one word so much as glancing this way can we find in anything he ever spoke, either to the multitudes, or to his disciples. Has any one of the apostles, or other inspired writers, left such an instruction upon record? No such thing.

No assertion of this kind is to be found in all the oracles of God. Who then are the men who are so much wiser than God—wise so far above that [which] is written?

6. Perhaps they will say that the reason of the thing requires such a restriction to be made. If it does, it must be on one of these two accounts; because, without such a restriction, the discourse would either be apparently absurd, or would contradict some other scripture. But this is not the case. It will plainly appear, when we come to examine the several particulars, that there is no absurdity at all in applying all which our Lord has here delivered to all mankind. Neither will it infer any contradiction to anything else he has delivered, nor to any other scripture whatever. Nay, it will farther appear that either all the parts of this discourse are to be applied to men in general, or no part; seeing they are all connected together, all joined as the stones in an arch, of which you cannot take one away, without destroying the whole fabric.

7. We may, lastly, observe, how our Lord teaches here. And surely, as at all times, so particularly at this, he speaks "as never man spoke." Not as the holy men of old; although they also spoke "as they were moved by the Holy Ghost." Not as Peter, or James, or John, or Paul: they were indeed wise master-builders in his Church; but still in this, in the degrees of heavenly wisdom, the servant is not as his Lord. No, nor even as himself at any other time, or on any other occasion. It does not appear that it was ever his design, at any other time or place, to lay down at once the whole plan of his religion; to give us a full prospect of Christianity; to describe at large the nature of that holiness, without which no man shall see the Lord. Particular branches of this he has indeed described, on a thousand different occasions; but never, besides here, did he give, of set purpose, a general view of the whole. Nay, we have nothing else of this kind in all the Bible; unless one should

except that short sketch of holiness delivered by God in those
Ten Words or Commandments to Moses, on Mount Sinai.
But even here how wide a difference is there between one and
the other! "Even that which was made glorious had no glory
in this respect, by reason of the glory that excels" (2 Cor. 3:10).

8. Above all, with what amazing love does the Son of God
here reveal his Father's will to man! He does not bring us again
"to the mount that burned with fire, nor unto blackness, and
darkness, and tempest." He does not speak as when he "thundered out of heaven"; when the Highest "gave his thunder,
hail-stones, and coals of fire." He now addresses us with his
still, small voice—"blessed," or happy, "are the poor in spirit."
Happy are the mourners, the meek, those that hunger after
righteousness, the merciful, the pure in heart. Happy in the
end, and in the way; happy in this life, and in life everlasting!
As if he had said, "Who is he that lusts to live, and would fain
see good days? Behold, I show you the thing which your soul
longs for! See the way you have so long sought in vain; the way
of pleasantness; the path to calm, joyous peace, to heaven below
and heaven above!"

9. At the same time, with what authority does he teach!
Well might they say, "Not as the scribes." Observe the manner
(but it cannot be expressed in words), the air, with which he
speaks! Not as Moses, the servant of God; not as Abraham,
his friend; not as any of the prophets; nor as any of the sons of
men. It is something more than human; more than can agree to
any created being. It speaks the Creator of all! A God, a God
appears! Yea, O ΩN, the Being of beings, JEHOVAH, the self-
existent, the Supreme, the God who is over all, blessed for ever!

10. This divine discourse, delivered in the most excellent
method, every subsequent part illustrating those that precede,
is commonly, and not improperly, divided into three principal
branches: the first, contained in the fifth; the second, in the

sixth; and the third, in the seventh chapter. In the first, the sum of all true religion is laid down in eight particulars, which are explained, and guarded against the false glosses of man, in the following parts of the fifth chapter. In the second are rules for that right intention which we are to preserve in all our outward actions, unmixed with worldly desires, or anxious cares for even the necessaries of life. In the third are cautions against the main hindrances of religion, closed with an application of the whole.

I. Blessed Are the Poor in Spirit

1. Our Lord, first, lays down the sum of all true religion in eight particulars, which he explains, and guards against the false glosses of men, to the end of the fifth chapter.

The Foundation of All

Some have supposed that he designed, in these, to point out the several stages of the Christian course; the steps which a Christian successively takes in his journey to the promised land; others, that all the particulars here set down belong at all times to every Christian. And why may we not allow both the one and the other? What inconsistency is there between them? It is undoubtedly true, that both poverty of spirit, and every other temper which is here mentioned, are at all times found, in a greater or less degree, in every real Christian. And it is equally true that real Christianity always begins in poverty of spirit, and goes on in the order here set down, till the "man of God is made perfect." We begin at the lowest of these gifts of God, yet so as not to relinquish this, when we are called of God to come up higher. But "whereunto we have already attained, we hold fast," while we press on to what is yet before, to the highest blessings of God in Christ Jesus.

2. The foundation of all is poverty of spirit. Here, therefore, our Lord begins: "Blessed," says he, "are the poor in spirit; for theirs is the kingdom of heaven." It may not improbably be supposed that our Lord looked on those who were round about him, and, observing that not many rich were there, but rather the poor of the world, took occasion from thence to make a transition from temporal to spiritual things. "Blessed," says he (or happy—so the word should be rendered, both in this and the following verses), "are the poor in spirit." He does not say they that are poor, as to outward circumstances—it being not impossible, that some of these may be as far from happiness as a monarch upon his throne; but "the poor in spirit"—they who, whatever their outward circumstances are, have that disposition of heart which is the first step to all real, substantial happiness, either in this world, or that which is to come.

The Poor in Spirit Are Not Those Who Love Poverty

3. Some have judged, that by the poor in spirit here, are meant those who love poverty; those who are free from covetousness, from the love of money; who fear, rather than desire, riches. Perhaps they have been induced so to judge, by wholly confining their thoughts to the very term; or by considering that weighty observation of St. Paul, that "the love of money is the root of all evil." And hence many have wholly divested themselves, not only of riches, but of all worldly goods. Hence also the vows of voluntary poverty seem to have arisen in the Romish Church; it being supposed, that so eminent a degree of this fundamental grace must be a large step toward the "kingdom of heaven."

But these do not seem to have observed, first, that the expression of St. Paul must be understood with some restriction; otherwise it is not true; for the love of money is not the root, the sole root, of all evil. There are a thousand other roots of evil in the world, as sad experience daily shows. His meaning can only be, it is the root of very many evils; perhaps of more than any single vice besides.

Secondly, that this sense of the expression "poor in spirit," will by no means suit our Lord's present design, which is to lay a general foundation whereon the whole fabric of Christianity may be built; a design which would be in no wise answered by guarding against one particular vice: so that, if even this were supposed to be one part of his meaning, it could not possibly be the whole

Thirdly, that it cannot be supposed to be any part of his meaning, unless we charge him with manifest tautology: seeing, if poverty of spirit were only freedom from covetousness, from the love of money, or the desire of riches, it would coincide with what he afterwards mentions, it would be only a branch of purity of heart.

The Poor in Spirit Are the Humble

4. Who then are "the poor in spirit"? Without question, the humble; they who know themselves; who are convinced of sin; those to whom God has given that first repentance, which is previous to faith in Christ.

One of these can no longer say, "I am rich, and increased in goods, and have need of nothing"; as now knowing, that he is "wretched, and poor, and miserable, and blind, and naked." He is convinced that he is spiritually poor indeed; having no spiritual good abiding in him. "In me," says he, "dwelleth no good thing," but whatsoever is evil and abominable. He has a deep sense of the loathsome leprosy of sin, which be brought with him from his mother's womb, which overspreads his whole soul, and totally corrupts every power and faculty thereof.

He sees more and more of the evil tempers which spring from that evil root; the pride and haughtiness of spirit, the

constant bias to think of himself more highly than he ought
to think; the vanity, the thirst after the esteem or honor that
cometh from men, the hatred or envy, the jealousy or revenge,
the anger, malice, or bitterness; the inbred enmity both against
God and man, which appears in ten thousand shapes; the love
of the world, the self-will, the foolish and hurtful desires, which
cleave to his inmost soul. He is conscious how deeply he has
offended by his tongue; if not by profane, immodest, untrue, or
unkind words, yet by discourse which was not "good to the use
of edifying," not "meet to minister grace to the hearers"; which,
consequently, was all corrupt in God's account, and grievous
to his Holy Spirit. His evil works are now likewise ever in his
sight: if he tells them, they are more than he is able to express.
He may as well think to number the drops of rain, the sands of
the sea, or the days of eternity.

5. His guilt is now also before his face: he knows the punishment he has deserved, were it only on account of his carnal
mind, the entire, universal corruption of his nature; how much
more, on account of all his evil desires and thoughts, of all his
sinful words and actions! He cannot doubt for a moment, but
the least of these deserves the damnation of hell—"the worm
that dieth not, and the fire that never shall be quenched."
Above all, the guilt of "not believing on the name of the only-
begotten Son of God" lies heavy upon him. How, says he, shall
I escape, who "neglect so great salvation!" "He that believes not
is condemned already," and "the wrath of God abides on him."

6. But what shall he give in exchange for his soul, which is
forfeited to the just vengeance of God? "Wherewithal shall he
come before the Lord?" How shall he pay him that he owes?
Were he from this moment to perform the most perfect obedience to every command of God, this would make no amends
for a single sin, for any one act of past disobedience; seeing
he owes God all the service he is able to perform, from this

moment to all eternity: could he pay this, it would make no manner of amends for what he ought to have done before. He sees himself therefore utterly helpless with regard to atoning for his past sins; utterly unable to make any amends to God, to pay any ransom for his own soul.

But if God would forgive him all that is past, on this one condition, that he should sin no more; that for the time to come he should entirely and constantly obey all his commands; he well knows that this would profit him nothing, being a condition he could never perform. He knows and feels that he is not able to obey even the outward commands of God; seeing these cannot be obeyed while his heart remains in its natural sinfulness and corruption; inasmuch as an evil tree cannot bring forth good fruit. But he cannot cleanse a sinful heart; with men this is impossible: so that he is utterly at a loss even how to begin walking in the path of God's commandments. He knows not how to get one step forward in the way. Encompassed with sin, and sorrow, and fear, and finding no way to escape, he can only cry out, "Lord, save, or I perish!"

7. Poverty of spirit then, as it implies the first step we take in running the race which is set before us, is a just sense of our inward and outward sins, and of our guilt and helplessness. This some have monstrously styled, "the virtue of humility"; thus teaching us to be proud of knowing we deserve damnation! But our Lord's expression is quite of another kind; conveying no idea to the hearer, but that of mere want, of naked sin, of helpless guilt and misery.

The Poor in Spirit Are the Helpless

8. The great apostle, where he endeavors to bring sinners to God, speaks in a manner just answerable to this. "The wrath of God," says he, "is revealed from heaven against all ungodliness and unrighteousness of men" (Rom. 1:18ff); a charge

which he immediately fixes on the heathen world, and thereby proves they are under the wrath of God. He next shows that the Jews were no better than they, and were therefore under the same condemnation; and all this, not in order to their attaining "the noble virtue of humility," but "that every mouth might be stopped, and all the world become guilty before God."

He proceeds to show that they were helpless as well as guilty, which is the plain purport of all those expressions: "Therefore by the deeds of the law there shall no flesh be justified"—"But now the righteousness of God, which is by faith of Jesus Christ, without the law, is manifested"—"We conclude, that a man is justified by faith, without the deeds of the law"—expressions all tending to the same point, even to "hide pride from man"; to humble him to the dust, without teaching him to reflect upon his humility as a virtue; to inspire him with that full, piercing conviction of his utter sinfulness, guilt, and helplessness, which casts the sinner, stripped of all, lost and undone, on his strong Helper, Jesus Christ the Righteous.

9. One cannot but observe here that Christianity begins just where heathen morality ends; poverty of spirit, conviction of sin, the renouncing ourselves, the not having our own righteousness (the very first point in the religion of Jesus Christ), leaving all pagan religion behind. This was ever hid from the wise men of this world; insomuch that the whole Roman language, even with all the improvements of the Augustan age, does not afford so much as a name for humility (the word from whence we borrow this, as is well known, bearing in Latin a quite different meaning); no, nor was one found in all the copious language of Greece, till it was made by the great apostle.

10. O that we may feel what they were not able to express! Sinner, awake! Know thyself! Know and feel, that you were "shapen in wickedness," and that "in sin did your mother conceive you"; and that you yourself have been heaping up sin

upon sin, ever since you could discern good from evil! Sink under the mighty hand of God, as guilty of death eternal; and cast off, renounce, abhor, all imagination of ever being able to help yourself! Be it all your hope to be washed in his blood, and renewed by his almighty Spirit, who himself "bare all our sins in his own body on the tree!" So shall you witness, "Happy are the poor in spirit: for theirs is the kingdom of heaven."

For Theirs Is the Kingdom of Heaven

11. This is that kingdom of heaven, or of God, which is within us; even "righteousness, and peace, and joy in the Holy Ghost." And what is "righteousness," but the life of God in the soul; the mind which was in Christ Jesus; the image of God stamped upon the heart, now renewed after the likeness of him that created it? What is it but the love of God, because he first loved us, and the love of all mankind for his sake?

And what is this "peace," the peace of God, but that calm serenity of soul, that sweet repose in the blood of Jesus, which leaves no doubt of our acceptance in him; which excludes all fear, but the loving filial fear of offending our Father which is in heaven?

This inward kingdom implies also "joy in the Holy Ghost"; who seals upon our hearts "the redemption which is in Jesus," the righteousness of Christ imputed to us "for the remission of the sins that are past"; who gives us now "the earnest of our inheritance," of the crown which the Lord, the righteous Judge, will give at that day. And well may this be termed, "the kingdom of heaven"; seeing it is heaven already opened in the soul; the first springing up of those rivers of pleasure which flow at God's right hand for evermore.

12. "Theirs is the kingdom of heaven." Whosoever you are, to whom God has given to be "poor in spirit," to feel yourself lost, you have a right thereto, through the gracious promise of

him who cannot lie. It is purchased for you by the blood of the Lamb. It is very nigh: you are on the brink of heaven! Another step, and you enter into the kingdom of righteousness, and peace, and joy!

Are you all sin? "Behold the Lamb of God, who taketh away the sin of the world!" All unholy? See your "Advocate with the Father, Jesus Christ the Righteous!" Are you unable to atone for the least of your sins? "He is the propitiation for" all your "sins." Now believe on the Lord Jesus Christ, and all your sins are blotted out! Are you totally unclean in soul and body? Here is the "fountain for sin and uncleanness!" "Arise, and wash away your sins!" Stagger no more at the promise through unbelief! Give glory to God! Dare to believe! Now cry out, from the ground of thy heart,

> Yes, I yield, I yield at last,
> Listen to thy speaking blood;
> Me with all my sins, I cast
> On my atoning God.

13. Then you learn of him to be "lowly of heart." And this is the true, genuine, Christian humility, which flows from a sense of the love of God, reconciled to us in Christ Jesus. Poverty of spirit, in this meaning of the word, begins where a sense of guilt and of the wrath of God ends; and is a continual sense of our total dependence on him, for every good thought, or word, or work; of our utter inability to all good, unless he "water us every moment"; and an abhorrence of the praise of men, knowing that all praise is due unto God only. With this is joined a loving shame, a tender humiliation before God, even for the sins which we know he has forgiven us, and for the sin which still remains in our hearts, although we know it is not imputed to our condemnation. Nevertheless, the conviction we feel of inbred sin is deeper and deeper every day.

The more we grow in grace, the more do we see of the desperate wickedness of our heart. The more we advance in the knowledge and love of God, through our Lord Jesus Christ (as great a mystery as this may appear to those who know not the power of God unto salvation), the more do we discern of our alienation from God, of the enmity that is in our carnal mind, and the necessity of our being entirely renewed in righteousness and true holiness.

II. Blessed Are Those Who Mourn

1. It is true, he has scarce any conception of this who now begins to know the inward kingdom of heaven. "In his prosperity he says, I shall never be moved; you, Lord, have made my hill so strong." Sin is so utterly bruised beneath his feet, that he can scarce believe it remains in him. Even temptation is silenced, and speaks not again: it cannot approach, but stands afar off. He is borne aloft in the chariots of joy and love: he soars, "as upon the wings of an eagle." But our Lord well knew that this triumphant state does not often continue long. He therefore presently subjoins, "Blessed are they that mourn; for they shall be comforted."

Mourning Not Worldly Troubles

2. Not that we can imagine this promise belongs to those who mourn only on some worldly account; who are in sorrow and heaviness merely on account of some worldly trouble or disappointment, such as the loss of their reputation or friends, or the impairing of their fortune. As little title to it have they who are afflicting themselves, through fear of some temporal evil; or who pine away with anxious care, or that desire of earthly things which "maketh the heart sick." Let us not think these "shall receive anything from the Lord": he is not in all

their thoughts. Therefore it is that they thus "walk in a vain shadow, and disquiet themselves in vain." "And this shall you have of my hand," says the Lord, "you shall lie down in sorrow."

Mourning for an Absent God

3. The mourners of whom our Lord here speaks are those that mourn on quite another account: they that mourn after God; after him in whom they did "rejoice with joy unspeakable," when he gave them to "taste the good," the pardoning "word, and the powers of the world to come." But he now "hides his face, and they are troubled." They cannot see him through the dark cloud. But they see temptation and sin, which they fondly supposed were gone never to return, arising again, following after them amain, and holding them in on every side. It is not strange if their soul is now disquieted within them, and trouble and heaviness take hold upon them. Nor will their great enemy fail to improve the occasion, to ask, "Where is now your God? Where is now the blessedness whereof you spoke? The beginning of the kingdom of heaven? Yea, has God said, 'Your sins are forgiven you'? Surely God has not said it. It was only a dream, a mere delusion, a creature of your own imagination. If your sins are forgiven, why are you thus? Can a pardoned sinner be thus unholy?"

And, if then, instead of immediately crying to God, they reason with him that is wiser than they, they will be in heaviness indeed, in sorrow of heart, in anguish not to be expressed. Nay even when God shines again upon the soul, and takes away all doubt of his past mercy, still he that is weak in faith may be tempted and troubled on account of what is to come; especially when inward sin revives, and thrusts sore at him that he may fall. Then may he again cry out,

I have a sin of fear, that when I've spun
My last thread, I shall perish on the shore!
Lest I should make shipwreck of the faith,
and my last state be worse than the first:
Lest all my bread of life should fail,
And I sink down unchanged to hell!

Recovering the Joy of His Countenance

4. Sure it is that this "affliction," for the present, "is not joyous, but grievous; nevertheless afterward it bringeth forth peaceable fruit unto them that are exercised thereby." Blessed, therefore, are they that thus mourn, if they "tarry the Lord's leisure," and suffer not themselves to be turned out of the way, by the miserable comforters of the world; if they resolutely reject all the comforts of sin, of folly, and vanity; all the idle diversions and amusements of the world; all the pleasures which "perish in the using," and which only tend to benumb and stupefy the soul, that it may neither be sensible of itself nor God.

Blessed are they who "follow on to know the Lord," and steadily refuse all other comfort. They shall be comforted by the consolations of his Spirit; by a fresh manifestation of his love; by such a witness of his accepting them in the Beloved, as shall never more be taken away from them. This "full assurance of faith" swallows up all doubt, as well as all tormenting fear; God now giving them a sure hope of an enduring substance, and "strong consolation through grace." Without disputing whether it be possible for any of those to "fall away, who were once enlightened and made partakers of the Holy Ghost," it suffices them to say, by the power now resting upon them, "Who shall separate us from the love of Christ? I am persuaded, that neither death nor life, nor things present nor things to come, nor height nor depth, shall be able to separate us from the love of God, which is in Christ Jesus our Lord" (Rom. 8:35–39).

5. This whole process, both of mourning for an absent God, and recovering the joy of his countenance, seems to be shadowed out in what our Lord spoke to his apostles the night before his passion: "Do you inquire of that I said, A little while, and you shall not see me: and again, a little while, and you shall see me? Verily, verily, I say unto you, that you shall weep and lament"; namely, when you do not see me; "but the world shall rejoice"; shall triumph over you, as though your hope were now come to an end. "And you shall be sorrowful," through doubt, through fear, through temptation, through vehement desire; "but your sorrow shall be turned into joy," by the return of him whom your soul loves.

"A woman when she is in travail has sorrow, because her hour is come. But as soon as she is delivered of the child, she remembers no more the anguish, for joy that a man is born into the world. And you now have sorrow"; you mourn and cannot be comforted; "but I will see you again; and your heart shall rejoice," with calm, inward joy, "and your joy no man takes from you" (John 16:19–22).

Mourning for the Sins of Mankind

6. But although this mourning is at an end, is lost in holy joy, by the return of the Comforter, yet is there another, and a blessed mourning it is, which abides in the children of God. They still mourn for the sins and miseries of mankind: they "weep with them that weep." They weep for them that weep not for themselves, for the sinners against their own souls. They mourn for the weakness and unfaithfulness of those that are, in some measure, saved from their sins. "Who is weak, and they are not weak? Who is offended, and they burn not?" They

are grieved for the dishonor continually done to the Majesty of heaven and earth.

At all times they have an awful sense of this, which brings a deep seriousness upon their spirit; a seriousness which is not a little increased, since the eyes of their understanding were opened, by their continually seeing the vast ocean of eternity, without a bottom or a shore, which has already swallowed up millions of millions of men, and is gaping to devour them that yet remain. They see here the house of God eternal in the heavens; there, hell and destruction without a covering; and thence feel the importance of every moment, which just appears, and is gone for ever!

Foolishness to the World, Wisdom of God

7. But all this wisdom of God is foolishness with the world. The whole affair of mourning and poverty of spirit is with them stupidity and dullness. Nay, it is well if they pass so favorable a judgment upon it; if they do not vote it to be mere moping and melancholy, if not downright lunacy and distraction. And it is no wonder at all that this judgment should be passed by those who know not God. Suppose, as two persons were walking together, one should suddenly stop, and with the strongest signs of fear and amazement, cry out, "On what a precipice do we stand! See, we are on the point of being dashed in pieces! Another step, and we fall into that huge abyss! Stop! I will not go on for all the world!" When the other, who seemed, to himself at least, equally sharp-sighted, looked forward and saw nothing of all this, what would he think of his companion, but that he was beside himself; that his head was out of order; that much religion (if he was not guilty of "much learning") had certainly made him mad!

8. But let not the children of God, "the mourners in Zion," be moved by any of these things. You, whose eyes are

enlightened, be not troubled by those who walk on still in darkness. You do not walk on in a vain shadow: God and eternity are real things. Heaven and hell are in very deed open before you; and you are on the edge of the great gulf. It has already swallowed up more than words can express; nations, and kindreds, and peoples, and tongues; and still yawns to devour, whether they see it or no, the giddy, miserable children of men. O cry aloud! Spare not! Lift up your voice to him who grasps both time and eternity, both for yourselves and your brethren, that you may be counted worthy to escape the destruction that comes as a whirlwind; that you may be brought safe through all the waves and storms into the haven where you would be! Weep for yourselves, till he wipes away the tears from your eyes. And even then, weep for the miseries that come upon the earth, till the Lord of all shall put a period to misery and sin, shall wipe away the tears from all faces, and "the knowledge of the Lord shall cover the earth, as the waters cover the sea."

DISCOURSE TWO

OF MEEKNESS, MERCY, AND LOVE

Blessed are the meek: for they shall inherit the earth. Blessed are they which do hunger and thirst after righteousness: for they shall be filled. Blessed are the merciful: for they shall obtain mercy.

—Matthew 5:5–7

I. Blessed Are the Meek

1. When "the winter is past," when "the time of singing is come, and the voice of the turtle is heard in the land"; when he that comforts the mourners is now returned, "that he may abide with them for ever"; when, at the brightness of his presence, the clouds disperse, the dark clouds of doubt and uncertainty, the storms of fear flee away, the waves of sorrow subside, and their spirit again rejoiceth in God their Savior; then is it that this word is eminently fulfilled; then those whom

he has comforted can bear witness: "blessed," or happy, "are the meek; for they shall inherit the earth."

Meekness Is Not Apathy

2. But who are "the meek"? Not those who grieve at nothing, because they know nothing; who are not discomposed at the evils that occur, because they discern not evil from good. Not those who are sheltered from the shocks of life by a stupid insensibility; who have, either by nature or art, the virtue of stocks and stones, and resent nothing, because they feel nothing. Brute philosophers are wholly unconcerned in this matter. Apathy is as far from meekness as from humanity. So that one would not easily conceive how any Christians of the purer ages, especially any of the Fathers of the Church, could confound these, and mistake one of the foulest errors of heathenism for a branch of true Christianity.

Meekness Is Not Lack of Zeal

3. Nor does Christian meekness imply the being without zeal for God, any more than it does ignorance or insensibility. No; it keeps clear of every extreme, whether in excess or defect. It does not destroy but balance the affections, which the God of nature never designed should be rooted out by grace, but only brought and kept under due regulations. It poises the mind aright. It holds an even scale, with regard to anger, and sorrow, and fear; preserving the mean in every circumstance of life, and not declining either to the right hand or the left.

Meekness Restrains Our Outward Acts

4. Meekness, therefore, seems properly to relate to ourselves. But it may be referred either to God or our neighbor. When this due composure of mind has reference to God, it is usually termed resignation; a calm acquiescence in whatsoever

is his will concerning us, even though it may not be pleasing to nature; saying continually, "It is the Lord; let him do what seemeth him good." When we consider it more strictly with regard to ourselves, we style it patience or contentedness. When it is exerted toward other men, then it is mildness to the good, and gentleness to the evil.

5. They who are truly meek can clearly discern what is evil; and they can also suffer it. They are sensible of everything of this kind, but still meekness holds the reins. They are exceeding "zealous for the Lord of hosts"; but their zeal is always guided by knowledge, and tempered, in every thought, and word, and work, with the love of man, as well as the love of God. They do not desire to extinguish any of the passions which God has for wise ends implanted in their nature; but they have the mastery of all. They hold them all in subjection, and employ them only in subservience to those ends. And thus even the harsher and more unpleasing passions are applicable to the noblest purposes; even hatred, and anger, and fear, when engaged against sin, and regulated by faith and love, are as walls and bulwarks to the soul, so that the wicked one cannot approach to hurt it.

6. It is evident, this divine temper is not only to abide but to increase in us day by day. Occasions of exercising, and thereby increasing it, will never be wanting while we remain upon earth. "We have need of patience, that after we have done" and suffered "the will of God, we may receive the promise." We have need of resignation, that we may in all circumstances say, "Not as I will, but as you will." And we have need of "gentleness toward all men"; but especially toward the evil and unthankful: otherwise we shall be overcome of evil, instead of overcoming evil with good.

Meekness Begins in the Heart

7. Nor does meekness restrain only the outward act, as the scribes and Pharisees taught of old, and the miserable teachers

who are not taught of God will not fail to do in all ages. Our Lord guards against this, and shows the true extent of it, in the following words: "Ye have heard that it was said by them of old time, Thou shalt not kill; and whosoever shall kill, shall be in danger of the judgment" (Matt. 5:21ff.). "But I say unto you, That whosoever is angry with his brother without a cause, shall be in danger of the judgment. And whosoever shall say to his brother, Raca, shall be in danger of the council. But whosoever shall say, Thou fool, shall be in danger of hell-fire."

8. Our Lord here ranks under the head of murder, even that anger which goes no farther than the heart; which does not show itself by an outward unkindness, no, not so much as a passionate word.

"Whosoever is angry with his brother," with any man living, seeing we are all brethren; whosoever feels any unkindness in his heart, any temper contrary to love; whosoever is angry without a cause, without a sufficient cause, or farther than that cause requires, ἔνοχος ἔσται, *shall be in danger of the judgment*; shall, in that moment, be obnoxious to the righteous judgment of God.

But would not one be inclined to prefer the reading of those copies which omit the word εἰχή, *without a cause*? Is it not entirely superfluous? For if anger at persons be a temper contrary to love, how can there be a cause, a sufficient cause for it—any that will justify it in the sight of God?

Anger at sin we allow. In this sense we may be angry, and yet we sin not. In this sense our Lord himself is once recorded to have been angry: "He looked round about upon them with anger, being grieved for the hardness of their hearts." He was grieved at the sinners, and angry at the sin. And this is undoubtedly right before God.

9. "And whosoever shall say to his brother, Raca"—whosoever shall give way to anger, so as to utter any contemptuous

word. It is observed by commentators that *Raca* is a Syriac word, which properly signifies "empty, vain, foolish," so that it is as inoffensive an expression as can well be used toward one at whom we are displeased. And yet, whosoever shall use this, as our Lord assures us, "shall be in danger of the council"; rather, shall be obnoxious thereto. He shall be liable to a severer sentence from the Judge of all the earth.

"But whosoever shall say, Thou fool"—whosoever shall so give place to the devil as to break out into reviling, into designedly reproachful and contumelious language, "shall be obnoxious to hell-fire"; shall, in that instant, be liable to the highest condemnation. It should be observed that our Lord describes all these as obnoxious to capital punishment. The first, to strangling, usually inflicted on those who were condemned in one of the inferior courts; the second, to stoning, which was frequently inflicted on those who were condemned by the great Council at Jerusalem; the third, to burning alive, inflicted only on the highest offenders, in the γέενναν, *valley of the sons of Hinnom*, from which that word is evidently taken which we translate "hell."

Outward and Inward Acts Must Agree

10. And whereas men naturally imagine that God will excuse their defect in some duties, for their exactness in others; our Lord next takes care to cut off that vain, though common imagination. He shows that it is impossible for any sinner to commute with God, who will not accept one duty for another, nor take a part of obedience for the whole. He warns us that the performing our duty to God will not excuse us from our duty to our neighbor; that works of piety, as they are called, will be so far from commending us to God, if we are wanting in charity, that, on the contrary, that want of charity will make all those works an abomination to the Lord.

"Therefore, if you bring your gift to the altar, and there remember that your brother has aught against you," on account of your unkind behavior toward him, of your calling him "Raca," or, "Thou fool," think not that your gift will atone for your anger; or that it will find any acceptance with God, so long as your conscience is defiled with the guilt of unrepented sin. "Leave there your gift before the altar, and go your way; first be reconciled to your brother" (at least do all that in you lies toward being reconciled), "and then come and offer your gift" (Matt. 5:23, 24).

11. And let there be no delay in what so nearly concerneth your soul. "Agree with your adversary quickly"—now; upon the spot—"while you are in the way with him"; if it be possible, before he go out of your sight. "Lest at any time the adversary deliver you to the judge"; lest he appeal to God, the Judge of all; "and the judge deliver you to the officer"; to Satan, the executioner of the wrath of God; "and you be cast into prison"; into hell, there to be reserved to the judgment of the great day: "Verily, I say unto you, You shall by no means come out thence, till you have paid the uttermost farthing." But this it is impossible for you ever to do, seeing you have nothing to pay. Therefore, if you are once in that prison, the smoke of your torment must "ascend up for ever and ever."

The Meek Shall Inherit the Earth

12. Meantime "the meek shall inherit the earth." Such is the foolishness of worldly wisdom! The wise of the world had warned them again and again—that if they did not resent such treatment, if they would tamely suffer themselves to be thus abused, there would be no living for them upon earth; that they would never be able to procure the common necessaries of life, nor to keep even what they had; that they could expect no peace, no quiet possession, no enjoyment of anything. Most

true, suppose there were no God in the world; or, suppose he did not concern himself with the children of men.

But "when God arises to judgment, and to help all the meek upon earth," how does he laugh all this heathen wisdom to scorn, and turn the "fierceness of man to his praise!" He takes a peculiar care to provide them with all things needful for life and godliness; he secures to them the provision he has made, in spite of the force, fraud, or malice of men; and what he secures he gives them richly to enjoy. It is sweet to them, be it little or much. As in patience they possess their souls, so they truly possess whatever God has given them. They are always content, always pleased with what they have. It pleases them because it pleases God: so that while their heart, their desire, their joy is in heaven, they may truly be said to "inherit the earth."

13. But there seems to be a yet farther meaning in these words, even that they shall have a more eminent part in "the new earth, wherein dwelleth righteousness"; in that inheritance, a general description of which (and the particulars we shall know hereafter) St. John has given in the twentieth chapter of the Revelation:

> And I saw an angel come down from heaven . . . and he laid hold on the dragon, that old serpent . . . and bound him a thousand years . . . And I saw the souls of them that were beheaded for the witness of Jesus, and for the word of God, and of them which had not worshipped the Beast, neither his image, neither had received his mark upon their foreheads or in their hands; and they lived and reigned with Christ a thousand years. But the rest of the dead lived not again, until the thousand years were finished. This is the first resurrection. Blessed and holy is he that has part in the first resurrection: on such

the second death has no power, but they shall be priests
of God and of Christ, and shall reign with him a thousand years (Rev. 20:1–6).

II. Blessed Are They Who Hunger and Thirst after Righteousness

1. Our Lord has hitherto been more immediately employed
in removing the hindrances of true religion: Such is pride, the
first, grand hindrance of all religion, which is taken away by
poverty of spirit; levity and thoughtlessness, which prevent any
religion from taking root in the soul, till they are removed by
holy mourning; such are anger, impatience, discontent, which
are all healed by Christian meekness. And when once these
hindrances are removed, these evil diseases of the soul, which
were continually raising false cravings therein, and filling it
with sickly appetites, the native appetite of a heaven-born
spirit returns; it hungers and thirsts after righteousness. And
"blessed are they which do hunger and thirst after righteousness; for they shall be filled."

An Ever-Increasing Hunger after the Image of God

2. Righteousness, as was observed before, is the image of
God, the mind which was in Christ Jesus. It is every holy and
heavenly temper in one; springing from, as well as terminating
in, the love of God, as our Father and Redeemer, and the love
of all men for his sake.

3. "Blessed are they which do hunger and thirst after"
this. In order fully to understand which expression, we should
observe, first, that hunger and thirst are the strongest of all our
bodily appetites. In like manner this hunger in the soul, this
thirst after the image of God, is the strongest of all our spiritual appetites, when it is once awakened in the heart. Yea, it

swallows up all the rest in that one great desire—to be renewed after the likeness of him that created us.

We should, secondly, observe, that from the time we begin to hunger and thirst, those appetites do not cease, but are more and more craving and importunate, till we either eat and drink, or die. And even so, from the time that we begin to hunger and thirst after the whole mind which was in Christ, these spiritual appetites do not cease, but cry after their food with more and more importunity; nor can they possibly cease, before they are satisfied, while there is any spiritual life remaining.

We may, thirdly, observe, that hunger and thirst are satisfied with nothing but meat and drink. If you would give to him that is hungry all the world beside, all the elegance of apparel, all the trappings of state, all the treasure upon earth, yea, thousands of gold and silver; if you would pay him ever so much honor—he regards it not: all these things are then of no account with him. He would still say, "These are not the things I want; give me food, or else I die." The very same is the case with every soul that truly hungers and thirsts after righteousness. He can find no comfort in anything but this: he can be satisfied with nothing else. Whatever you offer besides, it is lightly esteemed: whether it be riches, or honor, or pleasure; he still says, "This is not the thing which I want! Give me love, or else I die!"

Satisfied in Nothing Else

4. And it is as impossible to satisfy such a soul, a soul that is athirst for God, the living God, with what the world accounts religion, as with what they account happiness. The religion of the world implies three things: (1.) the doing no harm, the abstaining from outward sin; at least from such as is scandalous, as robbery, theft, common swearing, drunkenness; (2.) the doing good, the relieving the poor; the being charitable,

as it is called; (3.) the using the means of grace; at least the going to church and to the Lord's Supper. He in whom these three marks are found is termed by the world a religious man. But will this satisfy him who hungers after God? No: it is not food for his soul. He wants a religion of a nobler kind, a religion higher and deeper than this. He can no more feed on this poor, shallow, formal thing than he can "fill his belly with the east wind."

True, he is careful to abstain from the very appearance of evil; he is zealous of good works; he attends all the ordinances of God. But all this is not what he longs for. This is only the outside of that religion, which he insatiably hungers after. The knowledge of God in Christ Jesus; "the life which is hid with Christ in God"; the being "joined unto the Lord in one Spirit"; the having "fellowship with the Father and the Son"; the "walking in the light as God is in the light"; the being "purified even as He is pure"—this is the religion, the righteousness, he thirsts after: nor can he rest, till he thus rests in God.

For They Shall Be Filled

5. "Blessed are they who" thus "hunger and thirst after righteousness; for they shall be filled." They shall be filled with the things which they long for; even with righteousness and true holiness. God shall satisfy them with the blessings of his goodness, with the felicity of his chosen. He shall feed them with the bread of heaven, with the manna of his love. He shall give them to drink of his pleasures as out of the river, which he that drinks of shall never thirst, only for more and more of the water of life. This thirst shall endure for ever.

The painful thirst, the fond desire,
Thy joyous presence shall remove;

But my full soul shall still require
A whole eternity of love.

6. Whosoever then you are, to whom God has given to "hunger and thirst after righteousness," cry unto him that you may never lose that inestimable gift—that this divine appetite may never cease. If many rebuke you, and bid you hold your peace, regard them not; yea, cry so much the more, "Jesus, Master, have mercy on me!" "Let me not live, but to be holy as you are holy!" No more "spend your money for that which is not bread, nor your labor for that which satisfies not." Can't you hope to dig happiness out of the earth, to find it in the things of the world? O trample under foot all its pleasures, despise its honors, count its riches as dung and dross—yea, and all the things which are beneath the sun—"for the excellency of the knowledge of Christ Jesus," for the entire renewal of your soul in that image of God wherein it was originally created.

Beware of quenching that blessed hunger and thirst, by what the world calls religion; a religion of form, of outward show, which leaves the heart as earthly and sensual as ever. Let nothing satisfy you but the power of godliness, but a religion that is spirit and life; your dwelling in God and God in you; the being an inhabitant of eternity; the entering in by the blood of sprinkling "within the veil," and sitting "in heavenly places with Christ Jesus."

III. Blessed Are the Merciful

1. And the more they are filled with the life of God, the more tenderly will they be concerned for those who are still without God in the world, still dead in trespasses and sins. Nor shall this concern for others lose its reward. "Blessed are the merciful; for they shall obtain mercy."

The Merciful Love Their Neighbors as Themselves

The word used by our Lord more immediately implies the compassionate, the tenderhearted; those who, far from despising, earnestly grieve for, those that do not hunger after God. This eminent part of brotherly love is here, by a common figure, put for the whole; so that "the merciful," in the full sense of the term, are they who "love their neighbors as themselves."

2. Because of the vast importance of this love—without which, "though we spoke with the tongues of men and angels, though we had the gift of prophecy, and understood all mysteries, and all knowledge; though we had all faith, so as to remove mountains; yea, though we gave all our goods to feed the poor, and our very bodies to be burned, it would profit us nothing"—the wisdom of God has given us, by the apostle Paul, a full and particular account of it; by considering which we shall most clearly discern who are the merciful that shall obtain mercy.

Love Suffers Long

3. "Charity," or love (as it were to be wished it had been rendered throughout, being a far plainer and less ambiguous word), the love of our neighbor as Christ has loved us, "suffers long," is patient toward all men. It suffers all the weakness, ignorance, errors, infirmities, all the frowardness and littleness of faith, of the children of God; all the malice and wickedness of the children of the world. And it suffers all this, not only for a time, for a short season, but to the end; still feeding our enemy when he hungers; if he thirst, still giving him drink; thus continually "heaping coals of fire," of melting love, "upon his head."

Love Is Tender Affection

4. And in every step toward this desirable end, the "overcoming evil with good," "love is kind" (χρηστεύεται, a word

not easily translated): it is soft, mild, benign. It stands at the utmost distance from moroseness, from all harshness or sourness of spirit; and inspires the sufferer at once with the most amiable sweetness, and the most fervent and tender affection.

Love Envies Not

5. Consequently, "love envies not." It is impossible it should; it is directly opposite to that baneful temper. It cannot be that he who has this tender affection to all, who earnestly wishes all temporal and spiritual blessings, all good things in this world and the world to come, to every soul that God has made, should be pained at his bestowing any good gift on any child of man. If he has himself received the same, he does not grieve, but rejoice, that another partakes of the common benefit. If he has not, he blesses God that his brother at least has, and is herein happier than himself. And the greater his love, the more does he rejoice in the blessings of all mankind; the farther is he removed from every kind and degree of envy toward any creature.

Love Is Not Hasty to Judge

6. Love οὐ περπερεύεται, *vaunts not itself*; which coincides with the very next words; but rather (as the word likewise properly imports), is not rash or hasty in judging; it will not hastily condemn any one. It does not pass a severe sentence, on a slight or sudden view of things. It first weighs all the evidence, particularly that which is brought in favor of the accused. A true lover of his neighbor is not like the generality of men, who, even in cases of the nicest nature, "see a little, presume a great deal, and so jump to the conclusion." No: he proceeds with wariness and circumspection, taking heed to every step; willingly subscribing to that rule of the ancient heathen (O where will the modern Christian appear!):

"I am so far from lightly believing what one man says against another, that I will not easily believe what a man says against himself. I will always allow him second thoughts, and many times counsel too."

Love Is Not Puffed Up

7. It follows, love "is not puffed up." It does not incline or suffer any man "to think more highly of himself than he ought to think"; but rather to think soberly. Yea, it humbles the soul unto the dust. It destroys all high conceits, engendering pride; and makes us rejoice to be as nothing, to be little and vile, the lowest of all, the servant of all. They who are "kindly affectioned one to another with brotherly love," cannot but "in honor prefer one another." Those who, having the same love, are of one accord, do in lowliness of mind "each esteem other better than themselves."

This Love Does Not Behave Unseemly

8. "It does not behave itself unseemly." It is not rude, or willingly offensive to any. It "renders to all their due; fear to whom fear, honor to whom honor"; courtesy, civility, humanity to all the world; in their several degrees "honoring all men." A late writer defines good breeding, nay, the highest degree of it, politeness: "a continual desire to please, appearing in all the behavior."

But if so, there is none so well-bred as a Christian, a lover of all mankind. For he cannot but desire to "please all men for their good to edification." And this desire cannot be hid; it will necessarily appear in all his intercourse with men. For his "love is without dissimulation": it will appear in all his actions and conversation; yea, and will constrain him, though without guile, "to become all things to all men, if by any means he may save some."

Love Seeks Not Her Own

9. And in becoming all things to all men, "love seeks not her own." In striving to please all men, the lover of mankind has no eye at all to his own temporal advantage. He covets no man's silver, or gold, or apparel: he desires nothing but the salvation of their souls. Yea, in some sense, he may be said, not to seek his own spiritual, any more than temporal, advantage; for while he is on the full stretch to save their souls from death, he, as it were, forgets himself. He does not think of himself, so long as that zeal for the glory of God swallows him up. Nay, at some times he may almost seem, through an excess of love, to give up himself, both his soul and his body; while he cries out, with Moses, "O, this people have sinned a great sin; yet now, if you will forgive their sin . . . and if not, blot me out of the book which you have written" (Exod. 32:31, 32); or, with St. Paul, "I could wish that myself were accursed from Christ, for my brethren, my kinsmen according to the flesh!" (Rom. 9:3).

Love Is Not Provoked

10. No marvel that such "love is not provoked": οὐ παροξύνεται. Let it be observed, the word *easily*, strangely inserted in the translation, is not in the original: St. Paul's words are absolute. "Love is not provoked." It is not provoked to unkindness toward any one. Occasions indeed will frequently occur; outward provocations of various kinds; but love does not yield to provocation; it triumphs over all. In all trials it looketh unto Jesus, and is more than conqueror in his love.

It is not improbable that our translators inserted that word, as it were, to excuse the apostle; who, as they supposed, might otherwise appear to be wanting in the very love which he so beautifully describes. They seem to have supposed this from a phrase in the Acts of the Apostles; which is likewise very inaccurately translated. When Paul and Barnabas disagreed

concerning John, the translation runs thus, "And the contention was so sharp between them, that they departed asunder"
(Acts 15:39). This naturally induces the reader to suppose
that they were equally sharp therein; that St. Paul, who was
undoubtedly right, with regard to the point in question (it
being quite improper to take John with them again, who had
deserted them before), was as much provoked as Barnabas,
who gave such a proof of his anger as to leave the work for
which he had been set apart by the Holy Ghost.

But the original imports no such thing; nor does it affirm
that St. Paul was provoked at all. It simply says, καὶ ἐγένετο
παροξυσμὸς, "*And there was a sharpness,*" a paroxysm of anger;
in consequence of which Barnabas left St. Paul, took John, and
went his own way. Paul then "chose Silas and departed, being
recommended by the brethren to the grace of God" (which
is not said concerning Barnabas); "and he went through Syria
and Cilicia," as he had proposed, "confirming the churches"
(Acts 15:39–41). But to return.

Love Infers No Evil

11. Love prevents a thousand provocations which would
otherwise arise, because it "thinks no evil." Indeed the merciful
man cannot avoid knowing many things that are evil; he cannot
but see them with his own eyes, and hear them with his own
ears. For love does not put out his eyes, so that it is impossible
for him not to see that such things are done; neither does it
take away his understanding, any more than his senses, so that
he cannot but know that they are evil. For instance, when he
sees a man strike his neighbor, or hears him blaspheme God,
he cannot either question the thing done, or the words spoken,
or doubt of their being evil.

Yet, οὐ λογίζεται τὸ κακόν [*thinketh no evil*]. The word
λογίζεται, *thinketh*, does not refer either to our seeing and

hearing, or to the first and involuntary acts of our understanding; but to our willingly thinking what we need not; our inferring evil, where it does not appear; to our reasoning concerning things which we do not see; our supposing what we have neither seen nor heard. This is what true love absolutely destroys. It tears up, root and branch, all imagining what we have not known. It casts out all jealousies, all evil surmisings, all readiness to believe evil. It is frank, open, unsuspicious; and, as it cannot design, so neither does it fear, evil.

Love Rejoices Not in Iniquity

12. It "rejoices not in iniquity;" common as this is, even among those who bear the name of Christ, who scruple not to rejoice over their enemy, when he falls either into affliction, or error, or sin. Indeed, how hardly can they avoid this, who are zealously attached to any party! How difficult is it for them not to be pleased with any fault which they discover in those of the opposite party—with any real or supposed blemish, either in their principles or practice!

What warm defender of any cause is clear of these? Yea, who is so calm as to be altogether free? Who does not rejoice when his adversary makes a false step, which he thinks will advantage his own cause? Only a man of love. He alone weeps over either the sin or folly of his enemy, takes no pleasure in hearing or in repeating it, but rather desires that it may be forgotten for ever.

Love Rejoices in the Truth

13. But he "rejoiceth in the truth," wheresoever it is found; in "the truth which is after godliness;" bringing forth its proper fruit, holiness of heart, and holiness of conversation. He rejoices to find that even those who oppose him, whether with regard to opinions, or some points of practice, are nevertheless lovers

of God, and in other respects unreprovable. He is glad to hear good of them, and to speak all he can consistently with truth and justice. Indeed, good in general is his glory and joy, wherever diffused throughout the race of mankind. As a citizen of the world, he claims a share in the happiness of all the inhabitants of it. Because he is a man, he is not unconcerned in the welfare of any man; but enjoys whatsoever brings glory to God, and promotes peace and goodwill among men.

Love Covers All Things

14. This "love covers all things." (So, without all doubt, πάντα στέγει should be translated; for otherwise it would be the very same with πάντα ὑπομένει, *endures all things*). Because the merciful man rejoices not in iniquity, neither does he willingly make mention of it. Whatever evil he sees, hears, or knows, he nevertheless conceals, so far as he can without making himself "partaker of other men's sins." Wheresoever or with whomsoever he is, if he sees anything which he approves not, it goes not out of his lips, unless to the person concerned, if haply he may gain his brother.

So far is he from making the faults or failures of others the matter of his conversation, that of the absent he never does speak at all, unless he can speak well. A tale-bearer, a backbiter, a whisperer, an evil-speaker, is to him all one as a murderer. He would just as soon cut his neighbor's throat as thus murder his reputation. Just as soon would he think of diverting himself by setting fire to his neighbor's house as of thus "scattering abroad arrows, fire-brands, and death," and saying, "Am I not in sport?"

He makes only one exception. Sometimes he is convinced that it is for the glory of God, or (which comes to the same) the good of his neighbor, that an evil should not be covered. In this case, for the benefit of the innocent, he is constrained to declare the guilty. But even here, (1.) he will not speak at all till love, superior love, constrains him; (2.) he cannot do it from a general confused view of doing good, or promoting the glory of God, but from a clear sight of some particular end, some determinate good which he pursues; (3.) still he cannot speak unless he be fully convinced that this very means is necessary to that end; that the end cannot be answered, at least not so effectually, by any other way; (4.) he then does it with the utmost sorrow and reluctance; using it as the last and worst medicine, a desperate remedy in a desperate case, a kind of poison never to be used but to expel poison. Consequently, (5.) he uses it as sparingly as possible. And this he does with fear and trembling, lest he should transgress the law of love by speaking too much, more than he would have done by not speaking at all.

Love Believes All Things

15. Love "believes all things." It is always willing to think the best; to put the most favorable construction on everything. It is ever ready to believe whatever may tend to the advantage of any one's character. It is easily convinced of (what it earnestly desires) the innocence or integrity of any man; or, at least, of the sincerity of his repentance, if he had once erred from the way. It is glad to excuse whatever is amiss; to condemn the offender as little as possible; and to make all the allowance for human weakness which can be done without betraying the truth of God.

Love Hopes All Things

16. And when it can no longer believe, then love "hopes all things." Is any evil related of any man? Love hopes that the relation is not true, that the thing related was never done. Is it certain it was? "But perhaps it was not done with such circumstances as are related; so that, allowing the fact, there

is room to hope it was not so ill as it is represented." Was the action apparently undeniably evil? Love hopes the intention was not so. Is it clear the design was evil too? "Yet might it not spring from the settled temper of the heart, but from a start of passion, or from some vehement temptation, which hurried the man beyond himself"?

And even when it cannot be doubted, but all the actions, designs, and tempers are equally evil; still love hopes that God will at last make bare his arm, and get himself the victory; and that there shall be "joy in heaven over" this "one sinner that repents, more than over ninety and nine just persons that need no repentance."

Love Endures All Things

17. Lastly, it "endures all things." This completes the character of him that is truly merciful. He endures not some, not many, things only; not most, but absolutely all things. Whatever the injustice, the malice, the cruelty of men can inflict, he is able to suffer. He calls nothing intolerable; he never says of anything, "This is not to be borne." No; he can not only do, but suffer, all things through Christ which strengthens him. And all he suffers does not destroy his love, nor impair it in the least. It is proof against all. It is a flame that burns even in the midst of the great deep. "Many waters cannot quench" his "love, neither can the floods drown it." It triumphs over all. It "never fails," either in time or in eternity.

> In obedience to what heaven decrees,
> Knowledge shall fail, and prophecy shall cease;
> But lasting charity's more ample sway,
> Nor bound by time, nor subject to decay,
> In happy triumph shall for ever live,
> And endless good diffuse, and endless praise receive.

The Merciful Shall Obtain Mercy

So shall "the merciful obtain mercy;" not only by the blessing of God upon all their ways, by his now repaying the love they bear to their brethren a thousand fold into their own bosom; but likewise by "an exceeding and eternal weight of glory," in the "kingdom prepared for them from the beginning of the world."

18. For a little while you may say, "Woe is me, that I" am constrained to "dwell with Mesech, and to have my habitation among the tents of Kedar!" You may pour out your soul, and bemoan the loss of true, genuine love in the earth: Lost indeed!

You may well say (but not in the ancient sense), "See how these Christians love one another!" These Christian kingdoms, that are tearing out each other's hearts, desolating one another with fire and sword! These Christian armies, that are sending each by thousands, by ten thousands, quick into hell! These Christian nations, that are all on fire with intestine broils, party against party, faction against faction! These Christian cities, where deceit and fraud, oppression and wrong, yea, robbery and murder, go not out of their streets! These Christian families, torn asunder with envy, jealousy, anger, domestic jars, without number, without end! Yea, what is most dreadful, most to be lamented of all, these Christian Churches!—churches ("Tell it not in Gath"; but, alas, how can we hide it, either from Jews, Turks, or Pagans?) that bear the name of Christ, the Prince of Peace, and wage continual war with each other; that convert sinners by burning them alive; that are "drunk with the blood of the saints!"

Does this praise belong only to "Babylon the Great, the mother of harlots and abominations of the earth"? Nay, verily; but Reformed Churches (so called) have fairly learned to tread in her steps. Protestant Churches too know to persecute, when they have power in their hands, even unto blood. And, meanwhile, how do they also anathematize each other! Devote each other to the nethermost hell! What wrath, what contention, what malice, what bitterness, is everywhere found among them, even where they agree in essentials, and only differ in opinions, or in the circumstantials of religion! Who follows after only the "things that make for peace, and things wherewith one may edify another"? O God! How long? Shall thy promise fail?

Fear it not, ye little flock! Against hope, believe in hope! It is your Father's good pleasure yet to renew the face of the earth. Surely all these things shall come to an end, and the inhabitants of the earth shall learn righteousness. "Nation shall not lift up sword against nation, neither shall they know war any more." "The mountains of the Lord's house shall be established on the top of the mountains"; and "all the kingdoms of the earth shall become the kingdoms of our God." "They shall not" then "hurt or destroy in all his holy mountain"; but they shall call their "walls salvation, and their gates praise." They shall all be without spot or blemish, loving one another, even as Christ has loved us.

Be thou part of the first-fruits, if the harvest is not yet. Do thou love your neighbor as yourself. The Lord God fill your heart with such a love to every soul, that you may be ready to lay down your life for his sake! May your soul continually overflow with love, swallowing up every unkind and unholy temper, till he call you up into the region of love, there to reign with him for ever and ever!

IMITATORS OF CHRIST

Blessed are the pure in heart: for they shall see God. Blessed are the peacemakers: for they shall be called the children of God. Blessed are they which are persecuted for righteousness' sake: for theirs is the kingdom of heaven. Blessed are you, when men shall revile you, and persecute you, and shall say all manner of evil against you falsely, for my sake. Rejoice, and be exceeding glad: for great is your reward in heaven. For so persecuted they the prophets which were before you.

—Matthew 5:8–12

I. Blessed Are the Pure in Heart

1. How excellent things are spoken of the love of our neighbor! It is "the fulfilling of the law," "the end of the commandment." Without this, all we have, all we do, all we suffer, is of no value in the sight of God. But it is that love of our neighbor which springs from the love of God: otherwise itself is nothing worth. It behooves us, therefore, to examine

well upon what foundation our love of our neighbor stands; whether it is really built upon the love of God; whether we do "love him because he first loved us;" whether we are pure in heart: for this is the foundation which shall never be moved. "Blessed are the pure in heart: for they shall see God."

Purity in the Inward Parts

2. "The pure in heart" are they whose hearts God has "purified even as he is pure"; who are purified, through faith in the blood of Jesus, from every unholy affection; who, being "cleansed from all filthiness of flesh and spirit, perfect holiness in the" loving "fear of God." They are, through the power of his grace, purified from pride, by the deepest poverty of spirit; from anger, from every unkind or turbulent passion, by meekness and gentleness; from every desire but to please and enjoy God, to know and love him more and more, by that hunger and thirst after righteousness which now engrosses their whole soul: so that now they love the Lord their God with all their heart, and with all their soul, and mind, and strength.

3. But how little has this purity of heart been regarded by the false teachers of all ages! They have taught men barely to abstain from such outward impurities as God has forbidden by name; but they did not strike at the heart; and by not guarding against, they in effect countenanced, inward corruptions.

A remarkable instance of this, our Lord has given us in the following words: "Ye have heard, that it was said by them of old time, Thou shalt not commit adultery" (Matt. 5:27); and, in explaining this, those blind leaders of the blind only insist on men's abstaining from the outward act. "But I say unto you, whosoever looketh on a woman to lust after her has committed adultery with her already in his heart" (Matt. 5:28). For God requireth truth in the inward parts: he searches the heart, and tries the reins; and if you incline unto iniquity with your heart, the Lord will not hear you.

Allow No Occasion for Impurity

4. And God admits no excuse for retaining anything which is an occasion of impurity. Therefore, "if thy right eye offend thee, pluck it out, and cast it from thee: for it is profitable for thee that one of thy members should perish, and not that thy whole body should be cast into hell" (Matt. 5:29). If persons as dear to you as your right eye be an occasion of your thus offending God, a means of exciting unholy desire in your soul, delay not; forcibly separate from them. "And if thy right hand offend thee, cut it off, and cast it from thee: for it is profitable for thee that one of thy members should perish, and not that thy whole body should be cast into hell" (Matt. 5:30). If any who seem as necessary to you as thy right hand be an occasion of sin, of impure desire; even though it were never to go beyond the heart, never to break out in word or action; constrain yourself to an entire and final parting; cut them off at a stroke; give them up to God. Any loss, whether of pleasure, or substance, or friends, is preferable to the loss of your soul.

Two steps only it may not be improper to take before such an absolute and final separation. First, try whether the unclean spirit may not be driven out by fasting and prayer, and by carefully abstaining from every action, and word, and look, which you have found to be an occasion of evil. Secondly, if you are not by this means delivered, ask counsel of him that watches over your soul, or, at least, of some who have experience in the ways of God, touching the time and manner of that separation; but confer not with flesh and blood, lest you be "given up to a strong delusion to believe a lie."

Purity in Marriage

5. Nor may marriage itself, holy and honorable as it is, be used as a pretense for giving a loose to our desires. Indeed, "it has been said, Whosoever will put away his wife, let him give her a writing of divorcement." And then all was well; though he alleged no cause, but that he did not like her, or liked another better. "But I say unto you, that whosoever shall put away his wife, saving for the case of fornication" (that is, adultery; the word πορνεία signifying unchastity in general, either in the married or unmarried state), "causes her to commit adultery," if she marry again. "And whosoever shall marry her that is put away commits adultery" (Matt 5:31, 32).

All polygamy is clearly forbidden in these words, wherein our Lord expressly declares, that for any woman who has a husband alive, to marry again is adultery. By parity of reason, it is adultery for any man to marry again, so long as he has a wife alive, yea, although they were divorced; unless that divorce had been for the cause of adultery: in that only case there is no scripture which forbids to marry again.

They Shall See God

6. Such is the purity of heart which God requires, and works in those who believe on the Son of his love. And "blessed are" they who are thus "pure in heart; for they shall see God." He will "manifest himself unto them," not only "as he does not unto the world," but as he does not always to his own children. He will bless them with the clearest communications of his Spirit, the most intimate "fellowship with the Father and with the Son." He will cause his presence to go continually before them, and the light of his countenance to shine upon them. It is the ceaseless prayer of their heart, "I beseech you, show me your glory"; and they have the petition they ask of him.

They now see him by faith (the veil of the flesh being made as it were transparent), even in these his lowest works, in all that surrounds them, in all that God has created and made. They see him in the height above, and in the depth beneath; they see him filling all in all. The pure in heart see all things full of God. They see Him in the firmament of heaven; in the moon, walking in brightness; in the sun, when he rejoices as a giant to run his course. They see him "making the clouds his chariots, and walking upon the wings of the wind." They see him "preparing rain for the earth, and blessing the increase of it; giving grass for the cattle, and green herb for the use of man." They see the Creator of all, wisely governing all, and "upholding all things by the word of his power." "O Lord our Governor, how excellent is your name in all the world!"

7. In all his providences relating to themselves, to their souls or bodies, the pure in heart do more particularly see God. They see his hand ever over them for good; giving them all things in weight and measure, numbering the hairs of their head, making a hedge round about them and all that they have, and disposing all the circumstances of their life according to the depth both of his wisdom and mercy.

8. But in a more especial manner they see God in his ordinances. Whether they appear in the great congregation, to "pay him the honor due unto his name," "and worship him in the beauty of holiness"; or "enter into their closets," and there pour out their souls before their "Father which is in secret"; whether they search the oracles of God, or hear the ambassadors of Christ proclaiming glad tidings of salvation; or, by eating of that bread, and drinking of that cup, "show forth his death till he come" in the clouds of heaven—in all these his appointed ways, they find such a near approach as cannot be expressed. They see him, as it were, face to face, and "talk with

him, as a man talking with his friend—a fit preparation for those mansions above, wherein they shall see him as he is.

Purity in Discourse

9. But how far were they from seeing God, who, having heard "that it had been said by them of old time, Thou shalt not forswear thyself, but shalt perform unto the Lord thine oaths" (Matt. 5:33), interpreted it thus, Thou shalt not forswear thyself, when thou swearest by the Lord Jehovah. Thou "shalt perform unto the Lord" these your oaths"; but as to other oaths, he regards them not. So the Pharisees taught. They not only allowed all manner of swearing in common conversation; but accounted even forswearing a little thing, so they had not sworn by the peculiar name of God.

But our Lord here absolutely forbids all common swearing, as well as all false swearing; and shows the heinousness of both, by the same awful consideration, that every creature is God's, and he is everywhere present, in all, and over all. "I say unto you, Swear not at all; neither by heaven, for it is God's throne" (Matt. 5:34), and therefore, this is the same as to swear by him who sits upon the circle of the heavens; "nor by the earth; for it is his footstool" (Matt. 5:35), and he is as intimately present in earth as heaven. "Neither by Jerusalem; for it is the city of the great King"; and God is well known in her palaces. "Neither shall you swear by your head; because you can not make one hair white or black" (Matt. 5:36); because even this, it is plain, is not yours, but God's, the sole disposer of all in heaven and earth. "But let your communication" (Matt. 5:37), your conversation, your discourse with each other "be, Yea, yea; Nay, nay"; a bare, serious affirming or denying. "For whatsoever is more than these comes of evil": ἐκ τοῦ πονηροῦ ἐστίν, *is of the evil one*; proceeds from the devil, and is a mark of his children.

10. That our Lord does not here forbid the "swearing in judgment and truth," when we are required so to do by a magistrate, may appear: (1.) From the occasion of this part of his discourse—the abuse he was here reproving—which was false swearing and common swearing; the swearing before a magistrate being quite out of the question. (2.) From the very words wherein he forms the general conclusion: "Let your communication," or discourse, "be, Yea, yea; Nay, nay." (3.) From his own example; for he answered himself upon oath, when required by a magistrate. When the high priest said unto him, "I adjure you by the living God, that you tell us whether you are the Christ, the Son of God"; Jesus immediately answered in the affirmative, "You have said" (that is, the truth); "nevertheless" (or rather, moreover), "I say unto you, Hereafter shall ye see the Son of man sitting on the right hand of power, and coming in the clouds of heaven" (Matt. 26:63, 64). (4.) From the example of God, even the Father, who, "willing the more abundantly to show unto the heirs of promise the immutability of his counsel, confirmed it by an oath" (Heb. 6:17). (5.) From the example of St. Paul, who we think had the Spirit of God, and well understood the mind of his Master. "God is my witness," says he, to the Romans, "that without ceasing I make mention of you always in my prayers" (Rom. 1:9): to the Corinthians, "I call God to record upon my soul, that to spare you I came not as yet unto Corinth" (2 Cor. 1:23); and to the Philippians, "God is my record, how greatly I long after you in the affections of Jesus Christ" (Phil. 1:8). Hence it undeniably appears that, if the apostle knew the meaning of his Lord's words, they do not forbid swearing on weighty occasions, even to one another: how much less before a magistrate! And, lastly, from that assertion of the great apostle, concerning solemn swearing in general (which it is impossible he could have mentioned without any touch of blame, if his Lord had totally forbidden it): "Men

verily swear by the greater"; by one greater than themselves; "and an oath for confirmation is to them the end of all strife" (Heb. 6:16).

11. But the great lesson which our blessed Lord inculcates here, and which he illustrates by this example, is, that God is in all things, and that we are to see the Creator in the glass of every creature; that we should use and look upon nothing as separate from God, which indeed is a kind of practical atheism; but, with a true magnificence of thought, survey heaven and earth, and all that is therein, as contained by God in the hollow of his hand, who by his intimate presence holds them all in being, who pervades and actuates the whole created frame, and is, in a true sense, the soul of universe.

II. Blessed Are the Peacemakers

1. Thus far our Lord has been more directly employed in teaching the religion of the heart. He has shown what Christians are to be. He proceeds to show, what they are to do also—how inward holiness is to exert itself in our outward conversation. "Blessed," says he, "are the peacemakers; for they shall be called the children of God."

2. "The peacemakers"—the word in the original is οἱ εἰρηνοποιοί. It is well known that εἰρήνη, *peace*, in the sacred writings, implies all manner of good; every blessing that relates either to the soul or the body, to time or eternity. Accordingly, when St. Paul, in the titles of his epistles, wishes grace and peace to the Romans or the Corinthians, it is as if he had said, "As a fruit of the free, undeserved love and favor of God, may you enjoy all blessings, spiritual and temporal; all the good things which God hath prepared for them that love him."

Peacemakers Detest Strife and Promote Goodwill

3. Hence we may easily learn, in how wide a sense the term peacemakers is to be understood. In its literal meaning it implies those lovers of God and man who utterly detest and abhor all strife and debate, all variance and contention; and accordingly labor with all their might, either to prevent this fire of hell from being kindled, or, when it is kindled, from breaking out, or, when it is broke out, from spreading any farther. They endeavor to calm the stormy spirits of men, to quiet their turbulent passions, to soften the minds of contending parties, and, if possible, reconcile them to each other. They use all innocent arts, and employ all their strength, all the talents which God has given them, as well to preserve peace where it is, as to restore it where it is not.

It is the joy of their heart to promote, to confirm, to increase, mutual goodwill among men, but more especially among the children of God, however distinguished by things of smaller importance; that as they have all "one Lord, one faith," as they are all "called in one hope of their calling," so they may all "walk worthy of the vocation wherewith they are called; with all lowliness and meekness, with long-suffering, forbearing one another in love; endeavoring to keep the unity of the Spirit in the bond of peace."

Peacemakers Do Good to All

4. *Doing good on every occasion to all men.* But in the full extent of the word, a peacemaker is one that, as he has opportunity, "does good unto all men"; one that, being filled with the love of God and of all mankind, cannot confine the expressions of it to his own family, or friends, or acquaintance, or party, or to those of his own opinions—no, nor those who are partakers

of like precious faith; but steps over all these narrow bounds, that he may do good to every man, that he may, some way or other, manifest his love to neighbors and strangers, friends and enemies. He does good to them all, as he has opportunity, that is, on every possible occasion; "redeeming the time," in order thereto; "buying up every opportunity, improving every hour, losing no moment wherein he may profit another. He does good, not of one particular kind, but good in general, in every possible way; employing herein all his talents of every kind, all his powers and faculties of body and soul, all his fortune, his interest, his reputation; desiring only that when his Lord cometh he may say, "Well done, good and faithful servant!"

5. *Doing good to the bodies of men.* He does good, to the uttermost of his power, even to the bodies of all men. He rejoices to "deal his bread to the hungry," and to "cover the naked with a garment." Is any a stranger? He takes him in, and relieves him according to his necessities. Are any sick or in prison? He visits them, and administers such help as they stand most in need of. And all this he does, not as unto man; but remembering him that has said, "Inasmuch as you have done it unto one of the least of these my brethren, you have done it unto me."

6. *Doing good to the souls of men.* How much more does he rejoice if he can do any good to the soul of any man! This power, indeed, belongs unto God. It is he only that changes the heart, without which every other change is lighter than vanity. Nevertheless, it pleases him who worketh all in all, to help man chiefly by man; to convey his own power, and blessing, and love, through one man to another. Therefore, although it be certain that "the help which is done upon earth, God doth it himself"; yet has no man need, on this account to stand idle in his vineyard. The peace-maker cannot: he is ever laboring therein, and, as an instrument in God's hand, preparing the ground for his Master's use, or sowing the seed of the kingdom,

or watering what is already sown, if haply God may give the increase.

According to the measure of grace which he has received, he uses all diligence, either to reprove the gross sinner, to reclaim those who run on headlong in the broad way of destruction; or "to give light to them that sit in darkness," and are ready to "perish for lack of knowledge"; or to "support the weak, to lift up the hands that hang down, and the feeble knees"; or to bring back and heal that which was lame and turned out of the way. Nor is he less zealous to confirm those who are already striving to enter in at the straight gate; to strengthen those that stand, that they may "run with patience the race which is set before them"; to build up in their most holy faith those that know in whom they have believed; to exhort them to stir up the gift of God which is in them, that daily growing in grace, "an entrance may be ministered unto them abundantly into the everlasting kingdom of our Lord and Savior Jesus Christ."

For They Shall Be Called Children of God

7. "Blessed" are they who are thus continually employed in the work of faith and the labor of love; "for they shall be called," that is, shall be (a common Hebraism) "the children "of God." God shall continue unto them the Spirit of adoption, yea, shall pour it more abundantly into their hearts. He shall bless them with all the blessings of his children. He shall acknowledge them as sons before angels and men; "and, if sons, then heirs; heirs of God, and joint heirs with Christ."

III. Blessed Are They Who Are Persecuted for Righteousness' Sake

1. One would imagine such a person as has been above described, so full of genuine humility, so unaffectedly serious,

so mild and gentle, so free from all selfish design, so devoted
to God, and such an active lover of men, should be the darling
of mankind. But our Lord was better acquainted with human
nature in its present state. He therefore closes the character
of this man of God with showing him the treatment he is to
expect in the world. "Blessed," says he, "are they which are
persecuted for righteousness' sake; for theirs is the kingdom
of heaven."

The Righteous Will Be Persecuted

2. In order to understand this throughly, let us, first,
inquire, Who are they that are persecuted? And this we may
easily learn from St. Paul: "As of old, he that was born after the
flesh persecuted him that was born after the Spirit, even so it is
now" (Gal. 4:29). "Yea," says the apostle, "and all that will live
godly in Christ Jesus, shall suffer persecution" (2 Tim. 3:12).
The same we are taught by St. John: "Marvel not, my brethren,
if the world hate you. We know that we have passed from death
unto life, because we love the brethren" (1 John 3:13–14). As
if he had said, The brethren, the Christians, cannot be loved,
but by them who have passed from death unto life. And most
expressly by our Lord: "If the world hate you, you know that
it hated me before it hated you. If you were of the world, the
world would love its own; but because you are not of the world,
therefore the world hates you. Remember the word that I said
unto you, The servant is not greater than his lord. If they have
persecuted me, they will also persecute you" (John 15:18ff.).

By all these Scriptures it manifestly appears who they are
that are persecuted; namely, the righteous: he "that is born of
the Spirit," "all that will live godly in Christ Jesus," they that
are "passed from death unto life," those who are "not of the
world"; all those who are meek and lowly in heart, that mourn
for God, that hunger after his likeness; all that love God and

their neighbor, and therefore, as they have opportunity, do good unto all men.

They Are Persecuted for Righteousness' Sake

3. If it be, secondly, inquired, why they are persecuted, the answer is equally plain and obvious. It is "for righteousness' sake"; because they are righteous; because they are born after the Spirit; because they "will live godly in Christ Jesus;" because they "are not of the world." Whatever may be pretended, this is the real cause. Be their infirmities more or less, still, if it were not for this, they would be borne with, and the world would love its own.

They are persecuted, because they are *poor in spirit*; that is, say the world, "poor-spirited, mean, dastardly souls, good for nothing, not fit to live in the world"; because they *mourn*: "They are such dull, heavy, lumpish creatures, enough to sink anyone's spirits that sees them! They are mere death-heads; they kill innocent mirth, and spoil company wherever they come"; because they are *meek*: "Tame, passive fools, just fit to be trampled upon"; because they *hunger and thirst after righteousness*: "A parcel of hot-brained enthusiasts, gaping after they know not what, not content with rational religion, but running mad after raptures and inward feelings" because they are *merciful*, lovers of all, lovers of the evil and unthankful: "Encouraging all manner of wickedness; nay, tempting people to do mischief by impunity, and men who, it is to be feared, have their own religion still to seek; very loose in their principles"; because they are *pure in heart*: "Uncharitable creatures, that damn all the world, but those that are of their own sort! Blasphemous wretches, that pretend to make God a liar, to live without sin!"

Above all, because they are *peacemakers*; because they take all opportunities of doing good to all men. This is the grand reason why they have been persecuted in all ages, and will be till the restitution of all things:

If they would but keep their religion to themselves, it would be tolerable. But it is this spreading their errors, this infecting so many others, which is not to be endured. They do so much mischief in the world, that they ought to be tolerated no longer. It is true, the men do some things well enough; they relieve some of the poor: But this, too, is only done to gain the more to their party; and so, in effect, to do the more mischief!

Thus the men of the world sincerely think and speak. And the more the kingdom of God prevails, the more the peace-makers are enabled to propagate lowliness, meekness, and all other divine tempers, the more mischief is done, in their account. Consequently, the more are they enraged against the authors of this, and the more vehemently will they persecute them.

They Are Persecuted by the World

4. Let us, thirdly, inquire, Who are they that persecute them? St. Paul answers, "He that is born after the flesh"— everyone who is not "born of the Spirit," or, at least, desirous so to be; all that do not at least labor to "live godly in Christ Jesus"; all that are not "passed from death unto life," and, consequently, cannot "love the brethren"; "the world," that is, according to our Savior's account, they who "know not him that sent me; they who know not God, even the loving, pardoning God, by the teaching of his own Spirit.

The reason is plain: the spirit which is in the world is directly opposite to the Spirit which is of God. It must therefore needs be, that those who are of the world will be opposite to those who are of God. There is the utmost contrariety between them, in all their opinions, their desires, designs, and tempers. And hitherto the leopard and the kid cannot lie down in peace together. The proud, because he is proud, cannot but persecute the lowly; the light and airy, those that mourn. And so in every other kind; the unlikeness of disposition (were there no other) being a perpetual ground of enmity. Therefore, were it only on this account, all the servants of the devil will persecute the children of God.

They Will Be Persecuted under God's Wise Direction

5. Should it be inquired, fourthly, how they will persecute them, it may be answered in general, just in that manner and measure which the wise Disposer of all sees will be most for his glory—will tend most to his children's growth in grace, and the enlargement of his own kingdom. There is no one branch of God's government of the world which is more to be admired than this. His ear is never heavy to the threatenings of the persecutor, or the cry of the persecuted. His eye is ever open, and his hand stretched out to direct even the minutest circumstance. When the storm shall begin, how high it shall rise, which way it shall point its course, when and how it shall end, are all determined by his unerring wisdom. The ungodly are only a sword of his; an instrument which he uses as it pleases him, and which itself, when the gracious ends of his providence are answered, is cast into the fire.

At some rare times, as when Christianity was planted first, and while it was taking root in the earth; as also when the pure doctrine of Christ began to be planted again in our nation; God permitted the storm to rise high, and his children were called to resist unto blood. There was a peculiar reason why he suffered this with regard to the apostles, that their evidence might be the more unexceptionable. But from the annals of the church we learn another, and a far different reason, why he suffered the heavy persecutions which rose in the second and third centuries; namely, because "the mystery of iniquity" did so strongly "work"; because of the monstrous corruptions which even then reigned in the church: these God chastised, and at the same time strove to heal, by those severe but necessary visitations.

Perhaps the same observation may be made, with regard to the grand persecution in our own land. God had dealt very graciously with our nation. He had poured out various blessings upon us: he had given us peace abroad and at home; and a king, wise and good beyond his years; and, above all, he had caused the pure light of his gospel to arise and shine amongst us. But what return did he find? "He looked for righteousness; but behold a cry!"—a cry of oppression and wrong, of ambition and injustice, of malice, and fraud, and covetousness. Yea, the cry of those who even then expired in the flames entered into the ears of the Lord of Sabaoth. It was then God arose to maintain his own cause against those that held the truth in unrighteousness. Then he sold them into the hands of their persecutors, by a judgment mixed with mercy; an affliction to punish, and yet a medicine to heal, the grievous backslidings of his people.

6. But it is seldom God suffers the storm to rise so high as torture, or death, or bonds, or imprisonment. Whereas his children are frequently called to endure those lighter kinds of persecution; they frequently suffer the estrangement of kinsfolk, the loss of the friends that were as their own soul. They find the truth of their Lord's word (concerning the event, though not the design of his coming): "Suppose ye that I am come to give peace on earth? I tell you, Nay; but rather division" (Luke 12:51). And hence will naturally follow loss of business or employment, and consequently of substance. But all these circumstances likewise are under the wise direction of God, who allots to everyone what is most expedient for him.

The Righteous Will Be Reviled

7. But the persecution which attends all the children of God is that our Lord describes in the following words: "Blessed are you, when men shall revile you, and persecute you,"—shall persecute by reviling you—"and say all manner of evil against you, falsely, for my sake." This cannot fail; it is the very badge of our discipleship; it is one of the seals of our calling; it is a sure portion entailed on all the children of God: if we have it not, we are bastards and not sons. Straight through evil report, as well as good report, lies the only way to the kingdom. The meek, serious, humble, zealous lovers of God and man are of good report among their brethren; but of evil report with the world, who count and treat them "as the filth and offscouring of all things."

8. Indeed some have supposed that before the fullness of the Gentiles shall come in the scandal of the cross will cease; that God will cause Christians to be esteemed and loved, even by those who are as yet in their sins. Yea, and sure it is, that even now he at some times suspends the contempt as well as the fierceness of men: "he makes a man's enemies to be at peace with him for a season, and gives him favor with his bitterest persecutors."

But setting aside this exempt case, the scandal of the cross is not yet ceased; but a man may say still, "If I please men, I am not the servant of Christ. Let no man therefore regard that pleasing suggestion (pleasing doubtless to flesh and blood), that bad men only pretend to hate and despise them that are good, but do indeed love and esteem them in their hearts." Not so: they may employ them sometimes; but it is for their own profit. They may put confidence in them; for they know their ways are not like other men's. But still they love them not; unless so far as the Spirit of God may be striving with them.

Our Savior's words are express: "If you were of the world, the world would love its own; but because you are not of the world, therefore the world hates you." Yea (setting aside what exceptions may be made by the preventing grace or the peculiar providence, of God), it hates them as cordially and sincerely as ever it did their Master.

The Proper Response to Persecution

9. *Do not seek it out.* It remains only to inquire, How are the children of God to behave with regard to persecution? And, first, they ought not knowingly or designedly to bring it upon themselves. This is contrary, both to the example and advice of our Lord and all his apostles; who teach us not only not to seek, but to avoid it, as far as we can, without injuring our conscience; without giving up any part of that righteousness which we are to prefer before life itself. So our Lord expressly, "When they persecute you in this city, flee ye into another," which is indeed, when it can be taken, the most unexceptionable way of avoiding persecution.

10. *Do not think you can avoid it.* Yet think not that you can always avoid it, either by this or any other means. If ever that idle imagination steals into your heart, put it to flight by that earnest caution, "Remember the word that I said unto you, "The servant is not greater than his Lord. If they have persecuted me, they will also persecute you." "Be ye wise as serpents, and harmless as doves." But will this screen you from persecution? Not unless you have more wisdom than your Master, or more innocence than the Lamb of God.

Do not desire to avoid it. Neither desire to avoid it, to escape it wholly; for if you do, you are none of his. If you escape the persecution, you escape the blessing; the blessing of those who are persecuted for righteousness' sake. If you are not persecuted for righteousness' sake, you cannot enter into the kingdom of heaven. "If we suffer with him, we shall also reign with him. But if we deny him, he will also deny us."

11. *Rejoice in it.* Nay, rather, "rejoice and be exceeding glad," when men persecute you for his sake; when they persecute you by reviling you, and by "saying all manner of evil against you falsely"; which they will not fail to mix with every kind of persecution. They must blacken you to excuse themselves: "For so persecuted they the prophets which were before you!"— those who were most eminently holy in heart and life; yea, and all the righteous which ever have been from the beginning of the world. Rejoice, because by his mark also you know unto whom you belong. And, because great is your reward in heaven,"—the reward purchased by the blood of the covenant, and freely bestowed in proportion to your sufferings, as well as to your holiness of heart and life. Be exceeding glad"; knowing that "these light afflictions, which are but for a moment, work out for you a far more exceeding and eternal weight of glory."

12. *Persevere in meekness and love.* Meantime, let no persecution turn you out of the way of lowliness and meekness, of love and beneficence. "You have heard" indeed "that it has been said, An eye for an eye, and a tooth for a tooth" (Matt. 5:38); and your miserable teachers have hence allowed you to avenge yourselves, to return evil for evil. "But I say unto you, that you resist not evil." Not thus; not by returning it in kind. "But, rather than do this, "whosoever smites you on your right cheek, turn to him the other also. And if any man will sue you at the law, and take away your coat, let him have your cloak also. And whosoever shall compel you to go a mile, go with him two."

So invincible let your meekness be. And be your love suitable thereto. "Give to him that asks you, and from him that would borrow of you turn not away." Only give not away that which is another man's, that which is not your own. Therefore, (1.) Take care to owe no man anything: for what you owe is not your own, but another man's. (2.) Provide for those of your own household: this also God has required of you; and what is necessary to sustain them in life and godliness is also not your own. Then, (3.) give or lend all that remains, from day to day, or from year to year: only, first, seeing you can not give or lend to all, remember the household of faith.

13. *Love your enemies.* The meekness and love we are to feel, the kindness we are to show to them which persecute us for righteousness' sake, our blessed Lord describes farther in the following verses: O that they were graven upon our hearts! "You have heard that it has been said, You shall love your neighbor, and hate your enemy" (Matt. 5:43ff.). God indeed had said only the former part, "You shall love your neighbor"; the children of the devil had added the latter, "and hate your enemy." "But I say unto you": (1.) "Love your enemies." See that you bear a tender goodwill to those who are most bitter of spirit against you; who wish you all manner of evil. (2.) "Bless them that curse you." Are there any whose bitterness of spirit breaks forth in bitter words; who are continually cursing and reproaching you when you are present, and "saying all evil against you" when absent? So much the rather do you bless: in conversing with them use all mildness and softness of language. Reprove them, by repeating a better lesson before them; by showing them how they ought to have spoken. And, in speaking of them, say all the good you can, without violating the rules of truth and justice.

(3.) "Do good to them that hate you." Let your actions show, that you are as real in love as they in hatred. Return good for evil. "Be not overcome of evil, but overcome evil with good." (4). If you can do nothing more, at least "pray for them that despitefully use you and persecute you." You can never be disabled from doing this; nor can all their malice or violence hinder you. Pour out your souls to God, not only for those who did this once, but now repent. This is a little thing: "If thy brother, seven times a day, turn and say unto you, I repent" (Luke 17:4); that is, if, after ever so many relapses, he give you reason to believe that he is really and throughly changed; then you shall forgive him, so as to trust him, to put him in your bosom, as if he had never sinned against thee at all.

But pray for, wrestle with God for, those that do not repent, that now despitefully use you and persecute you. Thus far forgive them, "not until seven times only, but until seventy times seven" (Matt. 18:22). Whether they repent or no, yea, though they appear farther and farther from it, yet show them this instance of kindness: "That you may be the children," that you may approve yourselves the genuine children, "of your Father which is in heaven"; who shows his goodness by giving such blessings as they are capable of, even to his stubbornest enemies; "who makes his sun to rise on the evil and on the good, and sendeth rain on the just and on the unjust." "For if you love them which love you, what reward have you? Do not even the publicans the same?" (Matt. 5:46)—who pretend to no religion; whom you yourselves acknowledge to be without God in the world.

"And if you salute," show kindness in word or deed to "your brethren," your friends or kinsfolk, "only, what do you more than others?"—than those who have no religion at all? "Do not even the publicans so?" (Matt. 5:47). Nay, but follow a better pattern than them. In patience, in longsuffering, in mercy, in beneficence of every kind, to all, even to your bitterest persecutors; "be ye," Christians, "perfect," in kind, though not in degree, "even as your Father which is in heaven is perfect" (Matt. 5:48).

IV. Conclusion

Behold Christianity in its native form, as delivered by its great Author! This is the genuine religion of Jesus Christ! Such he presents it to him whose eyes are opened. See a picture of God, so far as he is imitable by man! A picture drawn by God's own hand: "Behold, you despisers, and wonder, and perish!" Or rather, wonder and adore! Rather cry out, "Is this the religion of Jesus of Nazareth the religion which I persecuted! Let me no more be found even to fight against God. Lord, what would you have me to do?" What beauty appears in the whole! How just a symmetry! What exact proportion in every part! How desirable is the happiness here described! How venerable, how lovely the holiness! This is the spirit of religion; the quintessence of it.

These are indeed the fundamentals of Christianity. O that we may not be hearers of it only!—"like a man beholding his own face in a glass, who goes his way, and straightway forgets what manner of man he was." Nay, but let us steadily "look into this perfect law of liberty, and continue therein." Let us not rest until every line thereof is transcribed into our own hearts. Let us watch, and pray, and believe, and love, and "strive for the mastery," till every part of it shall appear in our soul, graven there by the finger of God; till we are "holy as he which has called us is holy, perfect as our Father which is in heaven is perfect!"

SALT OF THE EARTH, LIGHT OF THE WORLD

Ye are the salt of the earth: but if the salt hath lost its savor, wherewith shall it be salted? It is thenceforth good for nothing but to be cast out, and trodden under foot of men. Ye are the light of the world. A city that is set on an hill cannot be hid. Neither do men light a candle and put it under a bushel, but on a candlestick; and it giveth light to all that are in the house. Let your light so shine before men that they may see your good works, and glorify your Father which is in heaven.
—Matthew 5:13–16

Introduction

1. The beauty of holiness, of that inward man of the heart which is renewed after the image of God, cannot but strike every eye which God has opened, every enlightened understanding. The ornament of a meek, humble, loving spirit will

at least excite the approbation of all those who are capable in any degree of discerning spiritual good and evil. From the hour men begin to emerge out of the darkness which covers the giddy, unthinking world, they cannot but perceive how desirable a thing it is to be thus transformed into the likeness of him that created us. This inward religion bears the shape of God so visibly impressed upon it, that a soul must be wholly immersed in flesh and blood when he can doubt of its divine original. We may say of this, in a secondary sense, even as of the Son of God himself, that it is the ἀπαύγασμα τῆς δόξης καὶ χαρακτὴρ τῆς ὑποστάσεως αὐτοῦ, *brightness of his glory, the express image of his person, the beaming forth of his eternal glory;* and yet so tempered and softened, that even the children of men may herein see God and live; χαρακτὴρ τῆς ὑποστάσεως αὐτοῦ, *the character, the stamp, the living impression, of his person,* who is the fountain of beauty and love, the original source of all excellency and perfection.

2. If religion, therefore, were carried no farther than this, they could have no doubt concerning it; they should have no objection against pursuing it with the whole ardor of their souls. "But why," say they, "is it clogged with other things? What need of loading it with doing and suffering? These are what damps the vigor of the soul, and sinks it down to earth again. Is it not enough to "follow after charity"; to soar upon the wings of love? Will it not suffice to worship God, who is a Spirit, with the spirit of our minds, without encumbering ourselves with outward things, or even thinking of them at all? Is it not better that the whole extent of our thought should be taken up with high and heavenly contemplation; and that instead of busying ourselves at all about externals, we should only commune with God in our hearts?

3. Many eminent men have spoken thus, have advised us "to cease from all outward action"; wholly to withdraw from

the world; to leave the body behind us; to abstract ourselves from all sensible things; to have no concern at all about outward religion, but to work all virtues in the will; as the far more excellent way, more perfective of the soul, as well as more acceptable to God.

4. It needed not that any should tell our Lord of this masterpiece of the wisdom from beneath, this fairest of all the devices wherewith Satan has ever perverted the right ways of the Lord! And O! what instruments has he found, from time to time, to employ in this his service, to wield this grand engine of hell against some of the most important truths of God!— men that would "deceive, if it were possible, the very elect," the men of faith and love; yea, that have for a season deceived and led away no inconsiderable number of them, who have fallen in all ages into the gilded snare, and hardly escaped with the skin of their teeth.

5. But has our Lord been wanting on his part? Has he not sufficiently guarded us against this pleasing delusion? Has he not armed us here with armor of proof against Satan "transformed into an angel of light"? Yea, verily: he here defends, in the clearest and strongest manner, the active, patient religion he had just described. What can be fuller and plainer than the words he immediately subjoins to what he had said of doing and suffering? "You are the salt of the earth: but if the salt have lost his savor, wherewith shall it be salted? It is thenceforth good for nothing but to be cast out, and trodden under foot of men. You are the light of the world. A city that is set on an hill cannot be hid. Neither do men light a candle and put it under a bushel, but on a candlestick; and it giveth light to all that are in the house. Let your light so shine before men, that they may see your good works, and glorify your Father which is in heaven."

In order fully to explain and enforce these important words, I shall endeavor to show, first, that Christianity is essentially a social religion, and that to turn it into a solitary one is to destroy it; secondly, that to conceal this religion is impossible, as well as utterly contrary to the design of its Author. I shall, thirdly, answer some objections; and conclude the whole with a practical application.

I. Christianity Is a Social Religion

1. First, I shall endeavor to show that Christianity is essentially a social religion; and that to turn it into a solitary religion is indeed to destroy it.

By Christianity I mean that method of worshipping God which is here revealed to man by Jesus Christ. When I say, "This is essentially a social religion," I mean not only that it cannot subsist so well, but that it cannot subsist at all, without society, without living and conversing with other men. And in showing this, I shall confine myself to those considerations which will arise from the very discourse before us. But if this be shown, then doubtless, to turn this religion into a solitary one is to destroy it.

The Proper Place for Solitude

Not that we can in any way condemn the intermixing solitude or retirement with society. This is not only allowable but expedient; nay, it is necessary, as daily experience shows, for everyone that either already is, or desires to be, a real Christian. It can hardly be that we should spend one entire day in a continued intercourse with men without suffering loss in our soul, and in some measure grieving the Holy Spirit of God. We have need daily to retire from the world, at least morning and evening, to converse with God, to commune more freely with our Father which is in secret. Nor indeed can a man of experience condemn even longer seasons of religious retirement, so they do not imply any neglect of the worldly employ wherein the providence of God has placed us.

2. Yet such retirement must not swallow up all our time; this would be to destroy, not advance, true religion. For, that the religion described by our Lord in the foregoing words cannot subsist without society, without our living and conversing with other men, is manifest from hence, that several of the most essential branches thereof can have no place if we have no intercourse with the world.

Christian Dispositions in the Context of Society

3. There is no disposition, for instance, which is more essential to Christianity than meekness. Now although this, as it implies resignation to God, or patience in pain and sickness, may subsist in a desert, in a hermit's cell, in total solitude; yet as it implies (which it no less necessarily does) mildness, gentleness, and long-suffering, it cannot possibly have a being, it has no place under heaven, without an intercourse with other men. So that to attempt turning this into a solitary virtue is to destroy it from the face of the earth.

4. Another necessary branch of true Christianity is peacemaking, or doing of good. That this is equally essential with any of the other parts of the religion of Jesus Christ, there can be no stronger argument to evince (and therefore it would be absurd to allege any other), than that it is here inserted in the original plan he has laid down of the fundamentals of his religion. Therefore, to set aside this is the same daring insult on the authority of our Great Master as to set aside mercifulness, purity of heart, or any other branch of his institution. But this is apparently set aside by all who call us to the wilderness; who recommend entire solitude either to the babes, or the young men, or the fathers in Christ. For will any man affirm that a solitary Christian (so called, though it is little less than a

contradiction in terms) can be a merciful man, that is, one that takes every opportunity of doing all good to all men? What can be more plain than that this fundamental branch of the religion of Jesus Christ cannot possibly subsist without society, without our living and conversing with other men?

5. "But is it not expedient, however," one might naturally ask, "to converse only with good men, only with those whom we know to be meek and merciful, holy of heart and holy of life? Is it not expedient to refrain from any conversation or intercourse with men of the opposite character, men who do not obey, perhaps do not believe, the gospel of our Lord Jesus Christ? The advice of St. Paul to the Christians at Corinth may seem to favor this: "I wrote unto you in an epistle not to company with fornicators" (1 Cor. 5:9). And it is certainly not advisable so to company with them, or with any of the workers of iniquity, as to have any particular familiarity, or any strictness of friendship with them. To contract or continue an intimacy with any such is no way expedient for a Christian. It must necessarily expose him to abundance of dangers and snares, out of which he can have no reasonable hope of deliverance.

But the apostle does not forbid us to have any intercourse at all, even with the men that know not God: "For then," says he, "ye must needs go out of the world," which he could never advise them to do. But, he subjoins, "If any man that is called a brother," that professes himself a Christian, "be a fornicator, or covetous, or an idolater, or a railer, or a drunkard, or an extortioner" (1 Cor. 5:11), now I have written unto you not to keep company with him; "with such an one, no not to eat." This must necessarily imply that we break off all familiarity, all intimacy of acquaintance with him. "Yet count him not," saith the apostle elsewhere, "as an enemy, but admonish him as a brother" (2 Thess. 3:15); plainly showing that even in such a case as this we are not to renounce all fellowship with him.

So that here is no advice to separate wholly, even from wicked men. Yea, these very words teach us quite the contrary.

6. Much more the words of our Lord; who is so far from directing us to break off all commerce with the world, that without it, according to his account of Christianity, we cannot be Christians at all. It would be easy to show that some intercourse even with ungodly and unholy men is absolutely needful, in order to the full exertion of every temper which he has described as the way of the kingdom; that it is indispensably necessary, in order to the complete exercise of poverty of spirit, of mourning, and of every other disposition which has a place here, in the genuine religion of Jesus Christ. Yea, it is necessary to the very being of several of them; of that meekness, for example, which, instead of demanding "an eye for an eye, or a tooth for a tooth," does "not resist evil," but causes us rather, when smitten "on the right cheek, to turn the other also"; of that mercifulness, whereby "we love our enemies, bless them that curse us, do good to them that hate us, and pray for them which despitefully use us and persecute us"; and of that complication of love and all holy tempers which is exercised in suffering for righteousness' sake. Now all these, it is clear, could have no being, were we to have no commerce with any but real Christians.

Salt of the Earth

7. Indeed were we wholly to separate ourselves from sinners, how could we possibly answer that character which our Lord gives us in these very words: "You" (Christians, you that are lowly, serious and meek; you that hunger after righteousness, that love God and man, that do good to all, and therefore suffer evil; you) "are the salt of the earth"? It is your very nature to season whatever is round about you. It is the nature of the divine savor which is in you, to spread to whatsoever you touch;

to diffuse itself, on every side, to all those among whom you are. This is the great reason why the providence of God has so mingled you together with other men, that whatever grace you have received of God may through you be communicated to others; that every holy temper, and word, and work of yours, may have an influence on them also. By this means a check will, in some measure, be given to the corruption which is in the world; and a small part, at least, saved from the general infection, and rendered holy and pure before God.

Savorless Salt

8. That we may the more diligently labor to season all we can with every holy and heavenly temper, our Lord proceeds to show the desperate state of those who do not impart the religion they have received; which indeed they cannot possibly fail to do, so long as it remains in their own hearts. "If the salt has lost its savor, wherewith shall it be salted? It is thenceforth good for nothing but to be cast out, and trodden under foot of men." If you who were holy and heavenly-minded, and consequently zealous of good works, have no longer that savor in yourselves, and do therefore no longer season others; if you are grown flat, insipid, dead, both careless of your own soul and useless to the souls of other men; wherewith shall you be salted? How shall you be recovered? What help? What hope? Can tasteless salt be restored to its savor? No; "it is thenceforth good for nothing but to be cast out," even as the mire in the streets, "and to be trodden under foot of men," to be overwhelmed with everlasting contempt.

If you had never known the Lord, there might have been hope, if you had never been "found in him." But what can you now say to that, his solemn declaration, just parallel to what he has here spoken? "Every branch in me that beareth not fruit, he, the Father, "taketh away. He that abideth in me, and I in him, bringeth forth much fruit." "If a man abide not in me," or do not bring forth fruit," "he is cast out as a branch, and withered; and men gather them," not to plant them again, but "to cast them into the fire" (John 15:2, 5, 6).

9. Toward those who have never tasted of the good word, God is indeed pitiful and of tender mercy. But justice takes place with regard to those who have tasted that the Lord is gracious, and have afterwards turned back "from the holy commandment" then "delivered to them." "For it is impossible for those who were once enlightened" (Heb. 6:4); in whose hearts God had once shined, to enlighten them with the knowledge of the glory of God in the face of Jesus Christ; "who have tasted of the heavenly gift" of redemption in his blood, the forgiveness of sins; "and were made partakers of the Holy Ghost," of lowliness, of meekness, and of the love of God and man shed abroad in their hearts by the Holy Ghost which was given unto them; and καὶ παραπεσόντας *have fallen away* (here is not a supposition, but a flat declaration of matter of fact), "to renew them again unto repentance; seeing they crucify to themselves the Son of God afresh, and put him to an open shame."

But that none may misunderstand these awful words, it should be carefully observed, (1.) who they are that are here spoken of; namely they, and they only, who were once thus "enlightened"; they only "who did taste of" that "heavenly gift, and were" thus "made partakers of the Holy Ghost." So that all who have not experienced these things are wholly unconcerned in this Scripture. (2.) What that falling away is which is here spoken of: it is an absolute, total apostasy. A believer may fall, and not fall away. He may fall and rise again. And if he should fall, even into sin, yet this case, dreadful as it is, is not desperate. For "we have an Advocate with the Father, Jesus Christ the righteous; and he is the propitiation for our sins." But let him above all things beware, lest his "heart be

hardened by the deceitfulness of sin;" lest he should sink lower
and lower, till he wholly fall away, till he become as salt that has
lost its savor. For if we thus sin wilfully, after we have received
the experimental "knowledge of the truth, there remains no
more sacrifice for sins; but a certain, fearful looking for of fiery
indignation, which shall devour the adversaries."

II. Christianity Cannot Be Concealed

1. "But although we may not wholly separate ourselves
from mankind, although it be granted we ought to season
them with the religion which God has wrought in our hearts,
yet may not this be done insensibly? May we not convey this
into others in a secret and almost imperceptible manner, so
that scarce anyone shall be able to observe how or when it is
done—even as salt conveys its own savor into that which is
seasoned thereby, without any noise, and without being liable
to any outward observation? And if so, although we do not
go out of the world, yet we may lie hid in it. We may thus far
keep our religion to ourselves; and not offend those whom we
cannot help."

2. Of this plausible reasoning of flesh and blood our Lord
was well aware also. And he has given a full answer to it in
those words which come now to be considered; in explaining
which, I shall endeavor to show, as I proposed to do in the
second place, that so long as true religion abides in our hearts,
it is impossible to conceal it, as well as absolutely contrary to
the design of its great Author.

A City Set on a Hill

And, first, it is impossible for any that have it, to conceal the
religion of Jesus Christ. This our Lord makes plain beyond all
contradiction, by a two-fold comparison: "You are the light of

the world: a city set upon an hill cannot be hid." You Christians "are the light of the world," with regard both to your tempers and actions. Your holiness makes you as conspicuous as the sun in the midst of heaven. As you cannot go out of the world, so neither can you stay in it without appearing to all mankind. You may not flee from men; and while you are among them, it is impossible to hide your lowliness and meekness, and those other dispositions whereby you aspire to be perfect as your Father which is in heaven is perfect. Love cannot be hid any more than light; and least of all, when it shines forth in action, when you exercise yourselves in the labor of love, in benefi-cence of every kind. As well may men think to hide a city, as to hide a Christian; yea, as well may they conceal a city set upon a hill, as a holy, zealous, active lover of God and man.

3. It is true, men who love darkness rather than light, because their deeds are evil, will take all possible pains to prove that the light which is in you is darkness. They will say evil, all manner of evil, falsely, of the good which is in you; they will lay to your charge that which is farthest from your thoughts, which is the very reverse of all you are, and all you do. And your patient continuance in well-doing, your meek suffering all things for the Lord's sake, your calm, humble joy in the midst of persecution, your unwearied labor to overcome evil with good, will make you still more visible and conspicuous than you were before.

4. So impossible it is, to keep our religion from being seen, unless we cast it away; so vain is the thought of hiding the light, unless by putting it out! Sure it is that a secret, unobserved reli-gion cannot be the religion of Jesus Christ. Whatever religion can be concealed, is not Christianity. If a Christian could be hid, he could not be compared to a city set upon an hill; to the light of the world, the sun shining from heaven, and seen by all the world below. Never, therefore, let it enter into the heart of

him whom God has renewed in the spirit of his mind, to hide that light, to keep his religion to himself; especially considering it is not only impossible to conceal true Christianity, but likewise absolutely contrary to the design of the great Author of it.

A Light Shining in the Darkness

5. This plainly appears from the following words: "Neither do men light a candle, to put it under a bushel." As if he had said, As men do not light a candle, only to cover and conceal it, so neither does God enlighten any soul with his glorious knowledge and love, to have it covered or concealed, either by prudence, falsely so called, or shame, or voluntary humility; to have it hid either in a desert, or in the world; either by avoiding men, or in conversing with them. "But they put it on a candlestick, and it giveth light to all that are in the house." In like manner, it is the design of God that every Christian should be in an open point of view; that he may give light to all around, that he may visibly express the religion of Jesus Christ.

6. Thus has God in all ages spoken to the world, not only by precept, but by example also. He has "not left himself without witness," in any nation where the sound of the gospel has gone forth, without a few who testified his truth by their lives as well as their words. These have been "as lights shining in a dark place." And from time to time they have been the means of enlightening some, of preserving a remnant, a little seed which was "counted unto the Lord for a generation." They have led a few poor sheep out of the darkness of the world, and guided their feet into the way of peace.

7. One might imagine that, where both Scripture and the reason of things speak so clearly and expressly, there could not be much advanced on the other side, at least not with any appearance of truth. But they who imagine thus know little of the depths of Satan. After all that Scripture and reason

have said, so exceeding plausible are the pretenses for solitary religion, for a Christian's going out of the world, or at least hiding himself in it, that we need all the wisdom of God to see through the snare, and all the power of God to escape it; so many and strong are the objections which have been brought against being social, open, active Christians.

III. Objections to Letting Our Light Shine

Religion Doesn't Lie in Outward Things

1. To answer these was the third thing which I proposed. And, first, it has been often objected, that religion does not lie in outward things, but in the heart, the inmost soul; that it is the union of the soul with God, the life of God in the soul of man; that outside religion is nothing worth; seeing God "delighteth not in burnt-offerings," in outward services, but a pure and holy heart is "the sacrifice he will not despise."

I answer: It is most true that the root of religion lies in the heart, in the inmost soul; that this is the union of the soul with God, the life of God in the soul of man. But if this root be really in the heart, it cannot but put forth branches. And these are the several instances of outward obedience, which partake of the same nature with the root; and consequently, are not only marks or signs, but substantial parts of religion.

It is also true that bare outside religion, which has no root in the heart, is nothing worth; that God delighteth not in such outward services, no more than in Jewish burnt-offerings; and that a pure and holy heart is a sacrifice with which he is always well pleased. But he is also well pleased with all that outward service which arises from the heart; with the sacrifice of our prayers (whether public or private), of our praises and thanksgivings; with the sacrifice of our goods, humbly devoted to him, and employed wholly to his glory; and with that of our bodies, which he peculiarly claims, which the apostle beseeches us, "by the mercies of God, to present unto him a living sacrifice, holy, acceptable to God."

Love Is All in All

2. A second objection, nearly related to this, is that love is all in all; that it is "the fulfilling of the law," "the end of the commandment," of every commandment of God; that all we do, and all we suffer, if we have not charity or love, profiteth us nothing; and therefore the apostle directs us to "follow after charity," and terms this "the more excellent way."

I answer: It is granted that the love of God and man, arising from faith unfeigned, is all in all, the fulfilling of the law, the end of every commandment of God. It is true that without this, whatever we do, whatever we suffer, profits us nothing. But it does not follow that love is all in such a sense as to supersede either faith or good works. It is "the fulfilling of the law," not by releasing us from, but by constraining us to obey it. It is "the end of the commandment," as every commandment leads to and centers in it. It is allowed that whatever we do or suffer without love, profits us nothing. But withal, whatever we do or suffer in love, though it were only the suffering reproach for Christ, or the giving a cup of cold water in his name, it shall in no wise lose its reward.

3. "But does not the apostle direct us to "follow after charity"? And does he not term it "a more excellent way"? He does direct us to "follow after charity"; but not after that alone. His words are, "follow after charity and desire spiritual gifts" (1 Cor. 14:1). Yea, "follow after charity"; and desire to spend and to be spent for your brethren. "Follow after charity"; and as you have opportunity, do good to all men.

In the same verse also wherein he terms this, the way of love, "a more excellent way," he directs the Corinthians to desire other gifts besides it; yea, to desire them earnestly. "Covet earnestly," says he, "the best gifts; and yet I show unto you a more excellent way" (1 Cor. 12:31). More excellent than what? Than the gifts of healing, of speaking with tongues, and of interpreting, mentioned in the preceding verse; but not more excellent than the way of obedience. Of this the apostle is not speaking; neither is he speaking of outward religion at all: so that this text is quite wide of the present question.

But suppose the apostle had been speaking of outward as well as inward religion, and comparing them together; suppose, in the comparison, he had given the preference ever so much to the latter; suppose he had preferred (as he justly might) a loving heart, before all outward works whatever; yet it would not follow that we were to reject either one or the other. No; God has joined them together from the beginning of the world; and let not man put them asunder.

Spiritual Worship Is Sufficient

4. "But God is a Spirit; and they that worship him, must worship him in spirit and in truth." And is not this enough? Nay, ought we not to employ the whole strength of our mind herein? Does not attending to outward things clog the soul, that it cannot soar aloft in holy contemplation? Does it not damp the vigor of our thought? Has it not a natural tendency to encumber and distract the mind? Whereas St. Paul would have us to be "without carefulness," and to "wait upon the Lord without distraction."

I answer, "God is a Spirit; and they that worship him, must worship him in spirit and in truth." Yea, and this is enough: we ought to employ the whole strength of our mind therein. But then I would ask, What is it to worship God, a Spirit, in spirit and in truth? Why, it is to worship him with our spirit; to worship him in that manner which none but spirits are capable

of. It is to believe in him as a wise, just, holy Being, of purer
eyes than to behold iniquity; and yet merciful, gracious, and
long-suffering; forgiving iniquity, and transgression and sin;
casting all our sins behind his back, and accepting us in the
Beloved. It is to love him, to delight in him, to desire him,
with all our heart, and mind, and soul, and strength; to imitate
him we love, by purifying ourselves, even as he is pure; and
to obey him whom we love, and in whom we believe, both
in thought, and word, and work. Consequently, one branch of
the worshipping God in spirit and in truth is the keeping his
outward commandments. To glorify him, therefore with our
bodies, as well as with our spirits; to go through outward work
with hearts lifted up to him; to make our daily employment a
sacrifice to God; to buy and sell, to eat and drink, to his glory—
this is worshipping God in spirit and in truth, as much as the
praying to him in a wilderness.

5. But if so, then contemplation is only one way of worshipping God in spirit and in truth. Therefore to give ourselves up
entirely to this would be to destroy many branches of spiritual
worship, all equally acceptable to God and equally profitable,
not hurtful, to the soul. For it is a great mistake to suppose that
an attention to those outward things, whereto the providence of
God hath called us, is any clog to a Christian, or any hindrance
at all to his always seeing him that is invisible. It does not at all
damp the ardor of his thought; it does not encumber or distract
his mind; it gives him no uneasy or hurtful care, who does it all
as unto the Lord; who has learned whatsoever he does, in word
or deed, to do all in the name of the Lord Jesus; having only
one eye of the soul, which moves round on outward things,
and one immovably fixed on God. Learn what this means, you
poor recluses, that you may clearly discern your own littleness
of faith: yea, that you may no longer judge others by yourselves,
go and learn what that means:

Thou, O Lord, in tender love
    Dost all my burdens bear;
Lift my heart to things above,
    And fix it ever there.
Calm on tumult's wheel I sit;
    Midst busy multitudes alone;
Sweetly waiting at thy feet
    Till all thy will he done.

Our Labor Has Been in Vain

6. But the grand objection is still behind. "We appeal," say they, "to experience. Our light did shine; we used outward things many years; and yet they profited nothing. We attended on all the ordinances; but we were no better for it; nor indeed anyone else. Nay, we were the worse; for we fancied ourselves Christians for so doing, when we knew not what Christianity meant."

I allow the fact: I allow that you and ten thousand more have thus abused the ordinances of God; mistaking the means for the end; supposing that the doing these, or some other outward works either, was the religion of Jesus Christ, or would be accepted in the place of it. But let the abuse be taken away, and the use remain. Now use all outward things, but use them with a constant eye to the renewal of your soul in righteousness and true holiness.

7. But this is not all: they affirm, "Experience likewise shows that the trying to do good is but lost labor. What does it avail to feed or clothe men's bodies if they are just dropping into everlasting fire? And what good can any man do to their souls? If these are changed, God does it himself. Besides, all men are either good, at least desirous so to be, or obstinately evil. Now the former have no need of us; let them ask help of God, and it shall be given them. And the latter will receive

no help from us. Nay, and our Lord forbids to "cast our pearls before swine."

I answer, (1.) whether they will finally be lost or saved, you are expressly commanded to feed the hungry, and clothe the naked. If you can, and do not, whatever becomes of them, you shall go away into everlasting fire. (2.) Though it is God only changes hearts, yet he generally does it by man. It is our part to do all that in us lies, as diligently as if we could change them ourselves, and then to leave the event to him. (3.) God, in answer to their prayers, builds up his children by each other in every good gift; nourishing and strengthening the whole "body by that which every joint supplieth." So that "the eye cannot say to the hand, I have no need of you"; no, nor even "the head to the feet, I have no need of you." Lastly, how are you assured that the persons before you are dogs or swine? Judge them not until you have tried. "How knowest thou, O man, but you may gain your brother," but you may, under God, save his soul from death? When he spurns your love, and blasphemes the good word, then it is time to give him up to God.

8. "We have tried; we have labored to reform sinners; and what did it avail? On many we could make no impression at all. And if some were changed for a while, yet their goodness was but as the morning dew, and they were soon as bad, nay, worse than ever: so that we only hurt them, and ourselves too; for our minds were hurried and discomposed, perhaps filled with anger instead of love. Therefore, we had better have kept our religion to ourselves."

It is very possible this fact also may be true; that you have tried to do good, and have not succeeded; yea, that those who seemed reformed, relapsed into sin, and their last state was worse than the first. And what marvel? Is the servant above his master? But how often did he strive to save sinners, and they would not hear; or when they had followed him awhile, they turned back as a dog to his vomit! But he did not therefore desist from striving to do good: no more should you, whatever your success be. It is your part to do as you are commanded: the event is in the hand of God. You are not accountable for this. Leave it to him, who orders all things well. "In the morning sow thy seed, and in the evening withhold not thy hand: for thou knowest not whether shall prosper" (Eccl. 11:6).

But the trial hurries and frets your own soul. Perhaps it did so for this very reason, because you thought you were accountable for the event, which no man is, nor indeed can be; or perhaps, because you were off your guard; you were not watchful over your own spirit. But this is no reason for disobeying God. Try again; but try more warily than before. Do good (as you forgive) "not seven times only, but until seventy times seven." Only be wiser by experience: attempt it every time more cautiously than before. Be more humbled before God, more deeply convinced that of yourself you can do nothing. Be more jealous over your own spirit; more gentle, and watchful unto prayer. Thus "cast your bread upon the waters, and you shall find it again after many days."

IV. That They May Glorify God in You

1. Notwithstanding all these plausible pretenses for hiding it, "let your light so shine before men, that they may see your good works, and glorify your Father which is in heaven." This is the practical application which our Lord himself makes of the foregoing considerations.

"Let your light so shine": your lowliness of heart; your gentleness, and meekness of wisdom; your serious, weighty concern for the things of eternity, and sorrow for the sins and miseries of men; your earnest desire of universal holiness, and full happiness in God; your tender goodwill to all mankind, and fervent love to your supreme Benefactor. Endeavor not to conceal this light, wherewith God has enlightened your soul; but let it shine before men, before all with whom you are, in the whole tenor of your conversation. Let it shine still more eminently in your actions, in your doing all possible good to all men; and in your suffering for righteousness' sake, while you "rejoice and are exceeding glad, knowing that great is your reward in heaven."

2. "Let your light so shine before men, that they may see your good works." So far let a Christian be from ever designing or desiring to conceal his religion! On the contrary, let it be your desire, not to conceal it; not to put the light under a bushel. Let it be your care to place it "on a candlestick, that it may give light to all that are in the house." Only take heed, not to seek your own praise herein, not to desire any honor to yourselves. But let it be your sole aim, that all who see your good works may "glorify your Father which is in heaven."

3. Be this your one ultimate end in all things. With this view, be plain, open, undisguised. Let your love be without dissimulation. Why should you hide fair, disinterested love? Let there be no guile found in your mouth: let your words be the genuine picture of your heart. Let there be no darkness or reservedness in your conversation, no disguise in your behavior. Leave this to those who have other designs in view; designs which will not bear the light. Be artless and simple to all mankind; that all may see the grace of God which is in you. And although some will harden their hearts, yet others will take knowledge that you have been with Jesus, and, by returning themselves to the great Bishop of their souls, "glorify your Father which is in heaven."

4. With this one design, that men may glorify God in you, go on in his name, and in the power of his might. Be not ashamed even to stand alone, so it be in the ways of God. Let

the light which is in your heart shine in all good works, both works of piety and works of mercy. And in order to enlarge your ability of doing good, renounce all superfluities. Cut off all unnecessary expense in food, in furniture, in apparel. Be a good steward of every gift of God, even of these his lowest gifts. Cut off all unnecessary expense of time, all needless or useless employments; and "whatsoever thy hand findeth to do, do it with thy might." In a word, be thou full of faith and love; do good; suffer evil. And herein be "steadfast, unmovable;" yea, "always abounding in the work of the Lord; forasmuch as you know that your labor is not in vain in the Lord."

THE LAW AND RIGHTEOUSNESS

Think not that I am come to destroy the law or the prophets: I am not come to destroy, but to fulfill. For verily I say unto you: Till heaven and earth pass, one jot or one tittle shall in no wise pass from the law, till all be fulfilled. Whosoever therefore shall break one of these least commandments, and shall teach men so, he shall be called the least in the kingdom of heaven: but whosoever shall do and teach them, the same shall be called great in the kingdom of heaven. For I say unto you: That except your righteousness shall exceed the righteousness of the scribes and Pharisees, you shall in no case enter into the kingdom of heaven.

—Matthew 5:17–20

Introduction

1. Among the multitude of reproaches which fell upon him who "was despised and rejected of men," it could not fail to be one, that he was a teacher of novelties, an introducer of a new religion. This might be affirmed with the more color because many of the expressions he had used were not common among the Jews: either they did not use them at all, or not in the same sense, not in so full and strong a meaning. Add to this, that the worshipping God "in spirit and in truth" must always appear a new religion to those who have hitherto known nothing but outside worship, nothing but the "form of godliness."

2. And it is not improbable, some might hope it was so, that he was abolishing the old religion, and bringing in another; one which, they might flatter themselves, would be an easier way to heaven. But our Lord refutes, in these words, both the vain hopes of the one, and the groundless calumnies of the other.

I shall consider them in the same order as they lie, taking each verse for a distinct head of discourse.

I. Jesus Came to Fulfill the Law

1. And first, "Think not that I am come to destroy the law, or the prophets: I am not come to destroy, but to fulfill."

Jesus Abolished the Ritual or Ceremonial Law

The ritual or ceremonial law, delivered by Moses to the children of Israel, containing all the injunctions and ordinances which related to the old sacrifices and service of the temple, our Lord indeed did come to destroy, to dissolve, and utterly abolish. To this bear all the apostles witness; not only Barnabas and Paul, who vehemently withstood those who taught that Christians ought "to keep the law of Moses" (Acts 15:5); not only St. Peter, who termed the insisting on this, on the observance of the ritual law, a "tempting God," and "putting a yoke upon the neck of the disciples, which neither our fathers," saith he, "nor we, were able to bear"; but all the apostles, elders, and brethren, being assembled with one accord (Acts 15:22), declared that to command them to keep this law was to "subvert their souls"; and that "it seemed good to the Holy Ghost" and to them, to lay no such burden upon them (Acts 15:28). This "handwriting of ordinances" our Lord did blot out, take away, and nail to his cross.

Jesus Fulfilled the Moral Law

2. But the moral law, contained in the Ten Commandments, and enforced by the prophets, he did not take away. It was not the design of his coming to revoke any part of this. This is a law which never can be broken, which stands fast as the faithful witness in heaven. The moral stands on an entirely different foundation from the ceremonial or ritual law, which was only designed for a temporary restraint upon a disobedient and stiff-necked people; whereas this was from the beginning of the world, being "written not on tables of stone," but on the hearts of all the children of men, when they came out of the hands of the Creator. And, however the letters once written by the finger of God are now in a great measure defaced by sin, yet can they not wholly be blotted out, while we have any consciousness of good and evil. Every part of this law must remain in force, upon all mankind, and in all ages; as not depending either on time or place, or any other circumstances liable to change, but on the nature of God and the nature of man, and their unchangeable relation to each other.

Jesus Fully Reveals the Law

3. "I am not come to destroy, but to fulfill." Some have conceived our Lord to mean, I am come to fulfill this by my entire and perfect obedience to it. And it cannot be doubted but he did, in this sense, fulfill every part of it. But this does not appear to be what he intends here, being foreign to the scope of his present discourse. Without question, his meaning in this place is (consistently with all that goes before and follows after), I am come to establish it in its fullness, in spite of all the glosses of men; I am come to place in a full and clear view whatsoever was dark or obscure therein; I am come to declare the true and full import of every part of it; to show the length and breadth, the entire extent of every commandment contained therein, and the height and depth, the inconceivable purity and spirituality of it in all its branches.

4. And this our Lord has abundantly performed in the preceding and subsequent parts of the discourse before us, in which he has not introduced a new religion into the world, but the same which was from the beginning: a religion the substance of which is, without question, as old as the creation, being coeval with man, and having proceeded from God at the very time when "man became a living soul" (the substance, I say; for some circumstances of it now relate to man as a fallen creature); a religion witnessed to both by the Law and by the Prophets, in all succeeding generations. Yet was it never so fully explained, nor so thoroughly understood till the great Author of it himself condescended to give mankind this authentic comment on all the essential branches of it; at the same time declaring it should never be changed, but remain in force to the end of the world.

II. The Law Will Be Fulfilled

1. "For verily I say unto you" (a solemn preface, which denotes both the importance and certainty of what is spoken), "Till heaven and earth pass, one jot or one tittle shall in no wise pass from the law till all be fulfilled."

Not One Part of the Law Will Pass Away

"One jot"—It is literally, not one iota, not the most inconsiderable vowel. *Or one tittle,* μία κερέα—one corner, or point of a consonant. It is a proverbial expression which signifies that no one commandment contained in the moral law, nor the least part of any one, however inconsiderable it might seem, should ever be disannulled.

Shall in no wise pass from the law, οὐ μὴ παρέλθῃ ἀπὸ τοῦ νόμου. The double negative, here used, strengthens the sense, so as to admit of no contradiction. And the word παρέλθῃ, *will pass,* it may be observed, is not barely future, declaring what will be, but has likewise the force of an imperative, ordering what shall be. It is a word of authority, expressing the sovereign will and power of him that spoke; of him whose word is the law of heaven and earth, and stands fast for ever and ever.

"One jot or one tittle shall in no wise pass till heaven and earth pass"; or as it is expressed immediately after, ἕως ἂν πάντα γένηται, *till all (or rather, all things) be fulfilled*; till the consummation of all things. Here is therefore no room for that poor evasion (with which some have delighted themselves greatly) that "no part of the law was to pass away till all the law was fulfilled: but it has been fulfilled by Christ, and therefore now must pass, for the gospel to be established." Not so; the word *all* does not mean all the law, but all things in the universe; as neither has the term fulfilled any reference to the law, but to all things in heaven and earth.

The Law and the Gospel Perfectly Agree

2. From all this we may learn that there is no contrariety at all between the law and the gospel; that there is no need for the law to pass away, in order to the establishing of the gospel. Indeed neither of them supersedes the other, but they agree perfectly well together. Yea, the very same words, considered in different respects, are parts both of the law and of the gospel. If they are considered as commandments, they are parts of the law: if as promises, of the gospel. Thus, "Thou shalt love the Lord thy God with all thy heart," when considered as a commandment, is a branch of the law; when regarded as a promise, is an essential part of the gospel; the gospel being no other than the commands of the law proposed by way of promises. Accordingly poverty of spirit, purity of heart, and whatever else is enjoined in the holy law of God, are no other, when viewed in a gospel light, than so many great and precious promises.

3. There is, therefore, the closest connection that can be conceived between the law and the gospel. On the one hand, the law continually makes way for, and points us to, the gospel; on the other, the gospel continually leads us to a more exact fulfilling of the law. The law, for instance, requires us to love God, to love our neighbor, to be meek, humble, or holy. We feel that we are not sufficient for these things; yea, that "with man this is impossible." But we see a promise of God, to give us that love, and to make us humble, meek, and holy. We lay hold of this gospel, of these glad tidings; it is done unto us according to our faith; and "the righteousness of the law is fulfilled in us," through faith which is in Christ Jesus.

We may yet farther observe that every command in holy writ is only a covered promise. For by that solemn declaration, "This is the covenant I will make after those days, saith the Lord; I will put my laws in your minds, and write them in your hearts," God has engaged to give whatsoever he commands. Does he command us then to "pray without ceasing"? To "rejoice evermore"? "To be holy as he is holy"? It is enough. He will work in us this very thing. It shall be unto us according to his word.

The Final Dispensation

4. But if these things are so, we cannot be at a loss what to think of those who in all ages of the Church, have undertaken to change or supersede some commands of God, as they professed, by the peculiar direction of his Spirit. Christ has here given us an infallible rule, whereby to judge of all such pretensions. Christianity, as it includes the whole moral law of God, both by way of injunction and of promise, if we will hear him, is designed of God to be the last of all his dispensations. There is no other to come after this. This is to endure till the consummation of all things. Of consequence, all such new revelations are of Satan, and not of God; and all pretenses to another more perfect dispensation fall to the ground of course. "Heaven and earth shall pass away," but this word "shall not pass away."

III. The Least and the Great in the Kingdom

1. "Whosoever therefore shall break one of these least commandments, and shall teach men so, he shall be called the least in the kingdom of heaven; but whosoever shall do and teach them, the same shall be called great in the kingdom of heaven."

Who are they that make "the preaching of the law" a character of reproach? Do they not see on whom their reproach must fall, on whose head it must light at last? Whosoever on this ground despises us, despises him that sent us. For did ever any man preach the law like him, even when he came not to condemn but to save the world; when he came purposely to "bring life and immortality to light through the gospel"? Can any preach the law more expressly, more rigorously, than Christ does in these words? And who is he that shall amend them? Who is he that shall instruct the Son of God how to preach? Who will teach him a better way of delivering the message which he has received of the Father?

The Least in the Kingdom

2. "Whosoever shall break one of these least commandments," or one of the least of these commandments. "These commandments," we may observe, is a term used by our Lord as equivalent with the law, or the law and the prophets, which is the same thing, seeing the prophets added nothing to the law, but only declared, explained, or enforced it, as they were moved by the Holy Ghost.

"Whosoever shall break one of these least commandments," especially if it be done willfully or presumptuously—

"One"; for "he that keepeth the whole law, and" thus "offends in one point, is guilty of all." The wrath of God abideth on him, as surely as if he had broken every one. So that no allowance is made for one darling lust; no reserve for one idol; no excuse for refraining from all besides, and only giving way to one bosom sin. What God demands is an entire obedience; we are to have an eye to all his commandments; otherwise we lose all the labor we take in keeping some, and our poor souls for ever and ever.

"One of these least," or one of the least of these commandments: here is another excuse cut off, whereby many, who
cannot deceive God, miserably deceive their own souls. "This
sin," says the sinner, "is it not a little one? Will not the Lord
spare me in this thing? Surely he will not be extreme to mark
this, since I do not offend in the greater matters of the law."
Vain hope! Speaking after the manner of men, we may term
these great, and those little commandments; but in reality
they are not so. If we use propriety of speech there is no such
thing as a little sin; every sin being a transgression of the
holy and perfect law, and an affront on the great Majesty of
heaven.

3. "And shall teach men so." In some sense it may be
said that whosoever openly breaks any commandment
teaches others the same; for example speaks, and many
times louder than precept. In this sense, it is apparent, every
open drunkard is a teacher of drunkenness; every sabbath-
breaker is constantly teaching his neighbor to profane the
day of the Lord. But this is not all: an habitual breaker of
the law is seldom content to stop here; he generally teaches
other men to do so too, by word as well as example; especially when he hardens his neck, and hates to be reproved.
Such a sinner soon commences an advocate for sin; he
defends what he is resolved not to forsake; he excuses the
sin which he will not leave, and thus directly teaches every
sin which he commits.

"He shall be called least in the kingdom of heaven"; that is,
shall have no part therein. He is a stranger to the kingdom of
heaven which is on earth; he has no portion in that inheritance;
no share of that "righteousness and peace and joy in the Holy
Ghost." Nor, by consequence can he have any part in the glory
which shall be revealed.

Those Who Teach Others to Break the Commandments

4. But if those who even thus break, and teach others to break "one of the least of these commandments shall be called least in the kingdom of heaven," shall have no part in the kingdom of Christ and of God; if even these shall be cast into "outer darkness, where is wailing and gnashing of teeth," then where will they appear whom our Lord chiefly and primarily intends in these words; they who, bearing the character of Teachers sent from God, do nevertheless themselves break his commandments; yea, and openly teach others so to do, being corrupt both in life and doctrine?

5. *Those living in wilful, habitual sin.* These are of several sorts. Of the first sort are they who live in some wilful, habitual sin. Now, if an ordinary sinner teaches by his example, how much more a sinful Minister, even if he does not attempt to defend, excuse, or extenuate his sin! If he does, he is a murderer indeed; yea, the murderer-general of his congregation! He peoples the regions of death. He is the choicest instrument of the prince of darkness. When he goes hence, "hell from beneath is moved to meet him at his coming." Nor can he sink into the bottomless pit without dragging a multitude after him.

6. *Those with no regard for sin or holiness.* Next to these are the good-natured, good sort of men: who live an easy, harmless life, neither troubling themselves with outward sin, nor with inward holiness; men who are remarkable neither one way nor the other, neither for religion nor irreligion, who are very regular both in public and private, but do not pretend to be any stricter than their neighbors. A Minister of this kind breaks not one, or a few only, of the least commandments of God; but all the great and weighty branches of his law which relate to the power of godliness, and all that require us to "pass the time of our sojourning in fear," to "work out our salvation

with fear and trembling"; to have our "loins always girt and our lights burning," to "strive," or agonize, "to enter in at the straight gate." And he teaches men so, by the whole form of his life, and the general tenor of his preaching, which uniformly tends to soothe those in their pleasing dream who imagine themselves Christians and are not; to persuade all who attend upon his ministry to sleep on and take their rest. No marvel, therefore, if both he and they that follow him wake together in everlasting burnings.

7. *Those who openly overthrow the law.* But above all these, in the highest rank of the enemies of the gospel of Christ, are they who openly and explicitly "judge the law" itself, and "speak evil of the law"; who teach men to break (λύση, *to dissolve, to loose, to untie the obligation of*) not one only, whether of the least, or of the greatest, but all the commandments at a stroke; who teach, without any cover, in so many words, "What did our Lord do with the law? He abolished it. There is but one duty, which is that of believing. All commands are unfit for our times. From any demand of the law, no man is obliged now to go one step, to give away one farthing, to eat or omit one morsel." This is, indeed, carrying matters with a high hand; this is withstanding our Lord to the face, and telling him that he understood not how to deliver the message on which he was sent. O Lord, lay not this sin to their charge! Father, forgive them, for they know not what they do!

8. The most surprising of all the circumstances that attend this strong delusion that they who are given up to it really believe that they honor Christ by overthrowing his law, and that they are magnifying his office, while they are destroying his doctrine! Yea, they honor him just as Judas did, when he said, "Hail, Master!" and kissed him. And he may as justly say to every one of them, "Betrayest thou the Son of Man

with a kiss?" It is no other than betraying him with a kiss, to talk of his blood, and take away his crown; to set light by any part of his law, under pretense of advancing his gospel. Nor, indeed, can anyone escape this charge, who preaches faith in any such manner as either directly or indirectly tends to set aside any branch of obedience; who preaches Christ so as to disannul, or weaken, in anywise, the least of the commandments of God.

The Greatest in the Kingdom

9. It is impossible, indeed, to have too high an esteem for "the faith of God's elect." And we must all declare, "By grace you are saved through faith; not of works, lest any man should boast." We must cry aloud to every penitent sinner, "Believe in the Lord Jesus Christ, and you shall be saved." But, at the same time, we must take care to let all men know, we esteem no faith but that which works by love (Gal. 5:6); and that we are not saved by faith, unless so far as we are delivered from the power as well as the guilt of sin. And when we say, "Believe, and you shall be saved;" we do not mean, "Believe, and you shall step from sin to heaven, without any holiness coming between; faith supplying the place of holiness"; but, "Believe, and you shall be holy; believe in the Lord Jesus, and you shall have peace and power together. You shall have power from him in whom you believe, to trample sin under your feet; power to love the Lord your God with all your heart, and to serve him with all your strength. You shall have power "by patient continuance in well-doing, to seek for glory, and honor, and immortality"; you shall both do and teach all the commandments of God, from the least even to the greatest. You shall teach them by your life as well as your words, and so "be called great in the kingdom of heaven."

IV. The Righteousness of the Scribes and Pharisees

1. Whatever other way we teach to the kingdom of heaven, to glory, honor, and immortality, be it called the way of faith, or by any other name, it is, in truth, the way to destruction. It will not bring a man peace at the last. For thus saith the Lord, "[Verily] I say unto you, That except your righteousness shall exceed the righteousness of the scribes and Pharisees, you shall in no case enter into the kingdom of heaven."

Scribes and Pharisees

The scribes, mentioned so often in the New Testament as some of the most constant and vehement opposers of our Lord, were not secretaries, or men employed in writing only, as that term might incline us to believe. Neither were they lawyers, in our common sense of the word; although the word νομικὸς, *related to the law, learned in the law*, is so rendered in our translation. Their employment had no affinity at all to that of a lawyer among us. They were conversant with the laws of God, and not with the laws of man. These were their study: it was their proper and peculiar business to read and expound the law and the prophets, particularly in the synagogues. They were the ordinary, stated preachers among the Jews. So that if the sense of the original word was attended to, we might render it, the Divines. For these were the men who made divinity their profession; and they were generally (as their name literally imports) men of letters; men of the greatest account for learning that were then in the Jewish nation.

2. The Pharisees were a very ancient sect, or body of men, among the Jews; originally so called from a Hebrew word which signifies to *separate* or *divide*. Not that they made any

formal separation from, or division in, the national church. They were only distinguished from others by greater strictness of life, by more exactness of conversation. For they were zealous of the law in the minutest points; paying tithes of mint, anise, and cummin. And hence they were held in honor of all the people, and generally esteemed the holiest of men.

Many of the scribes were of the sect of the Pharisees. Thus St. Paul himself, who was educated for a scribe, first at the university of Tarsus, and after that in Jerusalem, at the feet of Gamaliel (one of the most learned scribes or doctors of the law that were then in the nation), declares of himself before the Council, "I am a Pharisee, the son of a Pharisee" (Acts 23:6); and before King Agrippa, "After the straightest sect of our religion, I lived a Pharisee" (Acts 26:5). And the whole body of the scribes generally esteemed and acted in concert with the Pharisees. Hence we find our Savior so frequently coupling them together, as coming in many respects under the same consideration. In this place they seem to be mentioned together as the most eminent professors of religion; the former of whom were accounted the wisest; the latter, the holiest of men.

The Righteousness of the Scribes and Pharisees

3. What "the righteousness of the scribes and Pharisees" really was, it is not difficult to determine. Our Lord has preserved an authentic account which one of them gave of himself, and he is clear and full in describing his own righteousness; and cannot be supposed to have omitted any part of it. He went up indeed "into the temple to pray"; but was so intent upon his own virtues, that he forgot the design upon which he came. For it is remarkable, he does not properly pray at all; he only tells God how wise and good he was. "God, I thank thee that I am not as other men are, extortioners, unjust, adulterers; or even as this publican. I fast twice in the week; I

give tithes of all that I possess." His righteousness therefore consisted of three parts: First, saith he, "I am not as other men are." I am not an extortioner, not unjust, not an adulterer; not "even as this publican." Secondly, "I fast twice in the week." And, thirdly, "I give tithes of all that I possess."

"I am not as other men are." This is not a small point. It is not every man that can say this. It is as if he had said, "I do not suffer myself to be carried away by that great torrent, custom. I live not by custom, but by reason; not by the examples of men, but the word of God. I am not an extortioner, not unjust, not an adulterer; however common these sins are, even among those who are called the people of God (extortion, in particular, a kind of legal injustice, not punishable by any human law, the making gain of another's ignorance or necessity, having filled every corner of the land); nor even as this publican, not guilty of any open or presumptuous sin; not an outward sinner; but a fair, honest man of blameless life and conversation."

4. *"I fast twice in the week."* There is more implied in this, than we may at first be sensible of. All the stricter Pharisees observed the weekly fasts; namely, every Monday and Thursday. On the former day they fasted in memory of Moses receiving on that day (as their tradition taught) the two tables of stone written by the finger of God; on the latter, in memory of his casting them out of his hand, when he saw the people dancing round the golden calf. On these days, they took no sustenance at all, till three in the afternoon; the hour at which they began to offer up the evening sacrifice in the temple. Till that hour, it was their custom to remain in the temple, in some of the corners, apartments, or courts thereof, that they might be ready to assist at all the sacrifices, and to join in all the public prayers. The time between they were accustomed to employ, partly in private addresses to God, partly in searching the Scriptures, in reading the Law and the Prophets, and in meditating thereon.

Thus much is implied in, "I fast twice in the week," the second branch of the righteousness of a Pharisee.

5. *"I give tithes of all that I possess."* This the Pharisees did with the utmost exactness. They would not except the most inconsiderable thing; no, not mint, anise, and cummin. They would not keep back the least part of what they believed properly to belong to God; but gave a full tenth of their whole substance yearly, and of all their increase, whatsoever it was.

Yea, the stricter Pharisees (as has been often observed by those who are versed in the ancient Jewish writings), not content with giving one tenth of their substance to God in his priests and Levites, gave another tenth to God in the poor, and that continually. They gave the same proportion of all they had in alms as they were accustomed to give in tithes. And this likewise they adjusted with the utmost exactness; that they might not keep back any part, but might fully render unto God the things which were God's, as they accounted this to be. So that, upon the whole, they gave away, from year to year an entire fifth of all that they possessed.

6. *Honest, not hypocritical, righteousness.* This was "the righteousness of the scribes and Pharisees;" a righteousness which, in many respects, went far beyond the conception which many have been accustomed to entertain concerning it. But perhaps it will be said, "It was all false and feigned; for they were all a company of hypocrites." Some of them doubtless were; men who had really no religion at all, no fear of God, or desire to please him; who had no concern for the honor that cometh of God, but only for the praise of men. And these are they whom our Lord so severely condemns, so sharply reproves, on many occasions.

But we must not suppose, because many Pharisees were hypocrites, therefore all were so. Nor indeed is hypocrisy by any means essential to the character of a Pharisee. This is not the distinguishing mark of their sect. It is rather this, according to our Lord's account, "They trusted in themselves that they were righteous, and despised others." This is their genuine badge. But the Pharisee of this kind cannot be a hypocrite. He must be, in the common sense, sincere; otherwise he could not "trust in himself that he is righteous." The man who was here commending himself to God unquestionably thought himself righteous. Consequently, he was no hypocrite; he was not conscious to himself of any insincerity. He now spoke to God just what he thought, namely, that he was abundantly better than other men.

But the example of St. Paul, were there no other, is sufficient to put this out of all question. He could not only say, when he was a Christian, "Herein do I exercise myself, to have always a conscience void of offense toward God and toward men" (Acts 24:16); but even concerning the time when he was a Pharisee, "Men and brethren, I have lived in all good conscience before God until this day" (Acts 23:1). He was therefore sincere when he was a Pharisee, as well when he was a Christian. He was no more a hypocrite when he persecuted the Church than when he preached the faith which once he persecuted. Let this then be added to "the righteousness of the scribes and Pharisees"—a sincere belief that they are righteous, and in all things "doing God service."

Equaling the Righteousness of the Scribes and Pharisees

7. And yet, "except your righteousness," saith our Lord, "shall exceed the righteousness of the scribes and Pharisees, you shall in no case enter into the kingdom of heaven." A solemn and weighty declaration, and which it behooves all who are called by the name of Christ seriously and deeply to consider. But before we inquire how our righteousness may exceed theirs, let us examine whether at present we come up to it.

Are you willing to stem the tide? First, a Pharisee was "not as other men are." In externals he was singularly good. Are we so? Do we dare to be singular at all? Do we not rather swim with the stream? Do we not many times dispense with religion and reason together, because we would not look particular? Are we not often more afraid of being out of the fashion, than of being out of the way of salvation? Have we courage to stem the tide—to run counter to the world—"to obey God rather than man"? Otherwise, the Pharisee leaves us behind at the very first step. It is well if we overtake him any more.

But to come closer. Can we use his first plea with God, which is, in substance, "I do no harm: I live in no outward sin. I do nothing for which my own heart condemns me"? Do you not? Are you sure of that? Do you live in no practice for which your own heart condemns you? If you are not an adulterer, if you are not unchaste, either in word or deed, are you not unjust? The grand measure of justice, as well as of mercy, is, "Do unto others as thou wouldst they should do unto thee." Do you walk by this rule? Do you never do unto any what you would not they should do unto you? Nay, are you not grossly unjust? Are you not an extortioner? Do you not make a gain of anyone's ignorance or necessity; neither in buying nor selling?

Suppose you are engaged in trade: Do you demand, do you receive, no more than the real value of what you sell? Do you demand, do you receive, no more of the ignorant than of the knowing; of a little child, than of an experienced trader? If you do, why does not your heart condemn you? You are a barefaced extortioner! Do you demand no more than the usual price of goods of any who is in pressing want; who must have, and that without delay, the things which you only can furnish him with? If you do, this also is flat extortion. Indeed you do not come up to the righteousness of a Pharisee.

8. *Do you use every means of grace available?* A Pharisee, secondly (to express his sense in our common way), used all the means of grace. As he fasted often and much, twice in every week, so he attended all the sacrifices. He was constant in public and private prayer, and in reading and hearing the Scriptures. Do you go as far as this? Do you fast much and often—twice in the week? I fear not! Once, at least, "on all Fridays in the year"? (So our Church clearly and peremptorily enjoins all her members to do; to observe all these as well as the vigils and the forty days of Lent, as days of fasting or abstinence.) Do you fast twice in the year? I am afraid some among us cannot plead even this! Do you neglect no opportunity of attending and partaking of the Christian sacrifice? How many are they who call themselves Christians, and yet are utterly regardless of it—yet do not eat of that bread, or drink of that cup, for months, perhaps years, together?

Do you, every day, either hear the Scriptures, or read them and meditate thereon? Do you join in prayer with the great congregation, daily, if you have opportunity; if not, whenever you can; particularly on that day which you "remember to keep it holy"? Do you strive to "make opportunities"? Are you glad when they say unto you, "We will go into the house of the Lord"? Are you zealous of, and diligent in, private prayer? Do you suffer no day to pass without it? Rather are not some of you so far from spending therein (with the Pharisee) several hours in one day that you think one hour full enough, if not too much? Do you spend an hour in a day, or in a week, in praying to your Father which is in secret; yea, an hour in a month? Have you spent one hour together in private prayer ever since you were born? Ah, poor Christian! Shall not the Pharisee rise up in the judgment against you and condemn you? His righteousness is as far above yours as the heaven is above the earth!

9. *Are you abundant in good works?* The Pharisee, thirdly, paid tithes and gave alms of all that he possessed. And in how ample a manner! So that he was (as we phrase it) "a man that did much good." Do we come up to him here? Which of us is so abundant as he was in good works? Which of us gives a fifth of all his substance to God? Both of the principal and of the increase? Who of us out of (suppose) an hundred pounds a year, gives twenty to God and the poor; out of fifty, ten; and so in a larger or a smaller proportion? When shall our righteousness, in using all the means of grace, in attending all the ordinances of God, in avoiding evil and doing good, equal at least the righteousness of the scribes and Pharisees?

Exceeding the Righteousness of the Scribes and Pharisees

10. *Be righteous in all things.* Although if it only equaled theirs, what would that profit? "For verily I say unto you, except your righteousness shall exceed the righteousness of the scribes and Pharisees, you shall in no case enter into the kingdom of heaven." But how can it exceed theirs? Wherein does the righteousness of a Christian exceed that of a scribe or Pharisee? Christian righteousness exceeds theirs, first, in the extent of it. Most of the Pharisees, though they were rigorously exact in many things, yet were emboldened, by the traditions of the Elders, to dispense with others of equal importance. Thus they were extremely punctual in keeping the fourth commandment— they would not even rub an ear of corn on the Sabbath-day; but not at all in keeping the third, making little account of light, or even false, swearing. So that their righteousness was partial; whereas the righteousness of a real Christian is universal. He does not observe one, or some parts, of the law of God, and neglect the rest; but keeps all his commandments, loves them all, values them above gold or precious stones.

11. *Be righteous inwardly.* It may be, indeed, that some of the scribes and Pharisees endeavored to keep all the commandments, and consequently were, as touching the righteousness of the law, that is, according to the letter of it, blameless. But still the righteousness of a Christian exceeds all this righteousness of a scribe or Pharisee, by fulfilling the spirit as well as the letter of the law; by inward as well as outward obedience. In this, in the spirituality of it, it admits of no comparison. This is the point which our Lord has so largely proved, in the whole tenor of this discourse. Their righteousness was external only: Christian righteousness is in the inner man. The Pharisee "cleansed the outside of the cup and the platter"; the Christian is clean within. The Pharisee labored to present God with a good life; the Christian with a holy heart. The one shook off the leaves, perhaps the fruits, of sin; the other "lays the axe to the root," as not being content with the outward form of godliness, how exact soever it be, unless the life, the Spirit, the power of God unto salvation, be felt in the inmost soul.

Thus, to do no harm, to do good, to attend the ordinances of God (the righteousness of a Pharisee), are all external; whereas, on the contrary, poverty of spirit, mourning, meekness, hunger and thirst after righteousness, the love of our neighbor, and purity of heart, (the righteousness of a Christian), are all internal. And even peace-making (or doing good), and suffering for righteousness' sake, stand entitled to the blessings annexed to them, only as they imply these inward dispositions, as they spring from, exercise, and confirm them. So that whereas the righteousness of the scribes and Pharisees was external only, it may be said in some sense that the righteousness of a Christian is internal only. All his actions and sufferings being as nothing in themselves, being estimated before God only by the tempers from which they spring.

12. *Surpass the scribes and Pharisees in righteousness.* Whosoever therefore you are, who bearest the holy and venerable name of a Christian, see, first, that thy righteousness fall not short of the righteousness of the scribes and Pharisees. Be not thou "as other men are!" Dare to stand alone, to be "against example, singularly good." If you "follow a multitude" at all, it must be "to do evil." Let not custom or fashion be thy guide, but reason and religion. The practice of others is nothing to you: "every man must give an account of himself to God." Indeed, if you can save the soul of another, do; but at least save one, your own. Walk not in the path of death because it is broad, and many walk therein. Nay, by this very token you may know it. Is the way wherein you now walk, a broad, well-frequented, fashionable way? Then it infallibly leads to destruction. O be not thou "damned for company!" Cease from evil; fly from sin as from the face of a serpent! At least, do no harm. "He that committeth sin is of the devil." Be not thou found in that number. Touching outward sins, surely the grace of God is even now sufficient for thee. "Herein," at least, "exercise thyself to have a conscience void of offence toward God, and toward men."

Surpass the scribes and Pharisees in means of grace. Secondly, let not thy righteousness fall short of theirs with regard to the ordinances of God. If your labor or bodily strength will not allow of your fasting twice in the week, however, deal faithfully with your own soul, and fast as often as your strength will permit. Omit no public, no private opportunity of pouring out your soul in prayer. Neglect no occasion of eating that bread and drinking that cup which is the communion of the body and blood of Christ. Be diligent in searching the Scriptures: read as you may, and meditate therein day and night. Rejoice to embrace every opportunity of hearing "the word of reconciliation" declared by the "ambassadors of Christ," the "stewards of the mysteries of God." In using all the means of grace, in a constant and careful attendance on every ordinance of God, live up to (at least till you can't go beyond) "the righteousness of the scribes and Pharisees."

Surpass the scribes and Pharisees in means of good works. Thirdly, fall not short of a Pharisee in doing good. Give alms of all you do possess. Is any hungry? Feed him. Is he athirst? Give him drink. Naked? Cover him with a garment. If you have this world's goods, do not limit your beneficence to a scanty proportion. Be merciful to the uttermost of your power. Why not, even as this Pharisee? Now "make yourself friends," while the time is, "of the mammon of unrighteousness," that when you fail," when this earthly tabernacle is dissolved, "they may receive you into everlasting habitations."

13. But rest not here. Let your "righteousness exceed the righteousness of the scribes and Pharisees." Be not thou content to "keep the whole law, and offend in one point." Hold fast all his commandments, and all "false ways do thou utterly abhor." Do all the things whatsoever he has commanded, and that with all your might. You can do all things through Christ strengthening you; though without him you can do nothing.

Surpass the scribes and Pharisees in purity. Above all, let your righteousness exceed theirs in the purity and spirituality of it. What is the exactest form of religion to you; the most perfect outside righteousness? Go thou higher and deeper than all this! Let your religion be the religion of the heart. Be thou poor in spirit; little, and base, and mean, and vile in your own eyes; amazed and humbled to the dust at the "love of God which is in Christ Jesus thy Lord!" Be serious: let the whole stream of your thoughts, words, and works, be such as flows from the deepest conviction that you stand on the edge of the great gulf, you and all the children of men, just ready to drop in, either into everlasting glory, or everlasting burnings! Be meek: let your soul be filled with mildness, gentleness, patience, long-suffering toward all men; at the same time that all which is in you is athirst for God, the living God, longing to awake up after his likeness, and to be satisfied with it. Be thou a lover of God, and of all mankind. In this spirit, do and suffer all things. Thus "exceed the righteousness of the scribes and Pharisees," and you shall be "called great in the kingdom of heaven."

TRUE MERCY
AND TRUE PRAYER

Take heed that ye do not your alms before men, to be seen of them: otherwise ye have no reward of your Father which is in heaven. Therefore when thou doest thine alms, do not sound a trumpet before thee, as the hypocrites do in the synagogues and in the streets, that they may have glory of men. Verily I say unto you, They have their reward. But when thou doest alms, let not thy left hand know what thy right hand doeth: that thine alms may be in secret: and thy Father, which seeth in secret, himself shall reward thee openly.

And when thou prayest, thou shalt not be as the hypocrites are: for they love to pray standing in the synagogues and in the corners of the streets, that they may be seen of men. Verily I say unto you, They have their reward. But thou, when thou prayest, enter into thy closet, and when thou hast shut thy door, pray to thy Father which is in secret; and thy Father which seeth in secret, he shall reward thee openly. But

> *when ye pray, use not vain repetitions, as the heathen do: for they think that they shall be heard for their much speaking. Be not ye therefore like unto them: for your Father knoweth what things ye have need of, before you ask him. After this manner therefore pray ye:*

> > *Our Father which art in heaven, hallowed be thy name. Thy kingdom come. Thy will be done in earth, as it is in heaven. Give us this day our daily bread. And forgive us our debts as we forgive our debtors. And lead us not into temptation, but deliver us from evil: for thine is the kingdom, and the power, and the glory, for ever. Amen.*

> > *For if ye forgive men their trespasses, your heavenly Father will also forgive you: but if ye forgive not men their trespasses, neither will your Father forgive your trespasses.*
> > —Matthew 6:1–15

Introduction

1. In the preceding chapter our Lord has described inward religion in its various branches. He has laid before us those dispositions of soul which constitute real Christianity; the inward tempers contained in that "holiness, without which no man shall see the Lord"; the affections which, when flowing from their proper fountain, from a living faith in God through Christ Jesus, are intrinsically and essentially good, and acceptable to God. He proceeds to show, in this chapter, how all our actions likewise, even those that are indifferent in their own nature, may be made holy, and good and acceptable to God, by a pure and holy intention. Whatever is done without this, he largely declares, is of no value before God. Whereas whatever outward works are thus consecrated to God, they are, in his sight, of great price.

2. The necessity of this purity of intention, he shows, first, with regard to those which are usually accounted religious actions, and indeed are such when performed with a right intention. Some of these are commonly termed works of piety; the rest, works of charity or mercy. Of the latter sort, he particularly names almsgiving; of the former, prayer and fasting. But the directions given for these are equally to be applied to every work, whether of charity or mercy.

I. Secret Works of Mercy

Give for God's Honor Alone

1. And, first, with regard to works of mercy: "Take heed," says he,"that you do not your alms before men, to be seen of them, otherwise you have no reward of your Father which is in heaven." "That you do not your alms"; although this only is named, yet is every work of charity included, every thing which we give, or speak, or do, whereby our neighbor may be profited; whereby another man may receive any advantage, either in his body or soul. The feeding the hungry, the clothing the naked, the entertaining or assisting the stranger, the visiting those that are sick or in prison, the comforting the afflicted, the instructing the ignorant, the reproving the wicked, the exhorting and encouraging the well-doer; and if there be any other work of mercy, it is equally included in this direction.

2. "Take heed that you do not your alms before men, to be seen of them." The thing which is here forbidden is not barely the doing good in the sight of men; this circumstance alone, that others see what we do, makes the action neither worse nor better; but the doing it before men, "to be seen of them," with this view from this intention only. I say, from this intention only; for this may, in some cases, be a part of our intention; we

may design that some of our actions should be seen, and yet they may be acceptable to God. We may intend that our light should shine before men, when our conscience bears us witness in the Holy Ghost, that our ultimate end in designing they should see our good works "that they may glorify our Father which is in heaven."

But take heed that you do not the least thing with a view to your own glory. Take heed that a regard to the praise of men have no place at all in your works of mercy. If you seek your own glory, if you have any design to gain the honor that comes of men, whatever is done with this view is nothing worth; it is not done unto the Lord; he accepts it not; "you have no reward" for this "of our Father which is in heaven."

3. "Therefore when you do your alms, do not sound a trumpet before you, as the hypocrites do, in the synagogues and in the streets, that they may have praise of men." The word *synagogue* does not here mean a place of worship, but any place of public resort, such as the marketplace, or exchange. It was a common thing among the Jews, who were men of large fortunes, particularly among the Pharisees, to cause a trumpet to be sounded before them in the most public parts of the city, when they were about to give any considerable alms. The pretended reason for this was to call the poor together to receive it; but the real design, that they might have praise of men. But be not thou like unto them. Do not cause a trumpet to be sounded before you. Use no ostentation in doing good. Aim at the honor which comes of God only. They who seek the praise of men have their reward: they shall have no praise of God.

Giving Done in Secret

4. "But when you do alms, let not your left hand know what your right hand does." This is a proverbial expression, the

meaning of which is: do it in as secret a manner as is possible; as secret as is consistent with the doing it at all (for it must not be left undone; omit no opportunity of doing good, whether secretly or openly), and with the doing it in the most effectual manner. For here is also an exception to be made: when you are fully persuaded in your own mind, that by your not concealing the good which is done, either you will yourself be enabled, or others excited, to do the more good, then you may not conceal it. Then let your light appear, and "shine to all that are in the house." But, unless where the glory of God and the good of mankind oblige you to the contrary, act in as private and unobserved a manner as the nature of the thing will admit; "that your alms may be in secret; and your Father which sees in secret, he shall reward you openly"; perhaps in the present world, many instances of this stand recorded in all ages; but infallibly in the world to come, before the general assembly of men and angels.

II. Sincere Works of Piety

Pray for God's Honor Alone

1. From works of charity or mercy our Lord proceeds to those which are termed works of piety. "And when you pray," says he, "you shall not be as the hypocrites are; for they love to pray standing in the synagogues, and in the corners of the streets, that they may be seen of men." "You shall not be as the hypocrites are." Hypocrisy, then, or insincerity, is the first thing we are to guard against in prayer. Beware not to speak what you do not mean. Prayer is the lifting up of the heart to God: all words of prayer, without this, are mere hypocrisy. Whenever therefore you attempt to pray, see that it be your one design to commune with God, to lift up your heart to him,

to pour out your soul before him; not as the hypocrites, who love, or are wont, "to pray standing in the synagogues," the exchange, or marketplaces, "and in the corners of the streets," wherever the most people are, "that they may be seen of men." This was the sole design, the motive, and end, of the prayers which they there repeated. "Verily I say unto you, They have their reward." They are to expect none from your Father which is in heaven.

2. But it is not only the having an eye to the praise of men which cuts us off from any reward in heaven; which leaves us no room to expect the blessing of God upon our works, whether of piety or mercy. Purity of intention is equally destroyed by a view to any temporal reward whatever. If we repeat our prayers, if we attend the public worship of God, if we relieve the poor, with a view to gain or interest, it is not a whit more acceptable to God than if it were done with a view to praise. Any temporal view, any motive whatever on this side eternity, any design but that of promoting the glory of God, and the happiness of men for God's sake, makes every action, however fair it may appear to men, an abomination unto the Lord.

Praying Done in Secret

3. "But when you pray, enter into your closet, and when you have shut the door, pray to your Father which is in secret." There is a time when you are openly to glorify God, to pray, and praise him, in the great congregation. But when you desire more largely and more particularly to make your requests known unto God, whether it be in the evening, or in the morning or at noon-day, "enter into your closet, and shut the door." Use all the privacy you can. (Only leave it not undone, whether you have any closet, any privacy, or no. Pray to God, if it be possible, when none sees but he; but, if otherwise, pray to God.) Thus "pray to your Father which is in secret;" pour out

your heart before him; "and your Father which sees in secret, he shall reward you openly."

4. "But when you pray," even in secret, μὴ βατταλογήσητε *"use not vain repetitions, as the heathen do."* Do not use abundance of words without any meaning. Say not the same thing over and over again; think not the fruit of your prayers depends on the length of them, like the heathens; for "they think they shall be heard for their much speaking."

The thing here reproved is not simply the length, any more than the shortness, of our prayers; but, first, length without meaning; speaking much, and meaning little or nothing; the using (not all repetitions; for our Lord himself prayed thrice, repeating the same words; but) vain repetitions, as the heathens did, reciting the names of their gods, over and over; as they do among Christians (vulgarly so called), and not among the Papists only, who say over and over the same string of prayers, without ever feeling what they speak.

Secondly, the thinking to be heard for our much speaking, the fancying God measures prayers by their length, and is best pleased with those which contain the most words, which sound the longest in his ears. These are such instances of superstition and folly as all who are named by the name of Christ should leave to the heathens, to them on whom the glorious light of the gospel has never shined.

5. "Be not ye therefore like unto them." You who have tasted of the grace of God in Christ Jesus are throughly convinced, "your Father knows what things you have need of, before you ask him." So that the end of your praying is not to inform God, as though he knew not your wants already; but rather to inform yourselves; to fix the sense of those wants more deeply in your hearts, and the sense of your continual dependence on him who only is able to supply all your wants. It is not so much to move God, who is always more ready to give than you to

ask, as to move yourselves, that you may be willing and ready to receive the good things he has prepared for you.

III. The Lord's Prayer

1. After having taught the true nature and ends of prayer, our Lord subjoins an example of it; even that divine form of prayer which seems in this place to be proposed by way of pattern chiefly, as the model and standard of all our prayers: "After this manner therefore pray ye." Whereas, elsewhere he enjoins the use of these very words: "He said unto them, When you pray, say . . ." (Luke 11:2).

2. We may observe, in general, concerning this divine prayer, first, that it contains all we can reasonably or innocently pray for. There is nothing which we have need to ask of God, nothing which we can ask without offending him, which is not included, either directly or indirectly, in this comprehensive form. Secondly, that it contains all we can reasonably or innocently desire; whatever is for the glory of God, whatever is needful or profitable, not only for ourselves, but for every creature in heaven and earth. And, indeed, our prayers are the proper test of our desires; nothing being fit to have a place in our desires which is not fit to have a place in our prayers: what we may not pray for, neither should we desire. Thirdly, that it contains all our duty to God and man; whatsoever things are pure and holy, whatsoever God requires of the children of men, whatsoever is acceptable in his sight, whatsoever it is whereby we may profit our neighbor, being expressed or implied therein.

3. It consists of three parts: the preface, the petitions, and the doxology, or conclusion. The preface, "Our Father which art in heaven," lays a general foundation for prayer; comprising what we must first know of God, before we can pray in confidence of being heard. It likewise points out to us all those

tempers with which we are to approach to God, which are most essentially requisite, if we desire either our prayers or our lives should find acceptance with him.

The Preface

4. *"Our Father."* If he is a Father, then he is good; then he is loving, to his children. And here is the first and great reason for prayer. God is willing to bless; let us ask for a blessing. "Our Father"—our Creator; the Author of our being; he who raised us from the dust of the earth; who breathed into us the breath of life, and we became living souls. But if he made us, let us ask, and he will not withhold any good thing from the work of his own hands. "Our Father"—our Preserver; who, day by day, sustains the life he has given; of whose continuing love we now and every moment receive life and breath and all things. So much the more boldly let us come to him, and we shall "obtain mercy, and grace to help in time of need." Above all, the Father of our Lord Jesus Christ, and of all that believe in him; who justifies us "freely by his grace, through the redemption that is in Jesus"; who hath "blotted out all our sins, and healed all our infirmities"; who hath received us for his own children, by adoption and grace; and, "because" we "are sons, hath sent forth the Spirit of his Son into" our "hearts, crying, Abba, Father"; who "hath begotten us again of incorruptible seed," and "created us anew in Christ Jesus." Therefore we know that he heareth us always; therefore we pray to him without ceasing. We pray, because we love; and "we love him because he first loved us."

5. *"Our Father."* Not mine only who now cry unto him, but ours in the most extensive sense. The God and "Father of the spirits of all flesh;" the Father of angels and men: so the very heathens acknowledged him to be, πατὴρ ἀνδρῶν τε θεῶν τε, *The Father of the universe, of all the families both in heaven and earth.*

Therefore with him there is no respect of persons. He loves all that he has made. "He is loving unto every man, and his mercy is over all his works." And the Lord's delight is in them that fear him, and put their trust in his mercy; in them that trust in him through the Son of his love, knowing they are "accepted in the Beloved." But "if God so loved us, we ought also to love one another"; yea, all mankind; seeing "God so loved the world, that he gave his only-begotten Son," even to die the death, that they "might not perish, but have everlasting life."

6. *"Which art in heaven."* High and lifted up; God over all, blessed for ever: who, sitting on the circle of the heavens, beholdeth all things both in heaven and earth; whose eye pervades the whole sphere of created being; yea, and of uncreated night; unto whom "are known all his works", and all the works of every creature, not only "from the beginning of the world" (a poor, low, weak translation), but ἀπ αἰῶνος, *from all eternity*, from everlasting to everlasting; who constrains the host of heaven, as well as the children of men, to cry out with wonder and amazement: O the depth!—"the depth of the riches, both of the wisdom and of the knowledge of God!"

"Which art in heaven"—the Lord and Ruler of all, superintending and disposing all things; who art the King of kings, and Lord of lords, the blessed and only Potentate; who art strong and girded about with power, doing whatsoever pleaseth you; the Almighty; for whensoever you willest, to do is present with you.

"In heaven"—eminently there. Heaven is your throne, "the place where your honor" particularly "dwelleth." But not there alone; for you fill heaven and earth, the whole expanse of space. "Heaven and earth are full of your glory. Glory be to you, O Lord, most high!" Therefore should we "serve the Lord with fear, and rejoice unto him with reverence." Therefore should we think, speak, and act, as continually under the eye, in the immediate presence, of the Lord, the King.

The Petitions: For All Mankind

7. *"Hallowed be thy name."* This is the first of the six petitions, whereof the prayer itself is composed. The name of God is God himself; the nature of God, so far as it can be discovered to man. It means, therefore, together with his existence, all his attributes or perfections; his eternity, particularly signified by his great and incommunicable name, JEHOVAH, as the apostle John translates it: τὸ Ὦ λέγει Κύριος, ὁ θεός, ὁ ὢν καὶ ὁ ἦν καὶ ὁ ἐρχόμενος, *the Alpha and Omega, the beginning and the end; He which is, and which was, and which is to come*; His Fullness of Being, denoted by his other great name, I AM THAT I AM!

His omnipresence; his omnipotence; who is indeed the only Agent in the material world; all matter being essentially dull and inactive, and moving only as it is moved by the finger of God; and he is the spring of action in every creature, visible and invisible, which could neither act nor exist, without the continual influx and agency of his almighty power; his wisdom, clearly deduced from the things that are seen, from the goodly order of the universe; his Trinity in Unity, and Unity in Trinity, discovered to us in the very first line of his written word, literally, *the Gods created*, a plural noun joined with a verb of the singular number; as well as in every part of his subsequent revelations, given by the mouth of all his holy prophets and apostles; his essential purity and holiness; and, above all, his love, which is the very brightness of his glory.

In praying that God, or his name, may "be hallowed" or glorified, we pray that he may be known, such as he is, by all that are capable thereof, by all intelligent beings, and with affections suitable to that knowledge; that he may be duly

honored, and feared, and loved, by all in heaven above and in
the earth beneath; by all angels and men, whom for that end
he has made capable of knowing and loving him to eternity.

8. *"Thy kingdom come."* This has a close connection with
the preceding petition. In order that the name of God might
be hallowed, we pray that his kingdom, the kingdom of Christ,
may come. This kingdom then comes to a particular person,
when he "repents and believes the gospel"; when he is taught
of God, not only to know himself, but to know Jesus Christ
and him crucified. As "this is life eternal, to know the only
true God, and Jesus Christ whom he hath sent"; so it is the
kingdom of God begun below, set up in the believer's heart;
"the Lord God Omnipotent" then "reigneth," when he is
known through Christ Jesus. He takes unto himself his mighty
power, that he may subdue all things unto himself. He goes on
in the soul conquering and to conquer, till he has put all things
under his feet, till "every thought is brought into captivity to
the obedience of Christ."

When therefore God shall "give his Son the heathen for
his inheritance, and the uttermost parts of the earth for his
possession"; when "all kingdoms shall bow before him, and
all nations shall do him service"; when "the mountain of the
Lord's house," the Church of Christ, "shall be established in
the top of the mountains"; when "the fullness of the Gentiles
shall come in, and all Israel shall be saved"; then shall it be
seen that "the Lord is King, and has put on glorious apparel,"
appearing to every soul of man as King of kings, and Lord
of lords. And it is meet for all those who love his appearing,
to pray that he would hasten the time; that this his kingdom,
the kingdom of grace, may come quickly, and swallow up all
the kingdoms of the earth; that all mankind, receiving him for
their King, truly believing in his name, may be filled with righteousness, and peace, and joy, with holiness and happiness, till

they are removed hence into his heavenly kingdom, there to reign with him for ever and ever.

For this also we pray in those words, "Thy kingdom come." We pray for the coming of his everlasting kingdom, the kingdom of glory in heaven, which is the continuation and perfection of the kingdom of grace on earth. Consequently this, as well as the preceding petition, is offered up for the whole intelligent creation, who are all interested in this grand event, the final renovation of all things, by God's putting an end to misery and sin, to infirmity and death, taking all things into his own hands, and setting up the kingdom which endures throughout all ages.

Exactly answerable to this are those awful words in the prayer at the burial of the dead: "Beseeching thee, that it may please thee of thy gracious goodness, shortly to accomplish the number of thine elect, and to hasten thy kingdom: that we, with all those that are departed in the true faith of thy holy name, may have our perfect consummation and bliss, both in body and soul, in thy everlasting glory."

9. *"Thy will be done in earth, as it is in heaven."* This is the necessary and immediate consequence wherever the kingdom of God is come; wherever God dwells in the soul by faith, and Christ reigns in the heart by love.

It is probable many, perhaps the generality of men, at the first view of these words, are apt to imagine they are only an expression of, or petition for, resignation; for a readiness to suffer the will of God, whatsoever it be concerning us. And this is unquestionably a divine and excellent temper, a most precious gift of God. But this is not what we pray for in this petition; at least, not in the chief and primary sense of it. We pray, not so much for a passive as for an active conformity to the will of God, in saying, "Thy will be done in earth, as it is in heaven."

How is it done by the angels of God in heaven, those who now circle his throne rejoicing? They do it willingly; they love his commandments, and gladly hearken to his words. It is their meat and drink to do his will; it is their highest glory and joy. They do it continually; there is no interruption in their willing service. They rest not day nor night, but employ every hour (speaking after the manner of men; otherwise our measures of duration, days, and nights, and hours, have no place in eternity) in fulfilling his commands, in executing his designs, in performing the counsel of his will. And they do it perfectly. No sin, no defect belongs to angelic minds. It is true, "the stars are not pure in his sight," even the morning-stars that sing together before him. "In his sight," that is, in comparison of him, the very angels are not pure. But this does not imply that they are not pure in themselves. Doubtless they are; they are without spot and blameless. They are altogether devoted to his will, and perfectly obedient in all things.

If we view this in another light, we may observe, the angels of God in heaven do all the will of God. And they do nothing else, nothing but what they are absolutely assured is his will. Again they do all the will of God as he willeth; in the manner which pleases him, and no other. Yea, and they do this only because it is his will; for this end, and no other reason.

10. When therefore we pray that the will of God may "be done in earth as it is in heaven," the meaning is, that all the inhabitants of the earth, even the whole race of mankind, may do the will of their Father which is in heaven, as willingly as the holy angels; that these may do it continually, even as they, without any interruption of their willing service; yea, and that they may do it perfectly—that "the God of peace, through the blood of the everlasting covenant, may make them perfect in

every good work to do his will, and work in them all "which is well-pleasing in his sight."

In other words, we pray that we and all mankind may do the whole will of God in all things; and nothing else, not the least thing, but what is the holy and acceptable will of God. We pray that we may do the whole will of God as he willeth, in the manner that pleases him: And, lastly, that we may do it because it is his will; that this may be the sole reason and ground, the whole and only motive, of whatsoever we think, or whatsoever we speak or do.

The Petitions: For the Church of Christ

11. *"Give us this day our daily bread."* In the three former petitions we have been praying for all mankind. We come now more particularly to desire a supply for our own wants. Not that we are directed, even here, to confine our prayer altogether to ourselves; but this, and each of the following petitions, may be used for the whole Church of Christ upon earth.

By "bread" we may understand all things needful, whether for our souls or bodies; τὰ πρὸς ζωὴν καὶ εὐσέβειαν, *the things pertaining to life and godliness.* We understand not barely the outward bread, what our Lord terms "the meat which perishes"; but much more the spiritual bread, the grace of God, the food "which endures unto everlasting life." It was the judgment of many of the ancient Fathers that we are here to understand the sacramental bread also; daily received in the beginning by the whole Church of Christ, and highly esteemed, till the love of many waxed cold, as the grand channel whereby the grace of his Spirit was conveyed to the souls of all the children of God.

"Our daily bread." The word we render daily has been differently explained by different commentators. But the most plain and natural sense of it seems to be this, which is retained in almost all translations, as well ancient as modern—what is sufficient for this day; and so for each day as it succeeds.

12. "Give us." For we claim nothing of right, but only of free mercy. We deserve not the air we breathe, the earth that bears, or the sun that shines upon, us. All our desert, we own, is hell: but God loves us freely; therefore, we ask him to give what we can no more procure for ourselves than we can merit it at his hands.

Not that either the goodness or the power of God is a reason for us to stand idle. It is his will that we should use all diligence in all things, that we should employ our utmost endeavors, as much as if our success were the natural effect of our own wisdom and strength. And then, as though we had done nothing, we are to depend on him, the giver of every good and perfect gift.

"This day." For we are to take no thought for the morrow. For this very end has our wise Creator divided life into these little portions of time, so clearly separated from each other, that we might look on every day as a fresh gift of God, another life, which we may devote to his glory; and that every evening may be as the close of life, beyond which we are to see nothing but eternity.

13. *"And forgive us our trespasses, as we forgive them that trespass against us."* As nothing but sin can hinder the bounty of God from flowing forth upon every creature, so this petition naturally follows the former; that, all hindrances being removed, we may the more clearly trust in the God of love for every manner of thing which is good.

"Our trespasses." The word properly signifies our debts. Thus our sins are frequently represented in Scripture; every sin laying us under a fresh debt to God, to whom we already owe, as it were, ten thousand talents. What then can we answer when he shall say, "Pay me that thou owest"? We are utterly insolvent; we have nothing to pay; we have wasted all our substance. Therefore, if he deals with us according to the rigor of his law, if he exacts what he justly may, he must command us to be "bound hand and foot, and delivered over to the tormentors."

Indeed we are already bound hand and foot by the chains of our own sins. These, considered with regard to ourselves, are chains of iron and fetters of brass. They are wounds wherewith the world, the flesh, and the devil have gashed and mangled us all over. They are diseases that drink up our blood and spirits, that bring us down to the chambers of the grave. But considered, as they are here, with regard to God, they are debts, immense and numberless. Well, therefore, seeing we have nothing to pay, may we cry unto him that he would "frankly forgive" us all!

The word translated "forgive" implies either to forgive a debt, or to unloose a chain. And if we attain the former, the latter follows of course: if our debts are forgiven, the chains fall off our hands. As soon as ever, through the free grace of God in Christ, we "receive forgiveness of sins," we receive likewise "a lot among those which are sanctified, by faith which is in him." Sin has lost its power; it has no dominion over those who "are under grace," that is, in favor with God. As "there is now no condemnation for them that are in Christ Jesus," so they are freed from sin as well as from guilt. "The righteousness of the law is fulfilled in" them, and they "walk not after the flesh, but after the Spirit."

14. *"As we forgive them that trespass against us."* In these words our Lord clearly declares both on what condition, and in what degree or manner, we may look to be forgiven of God. All our trespasses and sins are forgiven us, if we forgive, and as we forgive, others. First, God forgives us if we forgive others. This is a point of the utmost importance. And our blessed Lord is so

jealous lest at any time we should let it slip out of our thoughts, that he not only inserts it in the body of his prayer, but presently after repeats it twice over. "If," saith he, "you forgive men their trespasses, your heavenly Father will also forgive you. But if you forgive not men their trespasses, neither will your Father forgive your trespasses" (Matt. 6:14, 15). Secondly, God forgives us as we forgive others. So that if any malice or bitterness, if any taint of unkindness or anger remains, if we do not clearly, fully, and from the heart, forgive all men their trespasses, we far cut short the forgiveness of our own—God cannot clearly and fully forgive us: he may show us some degree of mercy; but we will not suffer him to blot out all our sins, and forgive all our iniquities.

In the meantime, while we do not from our hearts forgive our neighbor his trespasses, what manner of prayer are we offering to God whenever we utter these words? We are indeed setting God at open defiance: we are daring him to do his worst. "Forgive us our trespasses, as we forgive them that trespass against us!" That is, in plain terms, "Do not thou forgive us at all; we desire no favor at thy hands. We pray that you will keep our sins in remembrance, and that your wrath may abide upon us." But can you seriously offer such a prayer to God? And has he not yet cast you quick into hell? O tempt him no longer! Now, even now, by his grace, forgive as you would be forgiven! Now have compassion on your fellow-servant, as God has had and will have pity on you!

15. *"And lead us not into temptation, but deliver us from evil."* [And] lead us not into temptation. The word translated "temptation" means trial of any kind. And so the English word temptation was formerly taken in an indifferent sense, although now it is usually understood of solicitation to sin. St. James uses the word in both these senses; first, in its general, then in its restrained, acceptation. He takes it in the former

sense when he saith, "Blessed is the man that endureth temptation; for when he is tried," or approved of God, "he shall receive the crown of life" (James 1:12, 13). He immediately adds, taking the word in the latter sense, "Let no man say when he is tempted, I am tempted of God; for God cannot be tempted with evil, neither tempteth he any man. But every man is tempted, when he is drawn away of his own lust," or desire, ἐξελκόμενος, *drawn out of God*, in whom alone he is safe, "and enticed"; caught as a fish with a bait. Then it is, when he is thus drawn away and enticed, that he properly "enters into temptation." Then temptation covers him as a cloud; it overspreads his whole soul. Then how hardly shall he escape out of the snare! Therefore, we beseech God "not to lead us into temptation," that is (seeing God tempteth no man), not to suffer us to be led into it.

"But deliver us from evil." Rather ἀπὸ τοῦ πονηροῦ, *"from the evil one."* Ὁ πονηροῦς is unquestionably "the wicked one," emphatically so called, the prince and god of this world, who works with mighty power in the children of disobedience. But all those who are the children of God by faith are delivered out of his hands. He may fight against them; and so he will. But he cannot conquer, unless they betray their own souls. He may torment for a time, but he cannot destroy; for God is on their side, who will not fail, in the end, to "avenge his own elect, that cry unto him day and night." Lord, when we are tempted, suffer us not to enter into temptation! Do thou make a way for us to escape, that the wicked one touch us not!

The Doxology

16. The conclusion of this divine prayer, commonly called the Doxology, is a solemn thanksgiving, a compendious acknowledgment of the attributes and works of God. "For thine is the kingdom"—the sovereign right of all things

that are or ever were created; yea, your kingdom is an everlasting kingdom, and your dominion endures throughout all ages. "The power"—the executive power whereby you govern all things in your everlasting kingdom, whereby you do whatsoever pleaseth you, in all places of your dominion. "And the glory"—the praise due from every creature, for your power, and the mightiness of your kingdom, and for all your wondrous works which you workest from everlasting, and shalt do, world without end, "for ever and ever! Amen!" So be it!

A Paraphrase on the Lord's Prayer. I believe it will not be unacceptable to the serious reader to subjoin "A Paraphrase on the Lord's Prayer":

> 1. Father of all, whose powerful voice
> Call'd forth this universal frame;
> Whose mercies over all rejoice,
> Through endless ages still the same
> Thou, by thy word, upholdest all;
> Thy bounteous love to all is show'd,
> Thou hear'st thy every creature's call.
> And fillest every mouth with good
>
> 2. In heaven thou reign'st, enthroned in light,
> Nature's expanse beneath thee spread;
> Earth, air, and sea before thy sight,
> And hell's deep gloom are open laid.
> Wisdom, and might, and love are thine:
> Prostrate before thy face we fall,
> Confess thine attributes divine,
> And hail the Soverign Lord of All.
>
> 3. Thee, sovereign Lord, let all confess
> That moves in earth, or air, or sky

Revere thy power, they goodness bless,
Tremble before thy piercing eye.
All ye who owe to Him your birth,
In praise your every hour employ:
Jehovah reigns! Be glad, O earth!
And shout, ye morning stars, for joy!

4. Son of thy Sire's eternal love,
Take to thyself thy mighty power;
Let all earth's sons thy mercy prove,
Let all thy bleeding grace adore.
The triumphs of thy love display;
In every heart reign thou alone;
Till all thy foes confess thy sway,
And glory ends what grace begun.

5. Spirit of grace, and health, and power,
Fountain of light and love below,
Abroad thine healing influence shower,
O'er all the nations let it flow.
Inflame our hearts with perfect love;
In us the work of faith fulfill;
So not heaven's hosts shall swifter move
Than we on earth to do thy will.

6. Father, 'tis thine each day to yield
Thy children's wants a fresh supply:
Thou cloth'st the lilies of the field,
And hearest the young ravens cry.
On thee we cast our care; we live
Through thee, who know'st our every need;
O feed us with thy grace, and give
Our souls this day the living bread!

7. Eternal, spotless Lamb of God,
Before the world's foundation slain,
Sprinkle us ever with thy blood;
O cleanse and keep us ever clean.
To every soul (all praise to Thee!)
Our heart full of compassion more:
And all mankind by this may see
God is in us; for God is love.

8. Giver and Lord of life, whose power
And guardian care for all are free;
To thee, in fierce temptation's hour,
From sin and Satan let us flee.
Thine, Lord, we are, and ours thou art;
In us be all thy goodness show'd;
Renew, enlarge, and fill our heart
With peace, and joy, and heaven, and God.

9. Blessing and honor, praise and love,
Co-equal, co-eternal Three,
In earth below, in heaven above,
By all thy works be paid to thee.
Thrice Holy! thine the kingdom is,
The power omnipotent is thine;
And when created nature dies,
Thy never-ceasing glories shine.

DISCOURSE SEVEN

TRUE FASTING

*Moreover when you fast, be not, as the hypocrites, of a sad
countenance. For they disfigure their faces, that they may
appear unto men to fast. Verily I say unto you, They have
their reward. But thou, when thou fastest, anoint thine head,
and wash thy face; that thou appear not unto men to fast,
but unto thy Father which is in secret: and thy Father, which
seeth in secret, shall reward thee openly.*

—Matthew 6:16–18

Introduction

1. It has been the endeavor of Satan, from the beginning
of the world, to put asunder what God has joined together; to
separate inward from outward religion; to set one of these at
variance with the other. And herein he has met with no small
success among those who were "ignorant of his devices."

Many, in all ages, having a zeal for God, but not according
to knowledge, have been strictly attached to the "righteousness

of the law," the performance of outward duties, but in the meantime wholly regardless of inward righteousness, "the righteousness which is of God by faith." And many have run into the opposite extreme, disregarding all outward duties, perhaps even "speaking evil of the law, and judging the law," so far as it enjoins the performance of them.

2. It is by this very device of Satan that faith and works have been so often set at variance with each other. And many who had a real zeal for God have, for a time, fallen into the snare on either hand. Some have magnified faith to the utter exclusion of good works, not only from being the cause of our justification (for we know that man is justified freely by the redemption which is in Jesus), but from being the necessary fruit of it, yea, from having any place in the religion of Jesus Christ. Others, eager to avoid this dangerous mistake, have run as much too far the contrary way; and either maintained that good works were the cause, at least the previous condition, of justification, or spoken of them as if they were all in all, the whole religion of Jesus Christ.

3. In the same manner have the end and the means of religion been set at variance with each other. Some well-meaning men have seemed to place all religion in attending the Prayers of the Church, in receiving the Lord's supper, in hearing sermons, and reading books of piety; neglecting, meantime, the end of all these, the love of God and their neighbor. And this very thing has confirmed others in the neglect, if not contempt, of the ordinances of God, so wretchedly abused to undermine and overthrow the very end they were designed to establish.

4. But of all the means of grace there is scarce any concerning which men have run into greater extremes, than that of which our Lord speaks in the above-mentioned words, I mean religious fasting. How have some exalted this beyond all Scripture and reason, and others utterly disregarded it; as

it were revenging themselves by undervaluing as much as the former had overvalued it! Those have spoken of it, as if it were all in all; if not the end itself, yet infallibly connected with it: these, as if it were just nothing, as if it were a fruitless labor, which had no relation at all thereto. Whereas it is certain the truth lies between them both. It is not all, nor yet is it nothing. It is not the end, but it is a precious means thereto; a means which God himself has ordained, and in which therefore, when it is duly used, he will surely give us his blessing.

In order to set this in the clearest light, I shall endeavor to show, first, what is the nature of fasting, and what the several sorts and degrees thereof; secondly, what are the reasons, grounds, and ends of it; thirdly, how we may answer the most plausible objections against it; and fourthly, in what manner it should be performed.

I. The Nature and Degrees of Fasting

The Nature of Fasting

1. I shall endeavor to show, first, what is the nature of fasting, and what the several sorts and degrees thereof. As to the nature of it, all the inspired writers, both in the Old Testament and the New, take the word to fast in one single sense, for not to eat, to abstain from food. This is so clear that it would be labor lost to quote the words of David, Nehemiah, Isaiah, and the prophets which followed, or of our Lord and his apostles; all agreeing in this, that to fast is to not eat for a time prescribed.

2. To this, other circumstances were usually joined by them of old, which had no necessary connection with it. Such were the neglect of their apparel; the laying aside those ornaments which they were accustomed to wear; the putting on mourning;

the strewing ashes upon their head; or wearing sackcloth next their skin. But we find little mention made in the New Testament of any of these indifferent circumstances. Nor does it appear that any stress was laid upon them by the Christians of the purer ages; however some penitents might voluntarily use them, as outward signs of inward humiliation. Much less did the apostles, or the Christians contemporary with them, beat or tear their own flesh: such discipline as this was not unbecoming the priests or worshippers of Baal. The gods of the heathens were but devils; and it was doubtless acceptable to their devil-god, when his priests (1 Kings 18:28) "cried aloud, and cut themselves after their manner, till the blood gushed out upon them": but it cannot be pleasing to him, nor become his followers, who "came not to destroy men's lives, but to save them."

The Degrees of Fasting

3. As to the degrees or measures of fasting, we have instances of some who have fasted several days together. So Moses, Elijah, and our blessed Lord, being endued with supernatural strength for that purpose, are recorded to have fasted, without intermission, "forty days and forty nights." But the time of fasting, more frequently mentioned in Scripture, is one day, from morning till evening. And this was the fast commonly observed among the ancient Christians. But beside these, they had also their half-fasts (*Semijejunia*, as Tertullian styles them) on the fourth and sixth days of the week (Wednesday and Friday), throughout the year; on which they took no sustenance till three in the afternoon, the time when they returned from the public service.

4. Nearly related to this is what our Church seems peculiarly to mean by the term "abstinence," which may be used when we cannot fast entirely, by reason of sickness or bodily weakness. This is the eating little; the abstaining in part; the

taking a smaller quantity of food than usual. I do not remember any scriptural instance of this. But neither can I condemn it; for the Scripture does not. It may have its use, and receive a blessing from God.

5. The lowest kind of fasting, if it can be called by that name, is the abstaining from pleasant food. Of this, we have several instances in Scripture, besides that of Daniel and his brethren, who from a peculiar consideration, namely, that they might "not defile themselves with the portion of the king's meat, nor with the wine which he drank" (a daily provision of which the king had appointed for them), requested and obtained, of the prince of the eunuchs, pulse to eat and water to drink (Daniel 1:8ff.). Perhaps from a mistaken imitation of this might spring the very ancient custom of abstaining from flesh and wine during such times as were set apart for fasting and abstinence; if it did not rather arise from a supposition that these were the most pleasant food, and a belief that it was proper to use what was least pleasing at those times of solemn approach to God.

Stated and Occasional Fasts

6. In the Jewish church there were some stated fasts. Such was the fast of the seventh month, appointed by God himself to be observed by all Israel under the severest penalty. "The LORD spoke unto Moses, saying, On the tenth day of this seventh month, there shall be a day of atonement: and ye shall afflict your souls, to make an atonement for you before the LORD your God. For whatsoever soul it be that shall not be afflicted in that same day, he shall be cut off from among his people" (Lev. 23:26ff.). In after-ages, several other stated fasts were added to these. So mention is made, by the prophet Zechariah, of the fast not only "of the seventh, but also of the fourth, of the fifth, and of the tenth month" (Zech. 8:19).

In the ancient Christian Church, there were likewise stated fasts, and those both annual and weekly. Of the former sort was that before Easter; observed by some for eight-and-forty hours; by others, for an entire week; by many, for two weeks; taking no sustenance till the evening of each day. Of the latter, those of the fourth and sixth days of the week, observed (as Epiphanius writes, remarking it as an undeniable fact) ἐν τῇ ὅλῃ τῇ οἰκουμένῃ, *in the whole habitable earth*; at least in every place where any Christians made their abode. The annual fasts in our Church are, "the forty days of Lent, the Ember days at the four seasons, the Rogation days, and the Vigils or Eves of several solemn festivals; the weekly, all Fridays in the year, except Christmas day."

But beside those which were fixed, in every nation fearing God there have always been occasional fasts, appointed from time to time, as the particular circumstances and occasions of each required. So when "the children of Moab, and the children of Ammon, came against Jehoshaphat to battle, Jehoshaphat set himself to seek the LORD, and proclaimed a fast throughout all Judah" (2 Chron. 20:1, 3). And so, "in the fifth year of Jehoiakim the son of Josiah, in the ninth month," when they were afraid of the king of Babylon, the princes of "Judah proclaimed a fast before the LORD to all the people of Jerusalem" (Jer. 36:9).

And, in like manner, particular persons, who take heed unto their ways, and desire to walk humbly and closely with God, will find frequent occasion for private seasons of thus afflicting their souls before their Father which is in secret. And it is to this kind of fasting that the directions here given do chiefly and primarily refer.

II. The Grounds, Reasons and Ends of Fasting

1. I proceed to show, in the second place, what are the grounds, the reasons, and ends of fasting.

Fasting as a Strong Emotional Response

And, first, men who are under strong emotions of mind, who are affected with any vehement passion, such as sorrow or fear, are often swallowed up therein, and even forget to eat their bread. At such seasons they have little regard for food, not even what is needful to sustain nature, much less for any delicacy or variety, being taken up with quite different thoughts. Thus when Saul said, "I am sore distressed; for the Philistines make war against me, and God is departed from me," it is recorded, "he had eaten no bread all the day, nor all the night" (1 Sam. 28:15, 20). Thus those who were in the ship with St. Paul, "when no small tempest lay upon them, and all hope that they should be saved was taken away," "continued fasting, having taken nothing," no regular meal, for fourteen days together (Acts 27:20, 33). And thus David, and all the men that were with him, when they heard that the people were fled from the battle, and that many of the people were fallen and dead, and Saul and Jonathan his son were dead also, "mourned, and wept, and fasted until even, for Saul and Jonathan, and for the house of Israel" (2 Sam. 1:12).

Nay, many times they whose minds are deeply engaged are impatient of any interruption, and even loathe their needful food, as diverting their thoughts from what they desire should engross their whole attention; even as Saul, when, on the occasion mentioned before, he had "fallen all along upon the earth, and there was no strength in him," yet said, "I will not eat," till "his servants, together with the woman, compelled him."

Fasting as Grief over One's Sin

2. Here, then, is the natural ground of fasting. One who is under deep affliction, overwhelmed with sorrow for sin, and a strong apprehension of the wrath of God, would, without

any rule, without knowing or considering whether it were a command of God or not, "forget to eat his bread," abstain not only from pleasant but even from needful food; like St. Paul, who, after he was led into Damascus, "was three days without sight, and did neither eat nor drink" (Acts 9:9).

Yea, when the storm rose high; "when an horrible dread overwhelmed" one who had been without God in the world, his soul would "loathe all manner of meat"; it would be unpleasing and irksome to him; he would be impatient of anything that should interrupt his ceaseless cry, "Lord, save or I perish."

How strongly is this expressed by our Church in the first part of the Homily on Fasting! "When men feel in themselves the heavy burden of sin, see damnation to be the reward of it, and behold, with the eye of their mind, the horror of hell, they tremble, they quake, and are inwardly touched with sorrowfulness of heart, and cannot but accuse themselves, and open their grief unto Almighty God, and call unto him for mercy. This being done seriously, their mind is so occupied [taken up], partly with sorrow and heaviness, partly with an earnest desire to be delivered from this danger of hell and damnation, that all desire of meat and drink is laid apart, and loathsomeness [or loathing] of all worldly things and pleasure cometh in place. So that nothing then liketh them more than to weep, to lament, to mourn, and both with words and behavior of body to show themselves weary of life."

Fasting as an Act of Abstinence

3. Another reason or ground of fasting is this: many of those who now fear God are deeply sensible how often they have sinned against him, by the abuse of these lawful things. They know how much they have sinned by excess of food; how long they have transgressed the holy law of God, with regard to temperance, if not sobriety too; how they have indulged their

sensual appetites, perhaps to the impairing even their bodily health, certainly to the no small hurt of their soul. For hereby they continually fed and increased that sprightly folly, that airiness of mind, that levity of temper, that gay inattention to things of the deepest concern, that giddiness and carelessness of spirit, which were no other than drunkenness of soul, which stupefied all their noblest faculties, no less than excess of wine or strong drink. To remove, therefore, the effect, they remove the cause. They keep at a distance from all excess. They abstain, as far as is possible, from what had well nigh plunged them in everlasting perdition. They often wholly refrain; always take care to be sparing and temperate in all things.

4. They likewise well remember how fullness of bread increased not only carelessness and levity of spirit, but also foolish and unholy desires, yea, unclean and vile affections. And this experience puts beyond all doubt. Even a genteel, regular sensuality is continually sensualizing the soul, and sinking it into a level with the beasts that perish. It cannot be expressed what an effect variety and delicacy of food have on the mind as well as the body; making it just ripe for every pleasure of sense, as soon as opportunity shall invite. Therefore, on this ground also, every wise man will refrain his soul, and keep it low; will wean it more and more from all those indulgences of the inferior appetites, which naturally tend to chain it down to earth, and to pollute as well as debase it. Here is another perpetual reason for fasting; to remove the food of lust and sensuality, to withdraw the incentives of foolish and hurtful desires, of vile and vain affections.

Fasting as a Means of Self-Punishment

5. Perhaps we need not altogether omit (although I know not if we should do well to lay any great stress upon it) another reason for fasting, which some good men have largely insisted

on; namely, the punishing themselves for having abused the good gifts of God, by sometimes wholly refraining from them; thus exercising a kind of holy revenge upon themselves, for their past folly and ingratitude, in turning the things which should have been for their health into an occasion of falling. They suppose David to have had an eye to this when he said, "I wept and chastened," or punished, "my soul with fasting"; and St. Paul, when he mentions "what revenge" godly sorrow occasioned in the Corinthians.

Fasting as a Help to Prayer

6. A fifth and more weighty reason for fasting is that it is a help to prayer; particularly when we set apart larger portions of time for private prayer. Then especially it is that God is often pleased to lift up the souls of his servants above all the things of earth, and sometimes to rap them up, as it were, into the third heavens. And it is chiefly, as it is a help to prayer, that it has so frequently been found a means, in the hand of God, of confirming and increasing, not one virtue, not chastity only (as some have idly imagined, without any ground either from Scripture, reason, or experience), but also seriousness of spirit, earnestness, sensibility and tenderness of conscience, deadness to the world, and consequently the love of God, and every holy and heavenly affection.

Fasting to Avert the Wrath of God

7. Not that there is any natural or necessary connection between fasting and the blessings God conveys thereby. But he will have mercy as he will have mercy; he will convey whatsoever seemeth him good by whatsoever means he is pleased to appoint. And he has, in all ages, appointed this to be a means of averting his wrath, and obtaining whatever blessings we, from time to time, stand in need of.

How powerful a means this is to avert the wrath of God, we may learn from the remarkable instance of Ahab. "There was none like him who did sell himself"—wholly give himself up, like a slave bought with money—"to work wickedness." Yet when he "rent his clothes, and put sackcloth upon his flesh, and fasted, and went softly, the word of the Lord came to Elijah, saying, "Seest thou how Ahab humbles himself before me? Because he humbles himself before me, I will not bring the evil in his days."

It was for this end, to avert the wrath of God, that Daniel sought God "with fasting, and sackcloth, and ashes." This appears from the whole tenor of his prayer, particularly from the solemn conclusion of it: "O Lord, according to all thy righteousness," or mercies, "let thy anger be turned away from thy holy mountain. Hear the prayer of thy servant, and cause thy face to shine upon thy sanctuary that is desolate. O Lord, hear; O Lord, forgive; O Lord, hearken and do, for thine own sake" (Dan. 9:3ff.).

8. But it is not only from the people of God that we learn, when his anger is moved, to seek him by fasting and prayer; but even from the heathens. When Jonah had declared, "Yet forty days and Nineveh shall be overthrown," the people of Nineveh proclaimed a fast, and put on sackcloth, from the greatest of them unto the least. "For the King of Nineveh arose from his throne, and laid his robe from him, and covered him with sackcloth, and sat in ashes. And he caused it to be proclaimed and published through Nineveh, Let neither man nor beast, herd nor flock, taste anything: let them not feed, nor drink water." (Not that the beast had sinned, or could repent; but that, by their example, man might be admonished, considering that, for his sin, the anger of God was hanging over all creatures.) "Who can tell if God will turn and repent, and turn away from his fierce anger, that we perish not?" And their labor was not

in vain. The fierce anger of God was turned away from them. "God saw their works" (the fruits of that repentance and faith which he had wrought in them by his prophet); "and God repented of the evil that he had said he would do unto them; and he did it not" (Jonah 3:4–10).

9. And it is a means not only of turning away the wrath of God, but also of obtaining whatever blessings we stand in need of. So, when the other tribes were smitten before the Benjamites, "all the children of Israel went up unto the house of God, and wept, and fasted that day until even"; and then the Lord said, "Go up" again; "for tomorrow I will deliver them into thine hand" (Judges 20:26, 28). So Samuel gathered all Israel together, when they were in bondage to the Philistines, "and they fasted on that day" before the Lord. And when "the Philistines drew near to battle against Israel, the Lord thundered" upon them "with a great thunder, and discomfited them; and they were smitten before Israel" (1 Sam. 7:6). So Ezra: "I proclaimed a fast at the river Ahava, that we might afflict ourselves before our God, to seek of him a right way for us, and for our little ones; and he was entreated of us" (Ezra 8:21). So Nehemiah: "I fasted and prayed before the God of heaven, and said, Prosper, I pray thee, thy servant this day, and grant him mercy in the sight of this man." And God granted him mercy in the sight of the king (Neh. 1:4–11).

Fasting to Seek God's Blessing

10. In like manner, the apostles always joined fasting with prayer when they desired the blessing of God on any important undertaking. Thus we read, "There were in the church that was at Antioch certain prophets and teachers . . . as they ministered to the Lord and fasted," doubtless for direction in this very affair, "the Holy Ghost said, Separate me Barnabas and Saul, for the work whereunto I have called them. And when they

had" a second time "fasted and prayed, and laid their hands on them, they sent them away" (Acts 13:1–3).

Thus also Paul and Barnabas themselves, as we read in the following chapter, when they "returned again to Lystra, Iconium, and Antioch, confirming the souls of the disciples, and when they had ordained them elders in every church, and had prayed with fasting, commended them to the Lord" (Acts 14:23).

Yea, that blessings are to be obtained in the use of this means, which are not otherwise attainable, our Lord expressly declares in his answer to his disciples, asking, "Why could not we cast him out? Jesus said unto them, Because of your unbelief: for verily I say unto you, If you have faith as a grain of mustard seed, you shall say unto this mountain, Remove hence to yonder place; and it shall remove; and nothing shall be impossible unto you. Howbeit, this kind" of devils "go not out but by prayer and fasting" (Matt. 17:19–21). These being the appointed means of attaining that faith whereby the very devils are subject unto you.

11. These were the appointed means: for it was not merely by the light of reason, or of natural conscience, as it is called, that the people of God have been, in all ages, directed to use fasting as a means to these ends; but they have been, from time to time, taught it of God himself, by clear and open revelations of his will. Such is that remarkable one by the prophet Joel: "Therefore saith the LORD, Turn you to me with all your heart, and with fasting, and with weeping, and with mourning: who knows if he will return and repent, and leave a blessing behind him? Blow the trumpet in Zion, sanctify a fast, call a solemn assembly: then will the LORD be jealous over his land, and will pity his people. Yea, I will send you corn, and wine, and oil: I will no more make you a reproach among the heathen" (Joel 2:12ff.).

Nor are they only temporal blessings which God directs his people to expect in the use of these means. For, at the same time that he promised to those who should seek him with fasting, and weeping, and mourning, "I will restore you the years which locust hath eaten, the cankerworm, and the caterpillar, and the palmerworm, my great army"; he subjoins, "So shall you eat and be satisfied, and praise the name of the Lord your God. You shall also know that I am in the midst of Israel, and that I am the Lord your God." And then immediately follows the great gospel promise, "I will pour out my Spirit upon all flesh; and your sons and your daughters shall prophesy, your old men shall dream dreams, and your young men shall see visions: and also upon the servants and upon the handmaids in those days will I pour out my Spirit" (Joel 2:28–29).

Fasting in Response to God's Command

12. Now whatsoever reasons there were to quicken those of old, in the zealous and constant discharge of this duty, they are of equal force still to quicken us. But above all these, we have a peculiar reason for being "in fastings often"; namely, the command of him by whose name we are called. He does not, indeed, in this place expressly enjoin either fasting, giving of alms, or prayer; but his directions how to fast, to give alms, and to pray, are of the same force with such injunctions. For the commanding us to do anything thus, is an unquestionable command to do that thing; seeing it is impossible to perform it thus, if it be not performed at all. Consequently, the saying, "Give alms, pray, fast" in such a manner, is a clear command to perform all those duties; as well as to perform them in that manner which shall in nowise lose its reward.

And this is a still farther motive and encouragement to the performance of this duty; even the promise which our Lord has graciously annexed to the due discharge of it: "Thy Father which seeth in secret shall reward thee openly." Such are the plain grounds, reasons, and ends of fasting; such our encouragement to persevere therein, notwithstanding abundance of objections which men, wiser than their Lord, have been continually raising against it.

III. Objections Against Fasting

It Is Better to Abstain from Sin

1. The most plausible of these I come now to consider. And, first, it has been frequently said, "Let a Christian fast from sin, and not from food: this is what God requires at his hands." So he does; but he requires the other also. Therefore this ought to be done, and that not left undone.

View your argument in its full dimensions; and you will easily judge of the strength of it:

If a Christian ought to abstain from sin, then he ought not to abstain from food:

But a Christian ought to abstain from sin.

Therefore he ought not to abstain from food:

That a Christian ought to abstain from sin is most true; but how does it follow from hence that he ought not to abstain from food? Yea, let him do both the one and the other. Let him, by the grace of God, always abstain from sin; and let him often abstain from food, for such reasons and ends as experience and Scripture plainly show to be answered thereby.

It Is Better to Abstain from Foolish Passions and Tempers

2. "But is it not better" (as it has, secondly, been objected), "to abstain from pride and vanity, from foolish and hurtful desires, from peevishness, and anger, and discontent, than from food"? Without question, it is. But here again we have need to

remind you of our Lord's words: "These things ought you to have done, and not to leave the other undone." And, indeed, the latter is only in order to the former; it is a means to that great end. We abstain from food with this view, that, by the grace of God conveyed into our souls through this outward means, in conjunction with all the other channels of his grace which he has appointed, we may be enabled to abstain from every passion and temper which is not pleasing in his sight. We refrain from the one, that, being endued with power from on high, we may be able to refrain from the other. So that your argument proves just the contrary to what you designed. It proves that we ought to fast. For if we ought to abstain from evil tempers and desires, then we ought thus to abstain from food; since these little instances of self-denial are the ways God has chosen, wherein to bestow that great salvation.

Fasting Has Not Proven Fruitful

3. "But we do not find it so in fact" (this is a third objection). "We have fasted much and often; but what did it avail? We were not a whit better; we found no blessing therein. Nay, we have found it an hindrance rather than a help. Instead of preventing anger, for instance, or fretfulness, it has been a means of increasing them to such a height, that we could neither bear others nor ourselves." This may very possibly be the case. It is possible either to fast or pray in such a manner as to make you much worse than before; more unhappy, and more unholy. Yet the fault does not lie in the means itself, but in the manner of using it. Use it still, but use it in a different manner. Do what God commands as he commands it; and then, doubtless, his promise shall not fail: his blessings shall be withheld no longer; but, when you fast in secret, "He that seeth in secret shall reward thee openly."

God Is Not Concerned with Our Fasting

4. "But is it not mere superstition" (so it has been, fourthly, objected), "to imagine that God regards such little things as these"? If you say it is, you condemn all the generations of God's children. But will you say, These were all weak, superstitious men? Can you be so hardy as to affirm this, both of Moses and Joshua, of Samuel and David, of Jehosaphat, Ezra, Nehemiah, and all the prophets yea, of a greater than all, the Son of God himself? It is certain, both our Master, and all these his servants, did imagine that fasting is not a little thing, and that he who is higher than the highest does regard it. Of the same judgment, it is plain, were all his apostles, after they were "filled with the Holy Ghost, and with wisdom." When they had the "unction of the Holy One, teaching them all things," they still approved themselves the ministers of God, "by fastings," as well as "by the armor of righteousness on the right hand and on the left." After "the bridegroom was taken from them, then did they fast in those days." Nor would they attempt anything (as we have seen above) wherein the glory of God was nearly concerned, such as the sending forth laborers into the harvest, without solemn fasting as well as prayer.

Then Shall We Not Fast Continually?

5. "But if fasting be indeed of so great importance, and attended with such a blessing, is it not best," say some, fifthly, "to fast always not to do it now and then, but to keep a continual fast to use as much abstinence, at all times, as our bodily strength will bear"? Let none be discouraged from doing this. By all means use as little and plain food, exercise as much self-denial herein, at all times, as your bodily strength will bear. And this may conduce, by the blessing of God, to several of the great ends above-mentioned. It

may be a considerable help, not only to chastity, but also to
heavenly-mindedness; to the weaning your affections from
things below, and setting them on things above. But this is
not fasting, scriptural fasting; it is never termed so in all the
Bible. It, in some measure, answers some of the ends thereof;
but still it is another thing. Practice it by all means; but not so
as thereby to set aside a command of God, and an instituted
means of averting his judgments, and obtaining the blessings
of his children.

6. Use continually then as much abstinence as you please;
which, taken thus, is no other than Christian temperance; but
this need not at all interfere with your observing solemn times
of fasting and prayer. For instance: your habitual abstinence
or temperance would not prevent your fasting in secret, if you
were suddenly overwhelmed with huge sorrow and remorse,
and with horrible fear and dismay. Such a situation of mind
would almost constrain you to fast; you would loathe your daily
food; you would scarce endure even to take such supplies as
were needful for the body, till God "lifted you up out of the
horrible pit, and set your feet upon a rock, and ordered your
goings." The same would be the case if you were in agony of
desire, vehemently wrestling with God for his blessing. You
would need none to instruct you not to eat bread till you had
obtained the request of your lips.

7. Again, had you been at Nineveh when it was proclaimed
throughout the city, "Let neither man nor beast, herd nor
flock, taste anything: let them not feed or drink water, but let
them cry mightily unto God"; would your continual fast have
been any reason for not bearing part in that general humiliation? Doubtless it would not. You would have been as much
concerned as any other not to taste food on that day.

No more would abstinence, or the observing a continual
fast, have excused any of the children of Israel from fasting on

the tenth day of the seventh month, that shall not be afflicted," shall not fast, "in that day, he shall be cut off from among his people."

Lastly, had you been with the brethren in Antioch, at the time when they fasted and prayed, before the sending forth of Barnabas and Saul, can you possibly imagine that your temperance or abstinence would have been a sufficient cause for not joining therein? Without doubt, if you had not, you would soon have been cut off from the Christian community. You would have deservedly been cast out from among them, as bringing confusion into the Church of God.

IV. How We Should Fast

Fast as Unto the Lord

1. I am, in the last place, to show in what manner we are to fast, that it may be an acceptable service unto the Lord. And, first, let it be done unto the Lord, with our eye singly fixed on him. Let our intention herein be this, and this alone, to glorify our Father which is in heaven; to express our sorrow and shame for our manifold transgressions of his holy law; to wait for an increase of purifying grace, drawing our affections to things above; to add seriousness and earnestness to our prayers; to avert the wrath of God, and to obtain all the great and precious promises which he has made to us in Jesus Christ.

Let us beware of mocking God, of turning our fast, as well as our prayers, into an abomination unto the Lord, by the mixture of any temporal view, particularly by seeking the praise of men. Against this our blessed Lord more peculiarly guards us in the words of the text. "Moreover when you fast, be you not as the hypocrites": such were too many who were called the people of God; "of a sad countenance"; sour, affectedly sad, putting their looks into a peculiar form. "For they disfigure their faces," not only by unnatural distortions, but also by covering them with dust and ashes; "that they may appear unto men to fast"; this is their chief, if not only design. "Verily, I say unto you, They have their reward"; even the admiration and praise of men. "But you, when you fast, anoint your head, and wash your face." Do as you are accustomed to do at other times; "that you appear not unto men to fast"; let this be no part of your intention; if they know it without any desire of yours, it matters not, you are neither the better nor the worse; "but unto your Father which is in secret: and your Father, which seeth in secret, shall reward you openly."

Await God's Unmerited Blessing

2. But, if we desire this reward, let us beware, secondly of fancying we merit anything of God by our fasting. We cannot be too often warned of this; inasmuch as a desire to "establish our own righteousness," to procure salvation of debt and not of grace, is so deeply rooted in all our hearts. Fasting is only a way which God has ordained, wherein we wait for his unmerited mercy; and wherein, without any desert of ours, he has promised freely to give us his blessing.

3. Not that we are to imagine the performing the bare outward act will receive any blessing from God. "Is it such a fast that I have chosen, saith the Lord; a day for a man to afflict his soul? Is it to bow down his head as a bulrush, and to spread sackcloth and ashes under him?" Are these outward acts, however strictly performed, all that is meant by a man's "afflicting his soul"? "Will thou call this a fast, and an acceptable day to the Lord?" No, surely: if it be a mere external service, it is all but lost labor. Such a performance may possibly afflict the body; but as to the soul, it profits nothing.

Proportion the Fast to Our Strength

4. Yea, the body may sometimes be afflicted too much, so as to be unfit for the works of our calling. This also we are diligently to guard against; for we ought to preserve our health, as a good gift of God. Therefore care is to be taken, whenever we fast, to proportion the fast to our strength. For we may not offer God murder for sacrifice, or destroy our bodies to help our souls.

But at these solemn seasons, we may, even in great weakness of body, avoid that other extreme, for which God condemns those who of old expostulated with him for not accepting their fasts. "Wherefore have we fasted, say they, and thou seest not? Behold, in the day of your fast you find pleasure, saith the Lord." If we cannot wholly abstain from food, we may, at least, abstain from pleasant food; and then we shall not seek his face in vain.

Afflict Our Souls as Well as Our Bodies

5. But let us take care to afflict our souls as well as our bodies. Let every season, either of public or private fasting, be a season of exercising all those holy affections which are implied in a broken and contrite heart. Let it be a season of devout mourning, of godly sorrow for sin; such a sorrow as that of the Corinthians, concerning which the apostle saith, "I rejoice, not that you were made sorry, but that you sorrowed to repentance. For you were made sorry after a godly manner, that you might receive damage by us in nothing. For godly sorrow"— ἡ κατὰ θεὸν λύπη, *the sorrow which is according to God*—which is a precious gift of his Spirit, lifting the soul to God from whom it flows, "worketh repentance to salvation, not to be repented of."

Yea, and let our sorrowing after a godly sort work in us the same inward and outward repentance; the same entire change of heart, renewed after the image of God, in righteousness and true holiness; and the same change of life, till we are holy as he is holy, in all manner of conversation. Let it work in us the same carefulness to be found in him, without spot and blameless; the same clearing of ourselves, by our lives rather than words, by our abstaining from all appearance of evil; the same indignation, vehement abhorrence of every sin; the same fear of our own deceitful hearts; the same desire to be in all things conformed to the holy and acceptable will of God; the same zeal for whatever may be a means of his glory, and of our growth in the knowledge of our Lord Jesus Christ; and the same revenge against Satan and all his works, against all filthiness both of flesh and Spirit (2 Cor. 7:9ff.).

Join Fervent Prayer to Fasting

6. And with fasting let us always join fervent prayer, pouring out our whole souls before God, confessing our sins with all their aggravations, humbling ourselves under his mighty hand, laying open before him all our wants, all our guiltiness and helplessness. This is a season for enlarging our prayers, both in behalf of ourselves and of our brethren. Let us now bewail the sins of our people; and cry aloud for the city of our God, that the Lord may build up Zion, and cause his face to shine on her desolations. Thus, we may observe, the men of God, in ancient times always joined prayer and fasting together; thus the apostles, in all the instances cited above; and thus our Lord joins them in the discourse before us.

Join Works of Mercy to Fasting

7. It remains only, in order to our observing such a fast as is acceptable to the Lord, that we add alms thereto; works of mercy, after our power, both to the bodies and souls of men: "with such sacrifices" also "God is well pleased." Thus the angel

declares to Cornelius, fasting and praying in his house, "Thy prayers and thine alms are come up for a memorial before God" (Acts 10:4). And this God himself expressly and largely declares:

> Is not this the fast that I have chosen? To loose the bands of wickedness, to undo the heavy burdens, to let the oppressed go free, and that you break every yoke? Is it not to deal your bread to the hungry, and that you bring the poor that are cast out to your house when you seest the naked, that you cover him; and that you hide not yourself from your own flesh? Then shall your light break forth as the morning, and your health shall spring forth speedily; and your righteousness shall go before you; the glory of the Lord shall be your reward. Then shall you call, and the Lord shall answer: you shall cry, and he shall say, Here I am. If, "when you fast, "you draw out your soul to the hungry, and satisfy the afflicted soul; then shall your light rise in obscurity, and your darkness be as the noon-day. And the Lord shall guide you continually, and satisfy your soul in drought, and make fat thy bones: And you shall be like a watered garden, and like a spring of water, whose waters fail not (Isa. 58:6–11).

DISCOURSE EIGHT

Heavenly Intentions for Earthly Endeavors

Lay not up for yourselves treasures upon earth, where moth and rust doth corrupt, and where thieves break through and steal: but lay up for yourselves treasures in heaven, where neither moth nor rust doth corrupt, and where thieves do not break through nor steal: For where your treasure is, there will your heart be also. The light of the body is the eye: if therefore thine eye be single, thy whole body shall be full of light. But if thine eye be evil, thy whole body shall be full of darkness. If therefore the light that is in thee be darkness, how great is that darkness!

—Matthew 6:19–23

Introduction

1. From those which are commonly termed religious
actions, and which are real branches of true religion where they
spring from a pure and holy intention and are performed in a
manner suitable thereto, our Lord proceeds to the actions of
common life, and shows that the same purity of intention is
as indispensably required in our ordinary business as in giving
alms, or fasting, or prayer.

And without question the same purity of intention "which
makes our alms and devotions acceptable must also make our
labor or employment a proper offering to God. If a man pursues
his business that he may raise himself to a state of honor and
riches in the world, he is no longer serving God in his employment, and has no more title to a reward from God than he
who gives alms that he may be seen, or prays that he may be
heard of men. For vain and earthly designs are no more allowable in our employments than in our alms and devotions. They
are not only evil when they mix with our good works," with
our religious actions, "but they have the same evil nature when
they enter into the common business of our employments. If it
were allowable to pursue them in our worldly employments, it
would be allowable to pursue them in our devotions. But as our
alms and devotions are not an acceptable service but when they
proceed from a pure intention, so our common employment
cannot be reckoned a service to him but when it is performed
with the same piety of heart."

2. This our blessed Lord declares in the liveliest manner
in those strong and comprehensive words which he explains,
enforces, and enlarges upon, throughout this whole chapter.
"The light of the body is the eye: if therefore your eye be
single, your whole body shall be full of light. But if your eye
be evil, your whole body shall be full of darkness." The eye

is the intention: what the eye is to the body, the intention is to the soul. As the one guides all the motions of the body, so does the other those of the soul. This eye of the soul is then said to be single when it looks at one thing only; when we have no other design but to "know God, and Jesus Christ whom he has sent"—to know him with suitable affections, loving him as he has loved us; to please God in all things; to serve God (as we love him) with all our heart and mind and soul and strength; and to enjoy God in all and above all things, in time and in eternity.

If Your Eye Be Single

You Shall Be Filled with the Light of Wisdom and Truth

3. "If your eye be" thus "single," thus fixed on God, "your whole body shall be full of light." "Your whole body"—all that is guided by the intention, as the body is by the eye. All you are, all you do, your desires, tempers, affections; your thoughts, and words, and actions. The whole of these "shall be full of light"; full of true divine knowledge. This is the first thing we may here understand by light. "In his light you shall see light." "He which of old commanded light to shine out of darkness, shall shine in your heart": he shall enlighten the eyes of your under-standing with the knowledge of the glory of God. His Spirit shall reveal unto you the deep things of God. The inspiration of the Holy One shall give you understanding, and cause you to know wisdom secretly. Yea, the anointing which you receive of him "shall abide in you and teach you of all things."

How does experience confirm this! Even after God has opened the eyes of our understanding, if we seek or desire anything else than God, how soon is our foolish heart dark-ened! Then clouds again rest upon our souls. Doubts and fears again overwhelm us. We are tossed to and fro, and know not what to do, or which is the path wherein we should go. But when we desire and seek nothing but God, clouds and doubts vanish away. We who "were sometime darkness are now light in the Lord." The night now shineth as the day and we find "the path of the upright is light." God showeth us the path wherein we should go, and maketh plain the way before our face.

You Shall Be Filled with the Light of Holiness

4. The second thing which we may here understand by light, is holiness. While you seek God in all things you shall find him in all, the fountain of all holiness, continually filling you with his own likeness, with justice, mercy, and truth. While you look unto Jesus and him alone you shall be filled with the mind that was in him. Your soul shall be renewed day by day after the image of him that created it. If the eye of thy mind be not removed from him, if you endure "as seeing him that is invisible," and seeking nothing else in heaven or earth, then as you behold the glory of the Lord, you shall be transformed "into the same image, from glory to glory, by the Spirit of the Lord."

And it is also a matter of daily experience that "by grace we are" thus "saved through faith." It is by faith that the eye of the mind is opened to see the light of the glorious love of God. And as long as it is steadily fixed thereon, on God in Christ, reconciling the world unto himself, we are more and more filled with the love of God and man, with meekness, gentleness, long-suffering; with all the fruits of holiness, which are, through Christ Jesus, to the glory of God the Father.

You Shall Be Filled with the Light of Happiness

5. This light which fills him who has a single eye implies, thirdly, happiness as well as holiness. Surely "light is sweet, and

a pleasant thing it is to see the sun:" But how much more to see the Sun of Righteousness continually shining upon the soul! And if there be any consolation in Christ, if any comfort of love, if any peace that passeth all understanding, if any rejoicing in hope of the glory of God, they all belong to him whose eye is single. Thus is his "whole body full of light." He walks in the light as God is in the light, rejoicing evermore, praying without ceasing, and in everything giving thanks, enjoying whatever is the will of God concerning him in Christ Jesus.

But If Your Eye Be Evil

6. "But if your eye be evil, your whole body shall be full of darkness." "If your eye be evil"—we see there is no medium between a single and an evil eye. If the eye be not single, then it is evil. If the intention in whatever we do be not singly to God, if we seek anything else, then our "mind and conscience are defiled."

Our eye therefore is evil if in anything we do we aim at any other end than God; if we have any view, but to know and to love God, to please and serve him in all things; if we have any other design than to enjoy God, to be happy in him both now and for ever.

You Shall Be Filled with Darkness

7. If your eye be not singly fixed on God, "your whole body shall be full of darkness." The veil shall still remain on your heart. Your mind shall be more and more blinded by "the God of this world," "lest the light of the glorious gospel of Christ should shine upon you." You will be full of ignorance and error touching the things of God, not being able to receive or discern them. And even when you have some desire to serve God, you will be full of uncertainty as to the manner of serving him;

finding doubts and difficulties on every side, and not seeing any way to escape.

You Shall Be Filled with Ungodliness

Yea, if your eye be not single, if you seek any of the things of earth, you shall be full of ungodliness and unrighteousness, your desires, tempers, affections, being all out of course, being all dark, and vile, and vain. And your conversation will be evil as well as your heart, not "seasoned with salt," or "meet to minister grace unto the hearers;" but idle, unprofitable, corrupt, grievous to the Holy Spirit of God.

You Shall Be Filled with Unrest

8. Both destruction and unhappiness are in thy ways; "for the way of peace hast thou not known." There is no peace, no settled, solid peace, for them that know not God. There is no true nor lasting content for any who do not seek him with their whole heart. While you aim at any of the things that perish, "all that cometh is vanity"; yea, not only vanity, but "vexation of spirit," and that both in the pursuit and the enjoyment also. You walk indeed in a vain shadow, and disquiet yourself in vain. You walk in darkness that may be felt. Sleep on; but you cannot take your rest. The dreams of life can give pain, and that you know; but ease they cannot give. There is no rest in this world or the world to come, but only in God, the center of spirits.

"If the light which is in you be darkness, how great is that darkness!" If the intention which ought to enlighten the whole soul, to fill it with knowledge, and love, and peace, and which in fact does so as long as it is single, as long as it aims at God alone—if this be darkness; if it aim at anything beside God, and consequently cover the soul with darkness instead of light, with ignorance and error, with sin and misery: O how great is that darkness! It is the very smoke which ascends out of the bottomless pit! It is the essential night which reigns in the lowest deep, in the land of the shadow of death!

Laying Up Treasures upon Earth

9. Therefore, "lay not up for yourselves treasures upon earth, where moth and rust doth corrupt, and where thieves break through and steal." If you do, it is plain your eye is evil; it is not singly fixed on God.

Heathens and Christians on Level Ground

With regard to most of the commandments of God, whether relating to the heart or life, the heathens of Africa or America stand much on a level with those that are called Christians. The Christians observe them (a few only being excepted) very near as much as the heathens. For instance: the generality of the natives of England, commonly called Christians, are as sober and as temperate as the generality of the heathens near the Cape of Good Hope. And so the Dutch or French Christians are as humble and as chaste as the Choctaw or Cherokee Indians. It is not easy to say, when we compare the bulk of the nations in Europe with those in America, whether the superiority lies on the one side or the other. At least the American has not much the advantage.

But we cannot affirm this with regard to the command now before us. Here the heathen has far the preeminence. He desires and seeks nothing more than plain food to eat and plain raiment to put on. And he seeks this only from day to day. He reserves, he lays up nothing; unless it be as much corn at one season of the year as he will need before that season returns. This command, therefore, the heathens, though they know it not, do constantly and punctually observe. They "lay up for themselves no treasures upon earth"; no stores of purple or fine linen, of gold or silver, which either "moth or rust may corrupt" or "thieves break through and steal."

But how do the Christians observe what they profess to receive as a command of the most high God? Not at all! Not in any degree; no more than if no such command had ever been given to man. Even the good Christians, as they are accounted by others as well as themselves, pay no manner of regard thereto. It might as well be still hid in its original Greek for any notice they take of it.

In what Christian city do you find one man of five hundred who makes the least scruple of laying up just as much treasure as he can—of increasing his goods just as far as he is able? There are indeed those who would not do this unjustly; there are many who will neither rob nor steal; and some who will not defraud their neighbor; nay, who will not gain either by his ignorance or necessity. But this is quite another point. Even these do not scruple the thing, but the manner of it. They do not scruple the "laying up treasures upon earth," but the laying them up by dishonesty. They do not start at disobeying Christ, but at a breach of heathen morality. So that even these honest men do no more obey this command than a highwayman or a house-breaker. Nay, they never designed to obey it. From their youth up it never entered into their thoughts. They were bred up by their Christian parents, masters, and friends, without any instruction at all concerning it; unless it were this—to break it as soon and as much as they could, and to continue breaking it to their lives' end.

10. There is no one instance of spiritual infatuation in the world which is more amazing than this. Most of these very men read or hear the Bible read, many of them every Lord's day. They have read or heard these words a hundred times, and yet never suspect that they are themselves condemned thereby, any more than by those which forbid parents to offer up their

sons or daughters unto Moloch. O that God would speak to these miserable self-deceivers with his own voice, his mighty voice! That they may at last awake out of the snare of the devil, and the scales may fall from their eyes!

What Is Not Here Forbidden

11. Do you ask what it is to "lay up treasures on earth"? It will be needful to examine this thoroughly. And let us, first, observe what is not forbidden in this command, that we may then clearly discern what is.

Paying our debts. We are not forbidden in this command, first, to "provide things honest in the sight of all men," to provide wherewith we may render unto all their due, whatsoever they can justly demand of us. So far from it that we are taught of God to "owe no man anything." We ought therefore to use all diligence in our calling, in order to owe no man anything: this being no other than a plain law of common justice which our Lord came "not to destroy but to fulfill."

Providing for our needs. Neither, secondly, does he here forbid the providing for ourselves such things as are needful for the body; a sufficiency of plain, wholesome food to eat, and clean raiment to put on. Yea, it is our duty, so far as God puts it into our power, to provide these things also; to the end we may "eat our own bread," and be burdensome to no man.

Providing for our household. Nor yet are we forbidden, thirdly, to provide for our children, and for those of our own household. This also it is our duty to do, even upon principles of heathen morality. Every man ought to provide the plain necessaries of life both for his own wife and children, and to put them into a capacity of providing these for themselves when he is gone hence and is no more seen. I say, of providing these, the plain necessaries of life; not delicacies, not superfluities; and that by their diligent labor; for it is no man's duty to furnish them any more than himself with the means either of luxury or idleness. But if any man provides not thus far for his own children (as well as for the widows of his own house, of whom primarily St. Paul is speaking in those well-known words to Timothy), he hath practically "denied the faith, and is worse than an infidel," or heathen.

Laying up what is needful for these things. Lastly, we are not forbidden, in these words, to lay up, from time to time what is needful for the carrying on our worldly business in such a measure and degree as is sufficient to answer the foregoing purposes—in such a measure as, first, to owe no man anything; secondly, to procure for ourselves the necessaries of life; and, thirdly, to furnish those of our own house with them while we live, and with the means of procuring them when we are gone to God.

What Is Here Forbidden

12. *Do not seek to be rich.* We may now clearly discern (unless we are unwilling to discern it) what that is which is forbidden here. It is the designedly procuring more of this world's goods than will answer the foregoing purposes; the laboring after a larger measure of worldly substance, a larger increase of gold and silver—the laying up any more than these ends require—is what is here expressly and absolutely forbidden. If the words have any meaning at all, it must be this; for they are capable of no other. Consequently, whoever he is that, owing no man anything, and having food and raiment for himself and his household, together with a sufficiency to carry on his worldly business so far as answers these reasonable purposes; whosoever, I say, being already in these circumstances, seeks a still larger portion on earth; he lives in an open habitual denial of the Lord that bought him. He has practically denied the faith, and is worse than an African or American "infidel."

13. Hear ye this, all you that dwell in the world, and love the world wherein you dwell. You may be "highly esteemed of men"; but you are "an abomination in the sight of God." How long shall your souls cleave to the dust? How long will you load yourselves with thick clay? When will you awake and see that the open, speculative heathens are nearer the kingdom of heaven than you? When will you be persuaded to choose the better part; that which cannot be taken away from you? When will you seek only to "lay up treasures in heaven," renouncing, dreading, abhorring all other?

If you aim at "laying up treasures on earth," you are not barely losing your time and spending your strength for that which is not bread, for what is the fruit if you succeed: you have murdered your own soul! You have extinguished the last spark of spiritual life therein! Now indeed, in the midst of life you are in death! You are a living man, but a dead Christian. "For where your treasure is, there will your heart be also." Your heart is sunk into the dust, your soul cleaveth to the ground. Your affections are set, not on things above, but on things of the earth; on poor husks that may poison, but cannot satisfy an everlasting spirit made for God. Your love, your joy, your desire, are all placed on the things which perish in the using. You have thrown away the treasure in heaven: God and Christ are lost! You have gained riches, and hell-fire!

14. O "how hardly shall they that have riches enter into the kingdom of God!" When our Lord's disciples were astonished at his speaking thus he was so far from retracting it that he repeated the same important truth in stronger terms than before. "It is easier for a camel to go through the eye of a needle, than for a rich man to enter into the kingdom of God." How hard is it for them whose very word is applauded not to be wise in their own eyes! How hard for them not to think themselves better than the poor, base, uneducated herd of men! How hard

not to seek happiness in their riches, or in things dependent upon them; in gratifying the desire of the flesh, the desire of the eye, or the pride of life! O ye rich, how can you escape the damnation of hell? Only, with God all things are possible!

15. And even if you do not succeed, what is the fruit of your endeavoring to lay up treasures on earth? "They that will be rich" (οἱ δὲ βουλόμενοι, *they that desire, that endeavor after it, whether they succeed or no*), "fall into a temptation and a snare," a gin, a trap of the devil; "and into many foolish and hurtful lusts"; ἐπιθυμίας ἀνοήτους *(harmful desires)*, desires with which reason has nothing to do; such as properly belong, not to rational and immortal beings, but only to the brute beasts which have no understanding; "which drown men in destruction and perdition," in present and eternal misery. Let us but open our eyes, and we may daily see the melancholy proofs of this—men who, desiring, resolving to be rich, coveting after money, the root of all evil, have already pierced themselves through with many sorrows, and anticipated the hell to which they are going!

The cautiousness with which the apostle here speaks is highly observable. He does not affirm this absolutely of the rich: for a man may possibly be rich, without any fault of his, by an overruling Providence, preventing his own choice. But he affirms it of (οἱ δὲ βουλόμενοι *(those who desire or seek to be rich)*. Riches, dangerous as they are, do not always "drown men in destruction and perdition"; but the desire of riches does— those who calmly desire and deliberately seek to attain them, whether they do, in fact, gain the world or no, do infallibly lose their own souls. These are they that sell him who bought them with his blood, for a few pieces of gold or silver. These enter into a covenant with death and hell; and their covenant shall stand. For they are daily making themselves meet to partake of their inheritance with the devil and his angels!

16. O who shall warn this generation of vipers to flee from the wrath to come! Not those who lie at their gate, or cringe at their feet, desiring to be fed with the crumbs that fall from their tables. Not those who court their favor or fear their frown: none of those who mind earthly things. But if there be a Christian upon earth, if there be a man who has overcome the world, who desires nothing but God, and fears none but him that is able to destroy both body and soul in hell; you, O man of God, speak and spare not; lift up thy voice like a trumpet! Cry aloud, and show these honorable sinners the desperate condition wherein they stand! It may be, one in a thousand may have ears to hear, may arise and shake himself from the dust; may break loose from these chains that bind him to the earth, and at length lay up treasures in heaven.

17. And if it should be that one of these, by the mighty power of God, awoke and asked, "What must I do to be saved?" the answer, according to the oracles of God, is clear, full, and express. God does not say to you, "Sell all that you have." Indeed he who sees the hearts of men saw it needful to enjoin this in one peculiar case, that of the young, rich ruler. But he never laid it down for a general rule to all rich men, in all succeeding generations. His general direction is, first, "Be not high minded." God sees not as man sees." He esteems you not for your riches, grandeur or equipage, for any qualification or accomplishment which is directly or indirectly owing to thy wealth, which can be bought or procured thereby. All these are with him as dung and dross: let them be so with you also.

Beware you think not yourself to be one jot wiser or better for all these things. Weigh yourself in another balance: estimate yourself only by the measure of faith and love which God has given you. If you have more of the knowledge and love of God than he, you are on this account, and no other, wiser and better, more valuable and honorable than him who is with the dogs of your flock. But if you have not this treasure those are more foolish, more vile, more truly contemptible, I will not say, than the lowest servant under your roof, but than the beggar laid at your gate, full of sores.

18. *Trust not in uncertain riches.* Secondly. "Trust not in uncertain riches." Trust not in them for help; and trust not in them for happiness.

First, trust not in them for help. You are miserably mistaken if you look for this in gold or silver. These are no more able to set you above the world than to set you above the devil. Know that both the world, and the prince of this world, laugh at all such preparations against them. These will little avail in the day of trouble—even if they remain in the trying hour. But it is not certain that they will; for how oft do they "make themselves wings and fly away!"

But if not, what support will they afford, even in the ordinary troubles of life? The desire of your eyes, the wife of your youth, your son, your only son, or the friend which was as your own soul, is taken away at a stroke. Will your riches re-animate the breathless clay, or call back its late inhabitant? Will they secure you from sickness, diseases, pain? Do these visit the poor only? Nay, he that feeds your flocks or tills your ground has less sickness and pain than you. He is more rarely visited by these unwelcome guests: and if they come there at all they are more easily driven away from the little cot than from the "cloud-topt palaces." And during the time that thy body is chastened with pain, or consumes away with pining sickness, how do thy treasures help thee? Let the poor heathen answer,

> *Ut lippum pictae tabulae, fomenta podugrum*
> *Auriculas citharae collecta sorde dolentes.*

[Such help as pictures to sore eyes afford,
As heap'd-up tables to their gouty lord.]

19. But there is at hand a greater trouble than all these. Thou art to die! You are to sink into dust; to return to the ground from which you were taken, to mix with common clay. Your body is to go to the earth as it was, while your spirit returns to God that gave it. And the time draws on: the years slide away with a swift though silent pace. Perhaps your day is far spent: the noon of life is past, and the evening shadows begin to rest upon you. You feel in yourself sure approaching decay. The springs of life wear away apace.

Now what help is there in your riches? Do they sweeten death? Do they endear that solemn hour? Quite the reverse. "O death, how bitter art thou to a man that liveth at rest in his possessions!" How unacceptable to him is that awful sentence, "This night shall thy soul be required of thee!" Or will they prevent the unwelcome stroke, or protract the dreadful hour? Can they deliver your soul that it should not see death? Can they restore the years that are past? Can they add to your appointed time a month, a day, an hour, a moment? Or will the good things you have chosen for your portion here follow you over the great gulf? Not so. Naked came you into this world; naked must you return.

*Linquenda tellus, et domus, et placens
Uxor; neque harum quas colis, arborum,
Te, praeter invisam cupressos,
Ulla brevem dominum sequetur!*

Thy lands, thy dome, thy pleasing wife,
These must thou quit; 'tis nature's doom.
No tree, whose culture charms thy life,
Save the sad cypress, waits thy tomb.
—Horace (Boscawen's translation)

Surely, were not these truths too plain to be observed, because they are too plain to be denied, no man that is to die could possibly trust for help in uncertain riches.

20. And trust not in them for happiness: for here also they will be found "deceitful upon the weights." Indeed this every reasonable man may infer from what has been observed already. For if neither thousands of gold and silver, nor any of the advantages or pleasures purchased thereby, can prevent our being miserable, it evidently follows they cannot make us happy. What happiness can they afford to him who in the midst of all is constrained to cry out,

> To my new courts sad though does still repair,
> And round my gilded roofs hangs hovering care.

Indeed experience is here so full, strong, and undeniable, that it makes all other arguments needless. Appeal we therefore to fact. Are the rich and great the only happy men? And is each of them more or less happy in proportion to his measure of riches? Are they happy at all? I had well nigh said, they are of all men most miserable! Rich man, for once, speak the truth from your heart. Speak, both for yourself, and for your brethren!

> Amidst our plenty something still,
> To me, to thee, to him is wanting!
> That cruel something unpossessed
> Corrodes and leavens all the rest.

Yea, and so it will, till thy wearisome days of vanity are shut up in the night of death.

Surely then, to trust in riches for happiness is the greatest folly of all that are under the sun! Are you not convinced of this? Is it possible you should still expect to find happiness in money or all it can procure? What! Can silver and gold, and eating and drinking, and horses and servants, and glittering apparel, and diversions and pleasures (as they are called) make you happy? They can as soon make you immortal!

21. These are all dead show. Regard them not. Trust thou in the living God; so shall you be safe under the shadow of the Almighty; his faithfulness and truth shall be your shield and buckler. He is a very present help in time of trouble; such an help as can never fail. Then shall you say, if all your other friends die, "The Lord liveth, and blessed be my strong helper!" He shall remember you when you liest sick upon your bed; when vain is the help of man. When all the things of earth can give no support, he will "make all your bed in your sickness." He will sweeten your pain; the consolations of God shall cause you to clap your hands in the flames. And even when this house of earth is well nigh shaken down, when it is just ready to drop into the dust, he will teach you to say, "O death, where is thy sting? O grave, where is thy victory? Thanks be unto God, who giveth" me "the victory, through" my "Lord Jesus Christ."

O trust in Him for happiness as well as for help. All the springs of happiness are in him. Trust in him, παρέχοντι πλουσίως πάντα εἰς ἀπόλαυσιν, *who giveth us all things richly to enjoy*, who, of his own rich and free mercy holds them out to us as in his own hand, that receiving them as his gift, and as pledges of his love, we may enjoy all that we possess. It is his love gives a relish to all we taste, puts life and sweetness into all, while every creature leads us up to the great Creator, and all earth is a scale to heaven. He transfuses the joys that are at his own right hand into all he bestows on his thankful children; who, having fellowship with the Father and his Son Jesus Christ, enjoy him in all and above all.

22. *Seek not to increase in goods.* Thirdly, seek not to increase in goods. "Lay not up for" yourself "treasures upon earth." This is a flat, positive command; full and clear as "thou shalt not

commit adultery." How then is it possible for a rich man to grow richer without denying the Lord that bought him? Yea, how can any man who has already the necessaries of life gain or aim at more, and be guiltless? "Lay not up," says our Lord, "treasures upon earth." If, in spite of this, you do and will lay up money or goods, which "moth or rust may corrupt, or thieves break through and steal"; if you will add house to house, or field to field, why do you call yourself a Christian? You do not obey Jesus Christ. You do not design it. Why do you name yourself by his name? "Why call you me, Lord, Lord," saith he himself, "and do not the things which I say?"

23. If you ask, "But what must we do with our goods, seeing we have more than we have occasion to use, if we must not lay them up? Must we throw them away?" I answer: If you threw them into the sea, if you were to cast them into the fire and consume them, they would be better bestowed than they are now. You cannot find so mischievous a manner of throwing them away as either the laying them up for your posterity or the laying them out upon yourselves in folly and superfluity. Of all possible methods of throwing them away, these two are the very worst; the most opposite to the gospel of Christ, and the most pernicious to your own soul.

How pernicious to your own soul the latter of these is has been excellently shown by a late writer:

> If we waste our money we are not only guilty of wasting a talent which God has given us, but we do ourselves this farther harm, we turn this useful talent into a powerful means of corrupting ourselves; because so far as it is spent wrong, so far it is spent in the support of some wrong temper, in gratifying some vain and unreasonable desires, which as Christians we are obliged to renounce.

As wit and fine parts cannot be only trifled away, but will expose those that have them to greater follies, so money cannot be only trifled away, but if it is not used according to reason and religion, will make people live a more silly and extravagant life than they would have done without it. If therefore you don't spend your money in doing good to others, you must spend it to the hurt of yourself. You act like one that refuses the cordial to his sick friend which he cannot drink himself without inflaming his blood. For this is the case of superfluous money, if you give it to those who want it is a cordial; if you spend it upon yourself in something that you do not want it only inflames and disorders your mind.

In using riches where they have no real use, nor we any real want, we only use them to our great hurt, in creating unreasonable desires, in nourishing ill tempers, in indulging in foolish passions, and supporting a vain turn of mind. For high eating and drinking, fine clothes and fine houses, state and equipage, gay pleasures and diversions, do all of them naturally hurt and disorder our heart. They are the food and nourishment of all the folly and weakness of our nature. They are all of them the support of something that ought not to be supported. They are contrary to that sobriety and piety of heart which relishes divine things. They are so many weights upon our mind, that makes us less able and less inclined to raise our thoughts and affections to things above.

So that money thus spent is not merely wasted or lost, but it is spent to bad purposes and miserable effects; to the corruption and disorder of our hearts; to the making us unable to follow the sublime doctrines of the gospel. It is but like keeping money from the poor to buy poison for ourselves.

24. Equally inexcusable are those who lay up what they do not need for any reasonable purposes:

> If a man had hands and eyes and feet that he could give to those that wanted them; if he should lock them up in a chest instead of giving them to his brethren that were blind and lame, should we not justly reckon him an inhuman wretch? If he should rather choose to amuse himself with hoarding them up than entitle himself to an eternal reward by giving them to those that wanted eyes and hands, might we not justly reckon him mad?
>
> Now money has very much the nature of eyes and feet. If therefore we lock it up in chests, while the poor and distressed want it for their necessary uses, we are not far from the cruelty of him that chooses rather to hoard up the hands and eyes than to give them to those that want them. If we choose to lay it up rather than to entitle ourselves to an eternal reward by disposing of our money well, we are guilty of his madness that rather chooses to lock up eyes and hands than to make himself for ever blessed by giving them to those that want them.

25. May not this be another reason why rich men shall so hardly enter into the kingdom of heaven? A vast majority of them are under a curse, under the peculiar curse of God; inasmuch as in the general tenor of their lives they are not only robbing God continually, embezzling and wasting their Lord's goods, and by that very means corrupting their own souls; but also robbing the poor, the hungry, the naked, wronging the widow and the fatherless, and making themselves accountable for all the want, affliction, and distress which they may but do not remove. Yea, does not the blood of all those who perish for want of what they either lay up or lay out needlessly, cry against

them from the earth? O what account will they give to him who is ready to judge both the quick and the dead!

Lay Up Treasures in Heaven

26. The true way of employing what you do not want your-selves you may, fourthly, learn from those words of our Lord which are the counterpart of what went before: "Lay up for yourselves treasures in heaven; where neither moth nor rust doth corrupt, and where thieves do not break through and steal." Put out whatever you can spare upon better security than this world can afford. Lay up your treasures in the bank of heaven; and God shall restore them in that day. "He that hath pity upon the poor lendeth unto the Lord, and look, what he layeth out, it shall be paid him again." "Place that," saith he, "unto my account. Howbeit, you owe me your own self besides!"

Give to the poor with a single eye, with an upright heart, and write, "So much given to God." For "Inasmuch as you did it unto one of the least of these my brethren, you have done it unto me."

This is the part of a "faithful and wise steward:" not to sell either his houses or lands, or principal stock, be it more or less, unless some peculiar circumstance should require it; and not to desire or endeavor to increase it, any more than to squander it away in vanity; but to employ it wholly to those wise and reasonable purposes for which his Lord has lodged it in his hands. The wise steward, after having provided his own household with what is needful for life and godliness, makes himself friends with all that remains from time to time of the "mammon of unrighteousness; that when he fails they may receive him into everlasting habitations," that whensoever his earthly tabernacle is dissolved, they who were before carried into Abraham's bosom, after having eaten his bread, and worn the fleece of his flock, and praised God for the consolation, may welcome him into paradise, and to "the house of God, eternal in the heavens."

27. We "charge" you, therefore, "who are rich in this world," as having authority from our great Lord and Master, ἀγαθοεργεῖν, *to be habitually doing good*, to live in a course of good works. "Be ye merciful as your Father which is in heaven is merciful," who does good, and ceases not. "Be ye merciful"— how far? After your power, with all the ability which God gives. Make this your only measure of doing good, not any beggarly maxims or customs of the world.

We charge you to "be rich in good works;" as you have much, to give plenteously. "Freely you have received; freely give"; so as to lay up no treasure but in heaven. Be ye "ready to distribute" to everyone according to his necessity. Disperse abroad, give to the poor; deal your bread to the hungry. Cover the naked with a garment, entertain the stranger, carry or send relief to them that are in prison. Heal the sick; not by miracle, but through the blessing of God upon your seasonable support. Let the blessing of him that was ready to perish through pining want come upon thee. Defend the oppressed, plead the cause of the fatherless, and make the widow's heart sing for joy.

28. We exhort you in the name of the Lord Jesus Christ to be "willing to communicate"; koinōnikós εἶναι, *to be of the same spirit* (though not in the same outward state) with those believers of ancient times, who remained steadfast ἐν τῇ κοινωνίᾳ, *in that blessed and holy fellowship*, wherein "none said that anything was his own, but they had all things common." Be a steward, a faithful and wise steward, of God and of the poor; differing from them in these two circumstances only, that your wants are first supplied out of the portion of your Lord's goods which remains in your hands, and that you have the blessedness of giving.

Thus "lay up for yourselves a good foundation," not in the world which now is, but rather "for the time to come, that you may lay hold on eternal life." The great foundation indeed of all the blessings of God, whether temporal or eternal, is the Lord Jesus Christ, his righteousness and blood, what he has done, and what he has suffered for us. And "other foundation," in this sense, "can no man lay"; no, not an apostle; no, not an angel from heaven. But through his merits, whatever we do in his name is a foundation for a good reward in the day when "every man shall receive his own reward, according to his own labor." Therefore "labor" thou "not for the meat that perishes, but for that which endures unto everlasting life." Therefore "whatsoever your hand" now "findeth to do, do it with your might." Therefore let—

No fair occasion pass undeeded by;
Snatching the golden moments as they fly,
Thou by few fleeting years ensure eternity!

"By patient continuance in well-doing, seek" thou "for glory and honor and immortality." In a constant, zealous performance of all good works, wait for that happy hour when the King shall say, "I was hungry, and you gave me meat; I was thirsty, and you gave me drink. I was a stranger, and you took me in; naked, and you clothed me. I was sick, and you visited me; I was in prison, and you came unto me. Come, you blessed of my Father, receive the kingdom prepared for you from the foundation of the world!"

WHICH MASTER DO YOU SERVE?

No man can serve two masters; for either he will hate the one, and love the other; or else he will hold to the one and despise the other. You cannot serve God and mammon. Therefore I say unto you, Take no thought for your life, what you shall eat, or what you shall drink; nor yet for your body, what you shall put on. Is not the life more than meat, and the body than raiment? Behold the fowls of the air: for they sow not, neither do they reap, nor gather into barns; yet your heavenly Father feedeth them. Are you not much better than they? Which of you by taking thought can add one cubit unto his stature? And why take you thought for raiment? Consider the lilies of the field, how they grow; they toil not, neither do they spin. And yet I say unto you, that even Solomon in all his glory was not arrayed like one of these.

Wherefore, if God so clothe the grass of the field, which today is, and tomorrow is cast into the oven, shall he not

much more clothe you, O you of little faith? Therefore take
no thought, saying, What shall we eat? or, What shall we
drink? or, Wherewithal shall we be clothed? (For after all
these things do the Gentiles seek.) For your heavenly Father
knows that you have need of all these things. But seek ye
first the kingdom of God, and his righteousness; and all these
things shall be added unto you. Take therefore no thought for
the morrow: for the morrow shall take thought for the things
of itself. Sufficient unto the day is the evil thereof.
—Matthew 6:24–34

You Cannot Serve Two Masters

1. It is recorded of the nations whom the King of Assyria, after he had carried Israel away into captivity, placed in the cities of Samaria, that "they feared the Lord, and served their own gods." "These nations," saith the inspired writer, "feared the Lord"; performed an outward service to him (a plain proof that they had a fear of God, though not according to knowledge); "and served their graven images, both their children, and their children's children: as did their fathers, so do they unto this day (2 Kings 17:33ff.).

How nearly does the practice of most modern Christians resemble this of the ancient heathens! "They fear the Lord"; they also perform an outward service to him, and hereby show they have some fear of God; but they likewise "serve their own gods." There are those who "teach them" as there were who taught the Assyrians, "the manner of the God of the land"; the God whose name the country bears to this day, and who was once worshipped there with a holy worship: "Howbeit," they do not serve him alone; they do not fear him enough for this. But "every nation maketh gods of their own: every nation in the cities wherein they dwell." "These nations fear the Lord";

they have not laid aside the outward form of worshipping him; but "they serve their graven images," silver and gold, the work of men's hands: money, pleasure, and praise, the gods of this world, more than divide their service with the God of Israel. This is the manner both of "their children and their children's children; as did their fathers, so do they unto this day."

2. But although, speaking in a loose way, after the common manner of men, those poor heathens were said to "fear the Lord," yet we may observe the Holy Ghost immediately adds, speaking according to the truth and real nature of things, "they fear not the Lord, neither do after the law and the commandment, which the Lord commanded the children of Jacob; with whom the Lord made a covenant, and charged them, saying, You shall not fear other gods, nor serve them. But the Lord your God you shall fear; and he shall deliver you out of the hand of all your enemies."

The same judgment is passed by the unerring Spirit of God, and indeed by all the eyes of whose understanding he has opened to discern the things of God, upon these poor Christians, commonly so called. If we speak according to the truth and real nature of things, "they fear not the Lord, neither do they serve him." For they do not "after the covenant the Lord has made with them, neither after the law and commandment which he has commanded them, saying, Thou shalt worship the Lord thy God, and him only shalt thou serve." "They serve other gods unto this day." And "no man can serve two masters."

3. How vain is it for any man to aim at this, to attempt the serving of two masters! Is it not easy to foresee what must be the unavoidable consequence of such an attempt? "Either he will hate the one, and love the other; or else he will hold to the one, and despise the other." The two parts of this sentence, although separately proposed, are to be understood in connection with each other; for the latter part is a consequence of

the former. He will naturally hold to him whom he loves. He will so cleave to him, as to perform to him a willing, faithful, and diligent service. And, in the meantime, he will so far at least despise the master he hates as to have little regard to his commands, and to obey them, if at all, in a slight and careless manner. Therefore, whatsoever the wise men of the world may suppose, "you cannot serve God and mammon."

4. Mammon was the name of one of the heathen gods, who was supposed to preside over riches. It is here understood of riches themselves; gold and silver; or, in general, money; and, by a common figure of speech, of all that may be purchased thereby; such as ease, honor, and sensual pleasure.

What Does It Mean to Serve God?

But what are we here to understand by serving God, and what by serving mammon?

Serving God Means Believing in Him

We cannot serve God unless we believe in him. This is the only true foundation of serving him. Therefore, believing in God, as "reconciling the world to himself through Christ Jesus," the believing in him, as a loving, pardoning God, is the first great branch of his service.

And thus to believe in God implies, to trust in him as our strength, without whom we can do nothing, who every moment endues us with power from on high, without which it is impossible to please him; as our help, our only help in time of trouble, who compasses us about with songs of deliverance; as our shield, our defender, and the lifter up of our head above all our enemies that are round about us.

It implies, to trust in God as our happiness; as the center of spirits; the only rest of our souls; the only good who is adequate to all our capacities, and sufficient to satisfy all the desires he has given us.

It implies (what is nearly allied to the other), to trust in God as our end; to have an eye to him in all things; to use all things only as means of enjoying him; wheresoever we are, or whatsoever we do, to see him that is invisible, looking on us well-pleased, and to refer all things to him in Christ Jesus.

Serving God Means Loving Him

5. Thus to believe is the first thing we are to understand by serving God. The second is, to love him. Now to love God in the manner the Scripture describes, in the manner God himself requires of us, and by requiring engages to work in us, is to love him as the ONE GOD; that is, "with all our heart, and with all our soul, and with all our mind, and with all our strength"; it is to desire God alone for his own sake; and nothing else, but with reference to him; to rejoice in God; to delight in the Lord; not only to seek, but find, happiness in him; to enjoy God as the chiefest among ten thousand; to rest in him, as our God and our all; in a word, to have such a possession of God as makes us always happy.

Serving God Means Imitating Him

6. A third thing we are to understand by serving God is to resemble or imitate him. So the ancient Father: *Optimus Dei cultus, imitari quem colis*—"It is the best worship or service of God, to imitate him you worship."

We here speak of imitating or resembling him in the spirit of our minds; for here the true Christian imitation of God begins. "God is a Spirit"; and they that imitate or resemble him must do it "in spirit and in truth."

Now God is love: therefore, they who resemble him in the spirit of their minds are transformed into the same image.

They are merciful even as he is merciful. Their soul is all love. They are kind, benevolent, compassionate, tender-hearted; and that not only to the good and gentle, but also to the froward. Yea, they are, like Him, loving unto every man, and their mercy extends to all his works.

Serving God Means Obeying Him

7. One thing more we are to understand by serving God, and that is, the obeying him; the glorifying him with our bodies, as well as with our spirits; the keeping his outward commandments; the zealously doing whatever he hath enjoined; the carefully avoiding whatever he hath forbidden; the performing all the ordinary actions of life with a single eye and a pure heart, offering them all in holy, fervent love, as sacrifices to God through Jesus Christ.

What Does It Mean to Serve Mammon?

Serving Mammon Means Trusting in Riches

8. Let us consider now what we are to understand, on the other hand, by serving mammon. And, first, it implies the trusting in riches, in money, or the things purchasable thereby, as our strength—the means whereby we shall perform whatever cause we have in hand; the trusting in them as our help—by which we look to be comforted in or delivered out of trouble.

It implies the trusting in the world for happiness; the supposing that "a man's life," the comfort of his life, "consisteth in the abundance of the things which he possesseth"; the looking for rest in the things that are seen; for content, in outward plenty; the expecting that satisfaction in the things of the world, which can never be found out of God.

And if we do this, we cannot but make the world our end; the ultimate end, if not of all, at least of many, of our undertakings, many of our actions and designs; in which we shall aim only at an increase of wealth, at the obtaining pleasure or praise, at the gaining a larger measure of temporal things, without any reference to things eternal.

Serving Mammon Means Loving the World

9. The serving mammon implies, secondly, loving the world; desiring it for its own sake; the placing our joy in the things thereof, and setting our hearts upon them; the seeking (what indeed it is impossible we should find) our happiness therein; the resting with the whole weight of our souls, upon the staff of this broken reed, although daily experience shows it cannot support, but will only "enter into our hand and pierce it."

Serving Mammon Means Conforming to the World

10. To resemble, to be conformed to the world, is a third thing we are to understand by serving mammon; to have not only designs, but desires, tempers, affections, suitable to those of the world; to be of an earthly, sensual mind, chained down to the things of earth; to be self-willed, inordinate lovers of ourselves; to think highly of our own attainments; to desire and delight in the praise of men; to fear, shun, and abhor reproach; to be impatient of reproof, easy to be provoked, and swift to return evil for evil.

Serving Mammon Means Obeying the World

11. To serve mammon is, lastly, to obey the world, by outwardly conforming to its maxims and customs; to walk as other men walk, in the common road, in the broad, smooth, beaten path; to be in the fashion; to follow a multitude; to do like the rest of our neighbors; that is, to do the will of the

flesh and the mind, to gratify our appetites and inclinations; to sacrifice to ourselves; aim at our own ease and pleasure, in the general course both of our words and actions.

Now what can be more undeniably clear than that we cannot thus serve God and mammon?

You Cannot Serve Both God and Mammon

You Cannot Serve Both Comfortably

12. Does not every man see that he cannot comfortably serve both? That to trim between God and the world is the sure way to be disappointed in both, and to have no rest either in one or the other? How uncomfortable a condition must he be in, who, having the fear but not the love of God—who, serving him, but not with all his heart—has only the toils and not the joys of religion? He has religion enough to make him miserable, but not enough to make him happy: his religion will not let him enjoy the world, and the world will not let him enjoy God. So that, by halting between both, he loses both; and has no peace either in God or the world.

You Cannot Serve Both Consistently

13. Does not every man see that he cannot serve both consistently with himself? What more glaring inconsistency can be conceived than must continually appear in his whole behavior, who is endeavoring to obey both these masters, striving to "serve God and mammon"? He is indeed a "sinner that goeth two ways"; one step forward and another backward. He is continually building up with one hand, and pulling down with the other. He loves sin, and he hates it. He is always seeking, and yet always fleeing from, God. He would, and he would not. He is not the same man for one day; no, not for an

hour together. He is a motley mixture of all sorts of contrarieties; a heap of contradictions jumbled in one. O be consistent with thyself one way or the other! Turn to the right hand or to the left. If mammon be God, serve thou him; if the Lord, then serve him. But never think of serving either at all, unless it be with your whole heart.

You Cannot Serve Both Without Being Contrary

14. Does not every reasonable, every thinking man see that he cannot possibly serve God and mammon? Because there is the most absolute contrariety, the most irreconcilable enmity between them. The contrariety between the most opposite things on earth, between fire and water, darkness and light, vanishes into nothing when compared to the contrariety between God and mammon. So that, in whatsoever respect you serve the one, you necessarily renounce the other.

Do you believe in God through Christ? Do you trust in him as your strength, your help, your shield, and your exceeding great reward; as your happiness, your end in all, above all things? Then you cannot trust in riches. It is absolutely impossible you should, so long as you have this faith in God. Do you thus trust in riches? Then you have denied the faith. You do not trust in the living God. Do you love God? Do you seek and find happiness in him? Then you cannot love the world, neither the things of the world. You are crucified to the world, and the world crucified to you.

Do you love the world? Are your affections set on things beneath? Do you seek happiness in earthly things? Then it is impossible you should love God. Then the love of the Father is not in you. Do you resemble God? Are you merciful, as your Father is merciful? Are you transformed, by the renewal of your mind, into the image of him that created you? Then you cannot be conformed to the present world. You have renounced all its affections and lusts. Are you conformed to the world? Does your soul still bear the image of the earthly? Then you are not renewed in the spirit of your mind. You do not bear the image of the heavenly.

Do you obey God? Are you zealous to do his will on earth as the angels do in heaven? Then it is impossible you should obey mammon. Then you set the world at open defiance. You trample its customs and maxims under foot, and will neither follow nor be led by them. Do you follow the world? Do you live like other men? Do you please men? Do you please yourself? Then you cannot be a servant of God. You are of your master and father, the devil.

Therefore, Take No Thought for Your Life

15. Therefore, "thou shalt worship the Lord thy God; and him only shalt thou serve." You shall lay aside all thoughts of obeying two masters, of serving God and mammon. You shall propose to yourself no end, no help, no happiness, but God. You shall seek nothing in earth or heaven but him. You shall aim at nothing, but to know, to love, and enjoy him. And because this is all your business below, the only view you can reasonably have, the one design you are to pursue in all things—"Therefore I say unto you" (as our Lord continues his discourse), "Take no thought for your life, what you shall eat, or what you shall drink; nor yet for your body, what you shall put on"—a deep and weighty direction, which it imports us well to consider and thoroughly to understand.

Not a Command to Be Thoughtless or Slothful

16. Our Lord does not here require that we should be utterly without thought, even touching the concerns of this life. A giddy, careless temper is at the farthest remove from

the whole religion of Jesus Christ. Neither does he require us to be "slothful in business," to be slack and dilatory therein. This, likewise, is contrary to the whole spirit and genius of his religion. A Christian abhors sloth as much as drunkenness; and flees from idleness as he does from adultery. He well knows that there is one kind of thought and care with which God is well pleased; which is absolutely needful for the due performance of those outward works unto which the providence of God has called him.

It is the will of God that every man should labor to eat his own bread; yea, and that every man should provide for his own, for them of his own household. It is likewise his will that we should "owe no man anything, but provide things honest in the sight of all men." But this cannot be done without taking some thought, without having some care upon our minds; yea, often, not without long and serious thought, not without much and earnest care. Consequently this care, to provide for ourselves and our household, this thought how to render to all their dues, our blessed Lord does not condemn. Yea, it is good and acceptable in the sight of God our Savior.

It is good and acceptable to God that we should so take thought concerning whatever we have in hand, as to have a clear comprehension of what we are about to do, and to plan our business before we enter upon it. And it is right that we should carefully consider, from time to time, what steps we are to take therein; as well as that we should prepare all things beforehand, for the carrying it on in the most effectual manner. This care, termed by some, "the care of the head," it was by no means our Lord's design to condemn.

But a Condemnation of Anxious Care

17. What he here condemns is the care of the heart; the anxious, uneasy care; the care that has torment; all such care

as does hurt, either to the soul or body. What he forbids is that care which, sad experience shows, wastes the blood and drinks up the spirits; which anticipates all the misery it fears, and comes to torment us before the time. He forbids only that care which poisons the blessings of today, by fear of what may be tomorrow; which cannot enjoy the present plenty, through apprehensions of future want. This care is not only a sore disease, a grievous sickness of soul, but also an heinous offence against God, a sin of the deepest dye. It is a high affront to the gracious Governor and wise Disposer of all things; necessarily implying that the great Judge does not do right; that he does not order all things well. It plainly implies that he is wanting, either in wisdom, if he does not know what things we stand in need of; or in goodness, if he does not provide those things for all who put their trust in him.

Beware, therefore, that you take not thought in this sense: Be ye anxiously careful for nothing. Take no uneasy thought; this is a plain, sure rule: uneasy care is unlawful care. With a single eye to God, do all that in you lies to provide things honest in the sight of all men. And then give up all into better hands; leave the whole event to God.

18. "Take no thought" of this kind, no uneasy thought, even "for your life, what you shall eat, or what you shall drink; nor yet for your body, what you shall put on. Is not the life more than meat, and the body than raiment?" If then God gave you life, the greater gift, will he not give you food to sustain it? If he hath given you the body, how can you doubt but he will give you raiment to cover it? More especially, if you give yourselves up to him, and serve him with your whole heart.

Behold the Birds and the Lilies

"Behold," see before your eyes, "the fowls of the air: for they sow not, neither do they reap, nor gather into barns"; and yet they lack nothing; "yet your heavenly Father feedeth them. Are you not much better than they?" You that are creatures capable of God, are you not of more account in the eyes of God of a higher rank in the scale of beings? "And which of you, by taking thought, can add one cubit to his stature?" What profit have you then from this anxious thought? It is every way fruitless and unavailing.

"And why take ye thought for raiment?" Have you not a daily reproof wherever you turn your eyes? "Consider the lilies of the field, how they grow; they toil not, neither do they spin; and yet I say unto you, that even Solomon in all his glory was not arrayed like one of these. Wherefore, if God so clothe the grass of the field, which today is, and tomorrow is cast into the oven" (is cut down, burned up, and seen no more), "shall he not much more clothe you, O you of little faith?" you, whom he made to endure for ever and ever, to be pictures of his own eternity! You are indeed of little faith; otherwise you could not doubt of his love and care; no, not for a moment.

Your Heavenly Fathers Knows Your Need

19. "Therefore take no thought, saying, What shall we eat," if we lay up no treasure upon earth? "What shall we drink," if we serve God with all our strength, if our eye be singly fixed on him? "Wherewithal shall we be clothed," if we are not conformed to the world, if we disoblige those by whom we might be profited? "For after all these things do the Gentiles seek," the heathens who know not God. But you are sensible. "Your heavenly Father knows that you have need of all these things." And he has pointed out to you an infallible way of being constantly supplied therewith: "Seek ye first the kingdom of God, and his righteousness; and all these things shall be added unto you."

Seek Ye First the Kingdom of God

Seek Him First

20. "Seek ye first the kingdom of God." Before you give place to any other thought or care, let it be your concern that the God and Father of our Lord Jesus Christ (who "gave his only begotten Son," to the end that, believing in him, "you might not perish, but have everlasting life") may reign in your heart, may manifest himself in your soul, and dwell and rule there; that he may "cast down every high thing which exalteth itself against the knowledge of God, and bring into captivity every thought to the obedience of Christ." Let God have the sole dominion over you. Let him reign without a rival. Let him possess all your heart, and rule alone. Let him be your one desire, your joy, your love; so that all that is within you may continually cry out, "The Lord God omnipotent reigneth."

Seek First His Righteousness

"Seek the kingdom of God, and his righteousness." Righteousness is the fruit of God's reigning in the heart. And what is righteousness, but love—the love of God and of all mankind, flowing from faith in Jesus Christ, and producing humbleness of mind, meekness, gentleness, longsuffering, patience, deadness to the world; and every right disposition of heart, toward God and toward man. And by these it produces all holy actions, whatsoever are lovely or of good report; whatsoever works of faith and labor of love are acceptable to God, and profitable to man.

"His righteousness." This is all his righteousness still: it is his own free gift to us, for the sake of Jesus Christ the righteous, through whom alone it is purchased for us. And it is his work; it is He alone that worketh it in us, by the inspiration of the Holy Spirit.

21. Perhaps the well observing this may give light to some other scriptures, which we have not always so clearly understood. St. Paul, speaking in his Epistle to the Romans concerning the unbelieving Jews, says, "They, being ignorant of God's righteousness, and going about to establish their own righteousness, have not submitted themselves unto the righteousness of God." I believe this may be one sense of the words: they were "ignorant of God's righteousness," not only of the righteousness of Christ, imputed to every believer, whereby all his sins are blotted out, and he is reconciled to the favor of God; but (which seems here to be more immediately understood) they were ignorant of that inward righteousness, of that holiness of heart, which is with the utmost propriety termed God's righteousness; as being both his own free gift through Christ, and his own work, by his almighty Spirit. And because they were "ignorant" of this, they "went about to establish their own righteousness." They labored to establish that outside righteousness which might very properly be termed their own. For neither was it wrought by the Spirit of God, nor was it owned or accepted of him. They might work this themselves, by their own natural strength; and when they had done, it was a stink in his nostrils. And yet, trusting in this, they would "not submit themselves unto the righteousness of God." Yea, they hardened themselves against that faith whereby alone it was possible to attain it.

"For Christ is the end of the law for righteousness to everyone that believeth." Christ, when he said, "It is finished!" put an end to that law—to the law of external rites and ceremonies, that he might bring in a better righteousness through his blood, by that one oblation of himself once offered, even the image of God, into the inmost soul of everyone that believeth.

Seek First His Kingdom

22. Nearly related to these are those words of the apostle, in his Epistle to the Philippians: "I count all things but dung that I may win Christ"; an entrance into his everlasting kingdom; "and be found in him," believing in him, "not having mine own righteousness, which is of the law, but that which is through the faith of Christ, the righteousness which is of God by faith." "Not having my own righteousness, which is of the law;" a barely external righteousness, the outside religion I formerly had, when I hoped to be accepted of God because I was, "touching the righteousness which is of the law, blameless"; "but that which is through the faith of Christ, the righteousness which is of God by faith" (Phil. 3:8–9); that holiness of heart, that renewal of the soul in all its desires, tempers, and affections, "which is of God" (it is the work of God, and not of man), "by faith"; through the faith of Christ, through the revelation of Jesus Christ in us, and by faith in his blood; whereby alone we obtain the remission of our sins, and an inheritance among those that are sanctified.

And All These Things will be Added

23. "Seek ye first" this "kingdom of God" in your hearts; this righteousness, which is the gift and work of God, the image of God renewed in your souls; "and all these things shall be added unto you;" all things needful for the body; such a measure of all as God sees most for the advancement of his kingdom. These shall be added, they shall be thrown in, over and above. In seeking the peace and the love of God, you shall not only find what you more immediately seek, even the kingdom that cannot be moved; but also what you seek not, not at all for its own sake, but only in reference to the other. You shall find in your way to the kingdom, all outward things,

so far as they are expedient for you. This care God hath taken upon himself: cast you all your care upon him. He knoweth your wants; and whatsoever is lacking he will not fail to supply.

Therefore, Take No Thought for Tomorrow

Do Not Be Consumed with Cares about Tomorrow

24. "Therefore take no thought for the morrow." Not only, take you no thought how to lay up treasures on earth, how to increase in worldly substance; take no thought how to procure more food than you can eat, or more raiment than you can put on, or more money than is required from day to day for the plain, reasonable purposes of life; but take no uneasy thought, even concerning those things which are absolutely needful for the body. Do not trouble yourself now, with thinking what you shall do at a season which is yet afar off. Perhaps that season will never come; or it will be no concern of yours; before then you will have passed through all the waves, and be landed in eternity. All those distant views do not belong to you, who are but a creature of a day. Nay, what have you to do with the morrow, more strictly speaking? Why should you perplex yourself without need? God provides for you today what is needful to sustain the life which he has given you. It is enough: give yourself up into his hands. If you live another day, he will provide for that also.

Do Not Be Neglectful Today in Light of Tomorrow

25. Above all, do not make the care of future things a pretense for neglecting present duty. This is the most fatal way of "taking thought for the morrow." And how common is it among men! Many, if we exhort them to keep a conscience void of offence, to abstain from what they are convinced is

evil, do not scruple to reply, "How then must we live? Must we not take care of ourselves and of our families?" And this they imagine to be a sufficient reason for continuing in known, wilful sin. They say, and perhaps think, they would serve God now, were it not that they should, by and by, lose their bread. They would prepare for eternity; but they are afraid of wanting the necessaries of life. So they serve the devil for a morsel of bread; they rush into hell for fear of want; they throw away their poor souls, lest they should, some time or other, fall short of what is needful for their bodies!

It is not strange that they who thus take the matter out of God's hand should be so often disappointed of the very things they seek; that, while they throw away heaven to secure the things of earth, they lose the one but do not gain the other. The jealous God, in the wise course of his providence, frequently suffers this. So that they who will not cast their care on God, who, taking thought for temporal things, have little concern for things eternal, lose the very portion which they have chosen. There is a visible blast on all their undertakings; whatsoever they do, it doth not prosper; insomuch that, after they have forsaken God for the world, they lose what they sought, as well as what they sought not: they fall short of the kingdom of God, and his righteousness; nor yet are other things added unto them.

Do Not Be Distracted by Fond Dreams of Tomorrow

26. There is another way of "taking thought for the morrow," which is equally forbidden in these words. It is possible to take thought in a wrong manner, even with regard to spiritual things; to be so careful about what may be by and by, as to neglect what is now required at our hands. How insensibly do we slide into this, if we are not continually watching unto prayer! How easily are we carried away, in a kind of waking dream, projecting distant schemes, and drawing fine

scenes in our own imagination! We think, what good we will do when we are in such a place, or when such a time is come! How useful we will be, how plenteous in good works, when we are easier in our circumstances! How earnestly we will serve God, when once such an hindrance is out of the way!

Do Not Be Deceived by Idealistic Views of Tomorrow

Or perhaps you are now in heaviness of soul: God, as it were, hides his face from you. You see little of the light of his countenance: You cannot taste his redeeming love. In such a temper of mind, how natural is it to say, "O how I will praise God when the light of his countenance shall be again lifted up upon my soul! How will I exhort others to praise him when his love is again shed abroad in my heart! Then I will do thus and thus: I will speak for God in all places: I will not be ashamed of the gospel of Christ. Then I will redeem the time: I will use to the uttermost every talent I have received." Do not believe thyself. You will not do it then, unless you do it now. "He that is faithful in that which is little," of whatsoever kind it be, whether it be worldly substance, or the fear or love of God, "will be faithful in that which is much." But if you now hide one talent in the earth, you will then hide five. That is, if ever they are given; but there is small reason to expect they ever will. Indeed "unto him that hath," that is, uses what he hath, "shall be given, and he shall have more abundantly. But from him that hath not," that is, uses not the grace which he hath already received, whether in a larger or smaller degree, "shall be taken away even that which he hath."

Do Not Be Discouraged by the Temptations of Tomorrow

27. And take no thought for the temptations of tomorrow. This also is a dangerous snare. Think not, "When such a temptation comes, what shall I do? How shall I stand? I feel I have

not power to resist. I am not able to conquer that enemy." Most
true: you have not now the power which you do not now stand
in need of. You are not able at this time to conquer that enemy;
and at this time he does not assault you. With the grace you
have now, you could not withstand the temptations which
you have not. But when the temptation comes, the grace will
come. In greater trials you will have greater strength. When
sufferings abound, the consolations of God will, in the same
proportion, abound also. So that, in every situation, the grace
of God will be sufficient for you. He does not suffer you "to be
tempted" today "above that you are able to bear"; and "in every
temptation he will make a way to escape." "As thy days, so thy
strength shall be."

Live Thou Today

28. "Let the morrow," therefore, "take thought for the
things of itself"; that is, when the morrow comes, then think
of it. Live thou today. Be it your earnest care to improve the
present hour. This is your own; and it is your all. The past is
as nothing, as though it had never been. The future is nothing
to you. It is not yours; perhaps it never will be. There is no
depending on what is yet to come; for you "know not what a
day may bring forth." Therefore, live today: lose not an hour.
Use this moment; for it is your portion.

"Who knoweth the things which have been before him, or
which shall be after him under the sun?" The generations that
were from the beginning of the world, where are they now?
Fled away: forgotten. They were; they lived their day; they
were shook off of the earth, as leaves off of their trees: they
mouldered away into common dust! Another and another race
succeeded; then they "followed the generation of their fathers,
and shall never more see the light." Now is thy turn upon the

earth. "Rejoice, O young man, in the days of thy youth! Enjoy the very, very now, by enjoying Him "whose years fail not." Now let your eye be singly fixed on Him in "whom is no variableness neither shadow of turning!" Now give Him your heart; now stay yourself on Him: now be thou holy, as he is holy. Now lay hold on the blessed opportunity of doing his acceptable and perfect will! Now rejoice to "suffer the loss of all things," so you may "win Christ!"

29. Gladly suffer today, for his name's sake, whatsoever he permits this day to come upon you. But look not at the sufferings of tomorrow. "Sufficient unto the day is the evil thereof." Evil it is, speaking after the manner of men; whether it be reproach or want, pain or sickness; but in the language of God, all is blessing. It is a precious balm, prepared by the wisdom of God, and variously dispensed among his children, according to the various sicknesses of their souls. And he gives in one day, sufficient for that day; proportioned to the want and strength of the patient. If, therefore, thou snatchest today what belongs to the morrow; if thou addest this to what is given thee already, it will be more than thou canst bear. This is the way not to heal, but to destroy thy own soul. Take, therefore, just as much as he gives you today. Today, do and suffer his will! Today, give up yourself, your body, soul, and spirit to God, through Christ Jesus; desiring nothing, but that God may be glorified in all you are, all you do, all you suffer; seeking nothing, but to know God, and his Son Jesus Christ, through the eternal Spirit; pursuing nothing, but to love him, to serve him, and to enjoy him at this hour, and to all eternity!

Now unto "God the Father, who hath made me and all the world;" unto "God the Son, who hath redeemed me and all mankind"; unto "God the Holy Ghost, who sanctifies me and all the elect people of God;" be honor and praise, majesty, and dominion, for ever and ever! Amen.

Hindrances to Holiness

Judge not, that ye be not judged. For with what judgment ye judge, ye shall be judged; and with what measure ye mete, it shall be measured to you again. And why beholdest thou the speck that is in thy brother's eye, but considerest not the beam that is in thine own eye? Or how wilt thou say to thy brother, Let me pull out the speck out of thine eye; and, behold, a beam is in thine own eye? Thou hypocrite, first cast out the beam out of thine own eye; and then thou shalt see clearly to cast out the speck out of thy brother's eye. Give not that which is holy unto the dogs, neither cast ye your pearls before swine; lest they trample them under their feet, and turn again and rend you.

Ask, and it shall be given you; seek, and ye shall find; knock, and it shall be opened unto you. For everyone that asketh, receiveth; and he that seeketh, findeth; and to him that knocketh, it shall be opened. Or what man is there of you,

who, if his son ask bread, will give him a stone? Or if he ask
a fish, will give him a serpent? If ye, then, being evil, know
how to give good gifts unto your children, how much more
shall your Father which is in heaven give good gifts to them
that ask him? Therefore all things whatsoever ye would that
men should do to you, do ye even so to them; for this is the law
and the prophets.

—Matthew 7:1–12

Introduction

1. Our blessed Lord, having now finished his main design, having first delivered the sum of true religion, carefully guarded against those glosses of men whereby they would make the Word of God of none effect; and having, next, laid down rules touching that right intention which we are to preserve in all our outward actions, now proceeds to point out the main hindrances of this religion, and concludes all with a suitable application.

2. In the fifth chapter, our great Teacher has fully described inward religion in its various branches. He has there laid before us those dispositions of soul which constitute real Christianity; the tempers contained in that "holiness, without which no man shall see the Lord"; the affections which, when flowing from their proper fountain, from a living faith in God through Christ Jesus, are intrinsically and essentially good, and acceptable to God. In the sixth he has shown how all our actions likewise, even those that are indifferent in their own nature, may be made holy, and good, and acceptable to God, by a pure and holy intention. Whatever is done without this he declares is of no value with God: whereas, whatever outward works are thus consecrated to God are, in his sight, of great price.

3. In the former part of this chapter, he points out the most common and most fatal hindrances of this holiness. In the latter, he exhorts us by various motives, to break through all, and secure that prize of our high calling.

Hindrance to Holiness: Judging

The Temptation for Children of God to Judge

4. The first hindrance he cautions us against is judging. "Judge not, that ye be not judged." Judge not others, that you be not judged of the Lord, that you bring not vengeance on your own heads. "For with what judgment ye judge, ye shall be judged; and with what measure ye mete, it shall be measured to you again"—a plain and equitable rule, whereby God permits you to determine for yourselves in what manner he shall deal with you in the judgment of the great day.

5. There is no station of life, nor any period of time, from the hour of our first repenting and believing the gospel till we are made perfect in love, wherein this caution is not needful for every child of God. For occasions of judging can never be wanting. And the temptations to it are innumerable; many whereof are so artfully disguised that we fall into the sin before we suspect any danger. And unspeakable are the mischiefs produced hereby—always to him that judges another, thus wounding his own soul, and exposing himself to the righteous judgment of God—and frequently to those who are judged, whose hands hang down, who are weakened and hindered in their course, if not wholly turned out of the way, and caused to turn back even to perdition. Yea, how often when this "root of bitterness springs up," are "many defiled thereby"; by reason whereof the way of truth itself is evil spoken of, and that worthy name blasphemed whereby we are called!

The Temptation for the World to Judge

6. Yet it does not appear that our Lord designed this caution only, or chiefly, for the children of God; but rather for the children of the world, for the men who know not God. These cannot but hear of those who are not of the world; who follow after the religion above described; who endeavor to be humble, serious, gentle, merciful, and pure in heart; who earnestly desire such measures of these holy tempers as they have not yet attained, and wait for them in doing all good to all men, and patiently suffering evil. Whoever go but thus far cannot be hid, no more than "a city set upon a hill." And why do not those who "see their good works glorify their Father which is in heaven"? What excuse have they for not treading in their steps—for not imitating their example and being followers of them, as they are also of Christ? Why, in order to provide an excuse for themselves, they condemn those whom they ought to imitate. They spend their time in finding out their neighbor's faults, instead of amending their own. They are so busied about others going out of the way, that themselves never come into it at all; at least, never get forward, never go beyond a poor dead form of godliness without the power.

The Call to Take Up Thy Cross

7. It is to these more especially that our Lord says, "Why beholdest thou the speck that is in thy brother's eye"—the infirmities, the mistakes, the imprudence, the weakness of the children of God—"but considerest not the beam that is in thine own eye"? Thou considerest not the damnable impenitence, the satanic pride, the accursed self-will, the idolatrous love of the world, which are in yourself, and which make your whole life an abomination to the Lord. Above all, with what supine carelessness and indifference are you dancing over the

mouth of hell! And "how then," with what grace, with what decency or modesty, "wilt thou say to thy brother, Let me pull out the speck out of thine eye";—the excess of zeal for God, the extreme of self-denial, the too great disengagement from worldly cares and employments, the desire to be day and night in prayer, or hearing the words of eternal life—"And behold a beam is in thine own eye!" Not a speck, like one of these.

"Thou hypocrite!" who pretendest to care for others, and hast no care for your own soul; who makest a show of zeal for the cause of God, when in truth thou neither love nor fear him! "First cast out the beam out of thine own eye." Cast out the beam of impenitence! Know thyself! See and feel thyself a sinner! Feel that your inward parts are very wickedness, that thou art altogether corrupt and abominable, and that the wrath of God abideth on thee! Cast out the beam of pride; abhor thyself; sink down as in dust and ashes; be more and more little, and mean, and base, and vile in thine own eyes! Cast out the beam of self-will! Learn what that means, "If any man will come after me, let him renounce himself." Deny thyself, and take up thy cross daily. Let thy whole soul cry out, "I came down from heaven,"—for so you did, you never-dying spirit, whether you know it or no—"not to do my own will, but the will of him that sent me." Cast out the beam of love of the world! Love not the world, neither the things of the world. Be thou crucified unto the world, and the world crucified unto thee. Only use the world, but enjoy God. Seek all thy happiness in him! Above all, cast out the grand beam, that supine carelessness and indifference!

Deeply consider, that "one thing is needful"; the one thing which you have scarce ever thought of. Know and feel, that thou art a poor, vile, guilty worm, quivering over the great gulf! What art thou? A sinner born to die; a leaf driven before the wind; a vapor ready to vanish away, just appearing, and then scattered into air, to be no more seen! See this! "And then shalt thou see clearly to cast out the speck out of thy brother's eye." Then, if you have leisure from the concerns of your own soul, you shall know how to correct your brother also.

The Command to Judge Not

8. But what is properly the meaning of this word, "Judge not"? What is the judging which is here forbidden? It is not the same as evil-speaking, although it is frequently joined therewith. Evil-speaking is the relating anything that is evil concerning an absent person; whereas judging may indifferently refer either to the absent or the present. Neither does it necessarily imply the speaking at all, but only the thinking evil of another. Not that all kind of thinking evil of others is that judging which our Lord condemns. If I see one commit robbery or murder, or hear him blaspheme the name of God, I cannot refrain from thinking ill of the robber or murderer. Yet this is not evil judging: there is no sin in this, nor anything contrary to tender affection.

9. *Do not condemn the innocent.* The thinking of another in a manner that is contrary to love is that judging which is here condemned; and this may be of various kinds. For, first, we may think another to blame when he is not. We may lay to his charge (at least in our own mind) the things of which he is not guilty; the words which he has never spoke, or the actions which he has never done. Or we may think his manner of acting was wrong, although in reality it was not. And even where nothing can justly be blamed, either in the thing itself or in the manner of doing it, we may suppose his intention was not good, and so condemn him on that ground, at the same time that he who searches the heart sees his simplicity and godly sincerity.

10. *Do not condemn the guilty.* But we may not only fall into the sin of judging by condemning the innocent; but also, secondly, by condemning the guilty to a higher degree than he deserves. This species of judging is likewise an offense against justice as well as mercy; and yet such an offense as nothing can secure us from but the strongest and tenderest affection. Without this we readily suppose one who is acknowledged to be in fault to be more in fault than he really is. We undervalue whatever good is found in him. Nay, we are not easily induced to believe that anything good can remain in him in whom we have found anything that is evil.

11. All this shows a manifest want of that love which οὐ λογίζεται κακόν, *thinketh no evil;* which never draws an unjust or unkind conclusion from any premises whatsoever. Love will not infer from a person's falling once into an act of open sin that he is accustomed so to do, that he is habitually guilty of it: And if he was habitually guilty once, love does not conclude he is so still, much less, that if he is now guilty of this, therefore he is guilty of other sins also. These evil reasonings all pertain to that sinful judging which our Lord here guards us against; and which we are in the highest degree concerned to avoid, if we love either God or our own souls.

12. *Do not condemn without evidence.* But supposing we do not condemn the innocent, neither the guilty any farther than they deserve; still we may not be altogether clear of the snare. For there is a third sort of sinful judging, which is the condemning any person at all where there is not sufficient evidence. And be the facts we suppose ever so true; yet that does not acquit us. For they ought not to have been supposed, but proved; and till they were, we ought to have formed no judgment. I say, till they were; for neither are we excused; although the facts admit of ever so strong proof, unless that proof be produced before we pass sentence, and compared

with the evidence on the other side. Nor can we be excused if ever we pass a full sentence before the accused has spoken for himself. Even a Jew might teach us this, as a mere lesson of justice abstracted from mercy and brotherly love. "Does our law," says Nicodemus, "judge any man before it hear him, and know what he doeth" (John 7:51). Yea, a heathen could reply, when the chief of the Jewish nation desired to have judgment against his prisoner, "It is not the manner of the Romans" to judge "any man, before he that is accused have the accusers face to face, and have license to answer for himself concerning the crime laid against him."

13. Indeed we could not easily fall into sinful judging were we only to observe that rule which another [Seneca] of those heathen Romans affirms to have been the measure of his own practice. "I am so far," says he, "from lightly believing every man's or any man's evidence against another, that I do not easily or immediately believe a man's evidence against himself. I always allow him second thoughts, and many times counsel too." Go, thou who art called a Christian, and do likewise, lest the heathen rise and condemn thee in that day!

14. But how rarely should we condemn or judge one another, at least how soon would that evil be remedied, were we to walk by that clear and express rule which our Lord himself has taught us! "If thy brother shall trespass against thee," or if you hear or believe that he has, "go and tell him of his fault, between him and you alone." This is the first step you are to take. "But if he will not hear, take with you one or two more, that in the mouth of two or three witnesses every word may be established." This is the second step. "If he neglect to hear them, tell it unto the church," either to the overseers thereof, or to the whole congregation. You have then done your part. Then think of it no more, but commend the whole to God.

Hindrance to Holiness: Giving Pearls to Pigs

15. But supposing you have by the grace of God "cast the beam out of thine own eye," and do now "clearly see the speck or the beam which is in thy brother's eye," yet beware you do not receive hurt yourself by endeavoring to help him. Still "give not that which is holy unto dogs." Do not lightly account any to be of this number; but if it evidently appear that they deserve the title, then "cast you not your pearls before swine." Beware of that zeal which is not according to knowledge. For this is another great hindrance in their way who would be "perfect as their heavenly Father is perfect." They who desire this cannot but desire that all mankind should partake of the common blessing. And when we ourselves first partake of the heavenly gift, the divine "evidence of things not seen," we wonder that all mankind do not see the things which we see so plainly; and make no doubt at all but we shall open the eyes of all we have any intercourse with. Hence we are for attacking all we meet without delay, and constraining them to see, whether they will or no. And by the ill success of this intemperate zeal, we often suffer in our own souls. To prevent this spending our strength in vain our Lord adds this needful caution (needful to all, but more especially to those who are now warm in their first love) "Give not that which is holy unto the dogs, neither cast ye your pearls before swine; lest they trample them under foot, and turn again and rend you."

Giving Away the Holy Thing

16. "Give not that which is holy unto the dogs." Beware of thinking that any deserve this appellation till there is full and incontestable proof, such as you can no longer resist. But when it is clearly and indisputably proved that they are unholy and wicked men, not only strangers to, but enemies to God, to all

righteousness and true holiness; "give not that which is holy," τὸ ἅγιον, *the holy thing*, emphatically so called, unto these. The holy, the peculiar doctrines of the gospel—such as were "hid from the ages and generations" of old, and are now made known to us only by the revelation of Jesus Christ and the inspiration of his Holy Spirit—are not to be prostituted unto these men, who know not if there be any Holy Ghost. Not indeed that the ambassadors of Christ can refrain from declaring them in the great congregation, wherein some of these may probably be; we must speak, whether men will hear or whether they will forbear; but this is not the case with private Christians. They do not bear that awful character; nor are they under any manner of obligation to force these great and glorious truths on them who contradict and blaspheme, who have a rooted enmity against them. Nay, they ought not so to do, but rather to lead them as they are able to bear. Do not begin a discourse with these upon remission of sins and the gift of the Holy Ghost; but talk with them in their own manner, and upon their own principles. With the rational, honorable, and unjust Epicure, reason of "righteousness, temperance, and judgment to come." This is the most probable way to make Felix tremble. Reserve higher subjects for men of higher attainments.

Prostituting Your Pearls

17. "Neither cast ye your pearls before swine." Be very unwilling to pass this judgment on any man. But if the fact be plain and undeniable, if it is clear beyond all dispute, if the swine do not endeavor to disguise themselves, but rather glory in their shame, making no pretense to purity either of heart or life, but working all uncleanness with greediness; then "cast" not your pearls before them. Talk not to them of the mysteries of the kingdom; of the things which eye hath not seen, nor ear heard; which of consequence, as they have no other inlets

of knowledge, no spiritual senses, it cannot enter into their hearts to conceive. Tell not them of the "exceeding great and precious promises" which God hath given us in the Son of his love. What conception can they have of being made partakers of the divine nature, who do not even desire to escape the corruption that is in the world through lust? Just as much knowledge as swine have of pearls, and as much relish as they have for them, so much relish have they for the deep things of God, so much knowledge of the mysteries of the gospel, who are immersed in the mire of this world, in worldly pleasures, desires, and cares.

O cast not those pearls before these, "lest they trample them under their feet!"—lest they utterly despise what they cannot understand, and speak evil of the things which they know not. Nay, it is probable this would not be the only inconvenience which would follow. It would not be strange if they were, according to their nature, to "turn again, and rend you"; if they were to return you evil for good, cursing for blessing, and hatred for your goodwill. Such is the enmity of the carnal mind against God and all the things of God. Such is the treatment you are to expect from these, if you offer them the unpardonable affront of endeavoring to save their souls from death, to pluck them as brands out of the burning.

Hindrance to Holiness: Failure to Ask

18. And yet you need not utterly despair even of these, who, for the present, "turn again and rend you." For if all your arguments and persuasives fail, there is yet another remedy left; and one that is frequently found effectual when no other method avails; this is prayer. Therefore whatever you desire or want, either for others or for your own soul, "ask, and it shall be given you; seek, and ye shall find; knock, and it shall be opened unto

you." The neglect of this is a third grand hindrance of holiness. Still we "have not, because we ask not."

Asking, Seeking, Knocking, and Finding

O how meek and gentle, how lowly in heart, how full of love both to God and men, might you have been at this day, if you had only asked; if you had continued instant in prayer! Therefore, now, at least, "ask, and it shall be given unto you." Ask, that you may thoroughly experience and perfectly practice the whole of that religion which our Lord has here so beautifully described. It shall then be given you, to be holy as he is holy, both in heart and in all manner of conversation. Seek, in the way he hath ordained, in searching the Scriptures, in hearing his word, in meditating thereon, in fasting, in partaking of the Supper of the Lord, and surely you shall find. You shall find that pearl of great price, that faith which overcomes the world, that peace which the world cannot give, that love which is the earnest of your inheritance. Knock; continue in prayer, and in every other way of the Lord. Be not weary or faint in your mind. Press on to the mark. Take no denial: let him not go until he bless you. And the door of mercy, of holiness, of heaven shall be opened unto you.

19. It is in compassion to the hardness of our hearts, so unready to believe the goodness of God, that our Lord is pleased to enlarge upon this head, and to repeat and confirm what he has spoken. "For everyone," saith he, "that asketh, receiveth"; so that none need come short of the blessing; "and he that seeketh," even everyone that seeketh, "findeth" the love and the image of God; "and to him that knocketh," to everyone that knocketh, the gate of righteousness shall be opened. So that here is no room for any to be discouraged, as though they might ask or seek or knock in vain. Only remember always to pray, to seek, to knock, and not to faint. And then the promise

stands sure. It is firm as the pillars of heaven—yea, more firm; for heaven and earth shall pass away; but his word shall not pass away.

Our Heavenly Father

20. To cut off every pretense for unbelief, our blessed Lord, in the following verses, illustrates yet farther what he had said, by an appeal to what passes in our own breasts. "What man," saith he, "is there of you, whom if his son ask bread, will give him a stone?" Will even natural affection permit you to refuse the reasonable request of one you love? "Or if he ask a fish, will he give him a serpent?" Will he give him hurtful instead of profitable things? So that even from what you feel and do yourselves you may receive the fullest assurance, as on the one hand that no ill effect can possibly attend your asking, so, on the other, that it will be attended with that good effect, a full supply of all your wants. For "if you, being evil, know how to give good gifts unto your children, how much more shall your Father which is in heaven," who is pure, unmixed, essential goodness, "give good things to them that ask him" or (as he expresses it on another occasion), "give the Holy Ghost to them that ask him?" In him are included all good things; all wisdom, peace, joy, love; the whole treasures of holiness and happiness; all that God has prepared for them that love him.

Hindrances Removed: Charity Towards All

21. But that your prayer may have its full weight with God, see that you be in charity with all men; for otherwise it is more likely to bring a curse than a blessing on your own head; nor can you expect to receive any blessing from God while you have not charity towards your neighbor. Therefore, let this hindrance be removed without delay. Confirm your love

towards one another, and towards all men. And love them, not in word only, but in deed and in truth. "Therefore all things whatsoever ye would that men should do to you, do ye even so to them; for this is the law and the prophets."

22. This is that royal law, that golden rule of mercy as well as justice, which even the heathen Emperor caused to be written over the gate of his palace; a rule which many believe to be naturally engraved on the mind of everyone that comes into the world. And thus much is certain, that it commends itself, as soon as heard, to every man's conscience and understanding; insomuch that no man can knowingly offend against it without carrying his condemnation in his own breast.

23. "This is the law and the prophets." Whatsoever is written in that law which God of old revealed to mankind, and whatsoever precepts God has given by his holy prophets which have been since the world began," they are all summed up in these few words, they are all contained in this short direction. And this, rightly understood, comprises the whole of that religion which our Lord came to establish upon earth.

24. It may be understood either in a positive or negative sense. If understood in a negative sense, the meaning is, "Whatever ye would not that men should do to you, do not ye unto them." Here is a plain rule, always ready at hand, always easy to be applied. In all cases relating to your neighbor, make his case your own. Suppose the circumstances to be changed, and yourself to be just as he is now. And then beware that you indulge no temper or thought, that no word pass out of your lips, that you take no step which you should have condemned in him, upon such a change of circumstances. If understood in a direct and positive sense, the plain meaning of it is, "Whatsoever you could reasonably desire of him, supposing yourself to be in his circumstances, that do, to the uttermost of your power, to every child of man."

25. To apply this in one or two obvious instances. It is clear to every man's own conscience, we would not that others should judge us, should causelessly or lightly think evil of us; much less would we that any should speak evil of us, should publish our real faults or infirmities. Apply this to yourself. Do not unto another what you would not he should do unto you; and you will never more judge your neighbor, never causelessly or lightly think evil of anyone; much less will you speak evil; you will never mention even the real fault of an absent person, unless so far as you are convinced it is absolutely needful for the good of other souls.

26. Again, we would that all men should love and esteem us, and behave towards us according to justice, mercy, and truth. And we may reasonably desire that they should do us all the good they can do without injuring themselves; yea, that in outward things (according to the known rule), their superfluities should give way to our conveniencies, their conveniencies to our necessities, and their necessities to our extremities. Now then, let us walk by the same rule: let us do unto all as we would they should do to us. Let us love and honor all men. Let justice, mercy, and truth govern all our minds and actions. Let our superfluities give way to our neighbor's conveniencies (and who then will have any superfluities left); our conveniencies to our neighbor's necessities; our necessities to his extremities.

27. This is pure and genuine morality. This do, and you shall live. "As many as walk by this rule, peace be to them, and mercy"; for they are "the Israel of God." But then be it observed, none can walk by this rule (nor ever did from the beginning of the world), none can love his neighbor as himself, unless he first love God. And none can love God unless he believe in Christ; unless he have redemption through his blood, and the Spirit of God bearing witness with his spirit that he is a child of God. Faith, therefore, is still the root of all, of present as well

as future salvation. Still we must say to every sinner, "Believe in the Lord Jesus Christ, and you shall be saved." You shall be saved now, that you may be saved for ever; saved on earth, that you may be saved in heaven. Believe in him, and your faith will work by love. You will love the Lord your God because he has loved you. You will love your neighbor as yourself. And then it will be thy glory and joy, to exert and increase this love; not barely by abstaining from what is contrary thereto, from every unkind thought, word, and action, but by showing all that kindness to every man which thou wouldst he should show unto you.

ENTER AT THE STRAIGHT GATE

Enter ye in at the straight gate: For wide is the gate, and broad is the way, which leadeth to destruction, and many there be which go in thereat: Because straight is the gate, and narrow is the way, which leadeth unto life, and few there be that find it.
—Matthew 7:13–14

Introduction

1. Our Lord, having warned us of the dangers which easily beset us at our first entrance upon real religion, the hindrances which naturally arise from within, from the wickedness of our own hearts; now proceeds to apprise us of the hindrances from without, particularly ill example and ill advice. By one or the other of these, thousands, who once ran well, have drawn back unto perdition; yea, many of those who were not novices in religion, who had made some progress in righteousness. His

caution, therefore, against these he presses upon us with all possible earnestness, and repeats again and again, in variety of expressions, lest by any means we should let it slip. Thus, effectually to guard us against the former, "Enter ye in," saith he, "at the straight gate: for wide is the gate, and broad is the way, that leadeth to destruction, and many there be which go in thereat: Because straight is the gate, and narrow is the way, which leadeth unto life, and few there be that find it." To secure us from the latter, "Beware," saith he, "of false prophets." We shall, at present, consider the former only.

2. "Enter ye in," saith our blessed Lord, "at the straight gate: for wide is the gate, and broad is the way, that leadeth to destruction, and many there be which go in thereat: because straight is the gate, and narrow is the way, which leadeth unto life, and few there be that find it."

3. In these words we may observe, first, the inseparable properties of the way to hell: "Wide is the gate, broad the way, that leadeth to destruction, and many there be that go in thereat"; secondly, the inseparable properties of the way to heaven: "Straight is that gate, and few there be that find it"; thirdly, a serious exhortation grounded thereon, "Enter ye in at the straight gate."

I. The Inseparable Properties of the Way to Hell

1. We may observe, first, the inseparable properties of the way to hell: "Wide is the gate, and broad is the way, that leadeth to destruction, and many there be that go in thereat."

Wide Is the Gate and Broad Is the Way

2. Wide indeed is the gate, and broad the way, that leadeth to destruction! For sin is the gate of hell, and wickedness the way to destruction. And how wide a gate is that of sin! How

broad is the way of wickedness! The "commandment" of God "is exceeding broad"; as extending not only to all our actions, but to every word which goeth out of our lips, yea, every thought that rises in our heart. And sin is equally broad with the commandment, seeing any breach of the commandment is sin. Yea, rather, it is a thousand times broader; since there is only one way of keeping the commandment; for we do not properly keep it, unless both the thing done, the manner of doing it, and all the other circumstances, are right: But there are a thousand ways of breaking every commandment; so that this gate is wide indeed.

3. To consider this a little more particularly: How wide do those parent-sins extend, from which all the rest derive their being—that carnal mind which is enmity against God, pride of heart, self-will, and love of the world! Can we fix any bounds to them? Do they not diffuse themselves through all our thoughts, and mingle with all our tempers? Are they not the leaven which leavens, more or less, the whole mass of our affections? May we not, on a close and faithful examination of ourselves, perceive these roots of bitterness continually springing up, infecting all our words, and tainting all our actions? And how innumerable an offspring do they bring forth, in every age and nation! Even enough to cover the whole earth with darkness and cruel habitations.

4. O who is able to reckon up their accursed fruits; to count all the sins, whether against God or our neighbor, not which imagination might paint, but which may be matter of daily, melancholy experience? Nor need we range over all the earth to find them. Survey any one kingdom, any single country, or city, or town; and how plenteous is this harvest! And let it not be one of those which are still overspread with Mahometan or Pagan darkness; but of those which name the name of Christ, which profess to see the light of his glorious gospel. Go no

farther than the kingdom to which we belong, the city wherein we are now. We call ourselves Christians; yea, and that of the purest sort: we are Protestants; Reformed Christians! But alas! who shall carry on the reformation of our opinions into our hearts and lives? Is there not a cause? For how innumerable are our sins—and those of the deepest dye! Do not the grossest abominations, of every kind, abound among us from day to day? Do not sins of every sort cover the land, as the waters cover the sea? Who can count them? Rather go and count the drops of rain, or the sands on the sea-shore. So "wide is the gate," so "broad is the way, that leadeth to destruction!"

Many There Are Who Enter

5. "And many there are who go in at" that gate; many who walk in that way; almost as many as go in at the gate of death, as sink into the chambers of the grave. For it cannot be denied (though neither can we acknowledge it but with shame and sorrow of heart) that even in this which is called a Christian country, the generality of every age and sex, of every profession and employment, of every rank and degree, high and low, rich and poor, are walking in the way of destruction. The far greater part of the inhabitants of this city, to this day, live in sin; in some palpable, habitual, known transgression of the law they profess to observe; yea, in some outward transgression, some gross, visible kind of ungodliness or unrighteousness; some open violation of their duty, either to God or man. These then, none can deny, are all in the way that leadeth to destruction.

Add to these, those who have a name indeed that they live, but were never yet alive to God; those that outwardly appear fair to men, but are inwardly full of all uncleanness; full of pride or vanity, of anger or revenge, of ambition or covetousness; lovers of themselves, lovers of the world, lovers of pleasure more than lovers of God. These, indeed, may be

highly esteemed of men; but they are an abomination to the
Lord. And how greatly will these saints of the world swell the
number of the children of hell! Yea, add all, whatever they be
in other respects, whether they have more or less of the form
of godliness, who, "being ignorant of God's righteousness, and
seeking to establish their own righteousness," as the ground of
their reconciliation to God and acceptance with him, of consequence have not "submitted themselves unto the righteousness
which is of God" by faith. Now, all these things joined together
in one, how terribly true is our Lord's assertion, "Wide is the
gate, and broad is the way, that leadeth to destruction, and
many there be who go in thereat!"

6. Nor does this only concern the vulgar herd—the poor,
base, stupid part of mankind. Men of eminence in the world,
men who have many fields and yoke of oxen, do not desire to
be excused from this. On the contrary, "many wise men after
the flesh," according to the human methods of judging, "many
mighty," in power, in courage, in riches, many "noble, are
called"; called into the broad way, by the world, the flesh, and
the devil; and they are not disobedient to that calling. Yea, the
higher they are raised in fortune and power, the deeper do they
sink into wickedness. The more blessings they have received
from God, the more sins do they commit; using their honor or
riches, their learning or wisdom, not as means of working out
their salvation, but rather of excelling in vice, and so insuring
their own destruction!

II. The Inseparable Properties of the Way to Heaven

1. And the very reason why many of these go on so securely
in the broad way is because it is broad; not considering that this
is the inseparable property of the way to destruction. "Many

there be," saith our Lord, "which go in thereat"; for the very reason why they should flee from it, even "because straight is the gate, and narrow the way that leadeth unto life, and few there be that find it."

Straight Is the Gate and Narrow Is the Way

2. This is an inseparable property of the way to heaven. So narrow is the way that leadeth unto life, unto life everlasting— so straight the gate—that nothing unclean, nothing unholy, can enter. No sinner can pass through that gate, until he is saved from all his sins. Not only from his outward sins, from his evil "conversation received by tradition from his fathers." It will not suffice, that he has "ceased to do evil" and "learned to do well." He must not only be saved from all sinful actions, and from all evil and useless discourse; but inwardly changed, thoroughly renewed in the spirit of his mind: otherwise he cannot pass through the gate of life, he cannot enter into glory.

3. For, "narrow is the way that leadeth unto life," the way of universal holiness. Narrow indeed is the way of poverty of spirit; the way of holy mourning; the way of meekness; and that of hungering and thirsting after righteousness. Narrow is the way of mercifulness; of love unfeigned; the way of purity of heart; of doing good unto all men; and of gladly suffering evil, all manner of evil, for righteousness' sake.

Few There Be That Find It

4. "And few there be that find it." Alas! How few find even the way of heathen honesty! How few are there that do nothing to another which they would not another should do unto them! How few that are clear, before God, from acts either of injustice or unkindness! How few that do not "offend with their tongue," that speak nothing unkind, nothing untrue!

What a small proportion of mankind are innocent even of outward transgressions! And how much smaller a proportion have their hearts right before God, clean and holy in his sight! Where are they, whom his all-searching eye discerns to be truly humble; to abhor themselves in dust and ashes, in the presence of God their Savior; to be deeply and steadily serious, feeling their wants, and "passing the time of their sojourning with fear"; truly meek and gentle, never "overcome of evil, but overcoming evil with good"; thoroughly athirst for God, and continually painting after a renewal in his likeness? How thinly are they scattered over the earth, whose souls are enlarged in love to all mankind; and who love God with all their strength; who have given him their hearts, and desire nothing else in earth or heaven! How few are those lovers of God and man that spend their whole strength in doing good unto all men; and are ready to suffer all things, yea, death itself, to save one soul from eternal death!

Hindrances to Entering the Narrow Gate

5. But while so few are found in the way of life, and so many in the way of destruction, there is great danger lest the torrent of example should bear us away with them. Even a single example, if it be always in our sight, is apt to make much impression upon us; especially when it has nature on its side, when it falls in with our own inclinations. How great then must be the force of so numerous examples, continually before our eyes; and all conspiring, together with our own hearts to carry us down the stream of nature! How difficult must it be to stem the tide, and to keep ourselves "unspotted in the world!"

6. *The wise man's appeal to our reason.* What heightens the difficulty still more is that they are not the rude and

senseless part of mankind, at least not these alone, who set us the example, who throng the downward way, but the polite, the well-bred, the genteel, the wise, the men who understand the world, the men of knowledge, of deep and various learning, the rational, the eloquent! These are all, or nearly all, against us. And how shall we stand against these? Do not their tongues drop manna; and have they not learned all the arts of soft persuasion—and of reasoning too; for these are versed in all controversies, and strife of words. It is therefore a small thing with them to prove, that the way is right, because it is broad; that he who follows a multitude cannot do evil, but only he who will not follow them; that your way must be wrong, because it is narrow, and because there are so few that find it. These will make it clear to a demonstration, that evil is good, and good is evil; that the way of holiness is the way of destruction, and the way of the world the only way to heaven.

7. *The powerful man's appeal to our fears.* O how can unlearned and ignorant men maintain their cause against such opponents! And yet these are not all with whom they must contend, however unequal to the task: for there are many mighty, and noble, and powerful men, as well as wise, in the road that leadeth to destruction; and these have a shorter way of confuting, than that of reason and argument. They usually apply, not to the understanding, but to the fears, of any that oppose them; a method that seldom fails of success, even where argument profits nothing, as lying level to the capacities of all men; for all can fear, whether they can reason or no. And all who have not a firm trust in God, a sure reliance both on his power and love, cannot but fear to give any disgust to those who have the power of the world in their hands. What wonder, therefore, if the example of these is a law to all who know not God.

8. *The rich man's appeal to our desires.* Many rich are likewise in the broad way. And these apply to the hopes of men, and to all their foolish desires, as strongly and effectually as the mighty and noble to their fears. So that hardly can you hold on in the way of the kingdom, unless you are dead to all below, unless you are crucified to the world, and the world crucified to you, unless you desire nothing more but God.

9. For how dark, how uncomfortable, how forbidding is the prospect on the opposite side! A straight gate! A narrow way! And few finding that gate! Few walking in the way! Besides, even those few are not wise men, not men of learning or eloquence. They are not able to reason either strongly or clearly: they cannot propose an argument to any advantage. They know not how to prove what they profess to believe; or to explain even what they say they experience. Surely such advocates as these will never recommend, but rather discredit, the cause they have espoused.

10. Add to this, that they are not noble, not honorable men. If they were, you might bear with their folly. They are men of no interest, no authority, of no account in the world. They are mean and base; low in life; and such as have no power, if they had the will, to hurt you. Therefore there is nothing at all to be feared from them; and there is nothing at all to hope: For the greater part of them may say, "Silver and gold have I none"; at least a very moderate share. Nay, some of them have scarce food to eat, or raiment to put on. For this reason, as well as because their ways are not like those of other men, they are everywhere spoken against, are despised, have their names cast out as evil, are variously persecuted, and treated as the filth and offscouring of the world. So that both your fears, your hopes, and all your desires (except those which you have immediately from God), yea, all your natural passions, continually incline you to return into the broad way.

III. The Exhortation: Strive to Enter In

Many Will Seek to Enter and Will Not Be Able

1. Therefore it is, that our Lord so earnestly exhorts, "Enter ye in at the straight gate." Or (as the same exhortation is elsewhere expressed), "Strive to enter in" (Ἀγωνίζεσθε εἰσελθεῖν, *strive as in an agony*). "For many," saith our Lord, "shall seek to enter in," indolently strive, "and shall not be able."

2. It is true, he intimates what may seem another reason for this, for their not being able to enter in, in the words which immediately follow these. For after he had said, "Many, I say unto you, will seek to enter in, and shall not be able," he subjoins, "When once the master of the house is risen up, and has shut to the door, and you begin to stand without,"— ἄρξησθε ἔξω ἑστάναι, rather, *you stand without*; for ἄρξησθε seems to be only an elegant expletive—"and to knock at the door, saying, Lord, Lord, open unto us; he shall answer and say unto you, I know you not: depart from me, all ye workers of iniquity" (Luke 13:24ff.).

3. It may appear, upon a transient view of these words, that their delaying to seek at all, rather than their manner of seeking, was the reason why they were not able to enter in. But it comes, in effect, to the same thing. They were, therefore, commanded to depart, because they had been "workers of iniquity"; because they had walked in the broad road; in other words, because they had not agonized to "enter in at the straight gate." Probably they did seek, before the door was shut; but that did not suffice. And they did strive, after the door was shut; but then it was too late.

So Today, Enter at the Straight Gate

4. Therefore strive ye now, in this your day, to "enter in at the straight gate." And in order thereto, settle it in your heart,

and let it be ever uppermost in your thoughts, that if you are
in a broad way, you are in the way that leadeth to destruction.
If many go with you, as sure as God is true, both they and you
are going to hell! If you are walking as the generality of men
walk, you are walking to the bottomless pit! Are many wise,
many rich, many mighty, or noble travelling with you in the
same way? By this token, without going any farther, you know
it does not lead to life. Here is a short, a plain, an infallible rule,
before you enter into particulars. In whatever profession you
are engaged, you must be singular, or be damned! The way to
hell has nothing singular in it; but the way to heaven is singularity all over. If you move but one step towards God, you are
not as other men are. But regard not this. It is far better to stand
alone, than to fall into the pit. Run, then, with patience the
race which is set before you, though your companions therein
are but few. They will not always be so. Yet a little while, and
you will "come to an innumerable company of angels, to the
general assembly and Church of the first-born, and to the
spirits of just men made perfect."

5. Now, then, "strive to enter in at the straight gate," being
penetrated with the deepest sense of the inexpressible danger
your soul is in, so long as you are in a broad way, so long as
you are void of poverty of spirit, and all that inward religion,
which the many, the rich, the wise, account madness. "Strive
to enter in"; being pierced with sorrow and shame for having
so long run on with the unthinking crowd, utterly neglecting,
if not despising, that "holiness without which no man can see
the Lord." Strive, as in an agony of holy fear, lest "a promise
being made you of entering into his rest," even that "rest which
remaineth for the people of God," you should nevertheless
"come short of it." Strive, in all the fervour of desire, with
"groanings which cannot be uttered. Strive by prayer without
ceasing; at all times, in all places, lifting up your heart to God,

and giving him no rest, till you "awake up after his likeness" and are "satisfied with it."

6. To conclude. "Strive to enter in at the straight gate," not only by this agony of soul, of conviction, of sorrow, of shame, of desire, of fear, of unceasing prayer; but likewise by ordering thy conversation aright, by walking with all thy strength in all the ways of God, the way of innocence, of piety, and of mercy. Abstain from all appearance of evil. Do all possible good to all men. Deny thyself, thy own will, in all things, and take up thy cross daily. Be ready to cut off thy right hand, to pluck out thy right eye and cast it from thee; to suffer the loss of goods, friends, health, all things on earth, so thou mayst enter into the kingdom of heaven!

BEWARE OF FALSE PROPHETS

Beware of false prophets, which come to you in sheep's clothing, but inwardly are ravenous wolves. You shall know them by their fruits. Do men gather grapes of thorns, or figs of thistles? Even so every good tree brings forth good fruit, but a corrupt tree brings forth evil fruit. A good tree cannot bring forth evil fruit, neither can a corrupt tree bring forth good fruit. Every tree that brings not forth good fruit is hewn down and cast into the fire. Wherefore by their fruits you shall know them.
—Matthew 7:15–20

Introduction

1. It is scarce possible to express or conceive what multitudes of souls run on to destruction, because they would not be persuaded to walk in a narrow way, even though it were the way to everlasting salvation. And the same thing we may still

observe daily. Such is the folly and madness of mankind, that thousands of men still rush on in the way to hell, only because it is a broad way. They walk in it themselves, because others do: because so many perish, they will add to the number. Such is the amazing influence of example over the weak, miserable children of men! It continually peoples the regions of death, and drowns numberless souls in everlasting perdition!

2. To warn mankind of this, to guard as many as possible against this spreading contagion, God has commanded his watchmen to cry aloud, and show the people the danger they are in. For this end he has sent his servants, the prophets, in their succeeding generations, to point out the narrow path, and exhort all men not to be conformed to this world. But what if the watchmen themselves fall into the snare against which they should warn others? What if "the prophets prophesy deceits"; if they "cause the people to err from the way"? What shall be done if they point out, as the way to eternal life, what is in truth the way to eternal death; and exhort others to walk, as they do themselves, in the broad, not the narrow way?

3. Is this an unheard-of, is it an uncommon thing? Nay, God knoweth it is not. The instances of it are almost innumerable. We may find them in every age and nation. But how terrible is this—when the ambassadors of God turn agents for the devil—when they who are commissioned to teach men the way to heaven do in fact teach them the way to hell! These are like the locusts of Egypt, "which eat up the residue that had escaped, that had remained after the hail." They devour even the residue of men that had escaped, that were not destroyed by ill example. It is not, therefore, without cause, that our wise and gracious Master so solemnly cautions us against them: "Beware," says he, "of false prophets,

which come to you in sheep's clothing, but inwardly they are ravening wolves."

4. A caution, this of the utmost importance. That it may the more effectually sink into our hearts, let us inquire, first, who these false prophets are; secondly, what appearance they put on; and, thirdly, how we may know what they really are, notwithstanding their fair appearance.

I. Who These False Prophets Are

1. We are, first, to inquire who these false prophets are. And this it is needful to do the more diligently, because these very men have so labored to "wrest this scripture to their own," though not only their own, "destruction." In order, therefore, to cut off all dispute, I shall raise no dust (as the manner of some is), neither use any loose, rhetorical exclamations, to deceive the hearts of the simple; but speak rough, plain truths, such as none can deny, who has either understanding or modesty left, and such truths as have the closest connection with the whole tenor of the preceding discourse: whereas too many have interpreted these words without any regard to all that went before; as if they bore no manner of relation to the sermon in the close of which they stand.

False Prophets Do Not Speak Truth

2. By prophets here (as in many other passages of Scripture, particularly in the New Testament) are meant, not those who foretell things to come, but those who speak in the name of God; those men who profess to be sent of God, to teach others the way to heaven. Those are false prophets, who teach a false way to heaven, a way which does not lead thither; or (which comes in the end to the same point), who do not teach the true.

False Prophets Do Not Teach the Narrow Way

3. Every broad way is infallibly a false one. Therefore this is one plain, sure rule: "They who teach men to walk in a broad way, a way that many walk in, are false prophets." Again: The true way to heaven is a narrow way. Therefore this is another plain, sure rule: "They who do not teach men to walk in a narrow way, to be singular, are false prophets."

4. To be more particular: The only true way to heaven is that pointed out in the preceding sermon. Therefore they are false prophets who do not teach men to walk in this way. Now the way to heaven pointed out in the preceding sermon is the way of lowliness, mourning, meekness, and holy desire, love of God and of our neighbor, doing good, and suffering evil for Christ's sake. They are, therefore, false prophets, who teach, as the way to heaven, any other way than this.

False Prophets Teach Another Way

5. It matters not what they call that other way. They may call it faith; or good works; or faith and works; or repentance; or repentance, faith, and new obedience. All these are good words: but if, under these, or any other terms whatever, they teach men any way distinct from this, they are properly false prophets.

6. How much more do they fall under that condemnation, who speak evil of this good way; but above all, they who teach the directly opposite way, the way of pride, of levity, of passion, of worldly desires, of loving pleasure more than God, of unkindness to our neighbor, of unconcern for good works, and suffering no evil, no persecution for righteousness' sake!

7. If it be asked, "Why, who ever did teach this, or who does teach it, as the way to heaven?" I answer, "Ten thousand wise

and honorable men; even all those, of whatever denomination, who encourage the proud, the trifler, the passionate, the lover of the world, the man of pleasure, the unjust or unkind, the easy, careless, harmless, useless creature, the man who suffers no reproach for righteousness' sake, to imagine he is in the way to heaven." These are false prophets in the highest sense of the word. These are traitors both to God and man. These are no other than the first-born of Satan; the eldest sons of Apollyon, the Destroyer. These are far above the rank of ordinary cut-throats; for they murder the souls of men. They are continually peopling the realms of night; and whenever they follow the poor souls whom they have destroyed, "hell shall be moved from beneath to meet them at their coming!"

II. How False Prophets Appear

1. But do they come now in their own shape? By no means. If it were so, they could not destroy. You would take the alarm, and flee for your life. Therefore they put on a quite contrary appearance (which was the second thing to be considered): "They come to you in sheep's clothing, although inwardly they are ravening wolves."

An Appearance of Harmlessness

2. "They come to you in sheep's clothing"; that is, with an appearance of harmlessness. They come in the most mild, inoffensive manner, without any mark or token of enmity. Who can imagine that these quiet creatures would do any hurt to any one? Perhaps they may not be so zealous and active in doing good as one would wish they were. However, you see no reason to suspect that they have even the desire to do any harm. But this is not all.

An Appearance of Usefulness

3. They come, secondly, with an appearance of usefulness. Indeed to this, to do good, they are particularly called. They are set apart for this very thing. They are particularly commissioned to watch over your soul, and to train you up to eternal life. It is their whole business, to "go about doing good, and healing those that are oppressed of the devil." And you have been always accustomed to look upon them in this light, as messengers of God, sent to bring you a blessing.

An Appearance of Religion

4. They come, thirdly, with an appearance of religion. All they do is for conscience' sake! They assure you, it is out of mere zeal for God, that they are making God a liar. It is out of pure concern for religion that they would destroy it root and branch. All they speak is only from a love of truth, and a fear lest it should suffer; and, it may be, from a regard for the Church, and a desire to defend her from all her enemies.

An Appearance of Love

5. Above all, they come with an appearance of love. They take all these pains, only for your good. They should not trouble themselves about you, but that they have a kindness for you. They will make large professions of their goodwill, of their concern for the danger you are in, and of their earnest desire to preserve you from error, from being entangled in new and mischievous doctrines. They should be very sorry to see one who means so well, hurried into any extreme, perplexed with strange and unintelligible notions, or deluded into enthusiasm. Therefore it is that they advise you to keep still, in the plain middle way; and to beware of "being righteous overmuch," lest you should "destroy yourself."

III. How We May Know What They Really Are

1. But how may we know what they really are, notwith-standing their fair appearance? This was the third thing into which it was proposed to inquire. Our blessed Lord saw how needful it was for all men to know false prophets, however disguised. He saw, likewise, how unable most men were to deduce a truth through a long train of consequences. He there-fore gives us a short and plain rule, easy to be understood by men of the meanest capacities, and easy to be applied upon all occasions: "You shall know them by their fruits."

The Fruits of Their Doctrine in Their Lives

2. Upon all occasions you may easily apply this rule. In order to know whether any who speak in the name of God are false or true prophets it is easy to observe, first, what are the fruits of their doctrine as to themselves? What effect has it had upon their lives? Are they holy and unblamable in all things? What effect has it had upon their hearts? Does it appear by the general tenor of their conversation that their tempers are holy, heavenly, divine; that the mind is in them which was in Christ Jesus? That they are meek, lowly, patient, lovers of God and man, and zealous of good works?

The Fruits of Their Doctrine to Their Hearers

3. You may easily observe, secondly, what are the fruits of their doctrine as to those that hear them—in many, at least, though not in all; for the apostles themselves did not convert all that heard them. Have these the mind that was in Christ? And do they walk as he also walked? And was it by hearing these men that they began so to do? Were they inwardly and outwardly wicked till they heard them? If so, it is a manifest proof that those are true prophets, teachers sent of God. But

if it is not so, if they do not effectually teach either themselves or others to love and serve God, it is a manifest proof that they are false prophets; that God has not sent them.

You Will Know Them by Their Fruit

4. A hard saying this! How few can bear it! This our Lord was sensible of, and therefore condescends to prove it at large by several clear and convincing arguments. "Do men," says he, "gather grapes of thorns, or figs of thistles?" (Matt. 7:16). Do you expect that these evil men should bring forth good fruit? As well might you expect that thorns should bring forth grapes, or that figs should grow upon thistles! "Every good tree brings forth good fruit; but a corrupt tree brings forth evil fruit" (Matt. 5:17). Every true prophet, every teacher whom I have sent, brings forth the good fruit of holiness. But a false prophet, a teacher whom I have not sent, brings forth only sin and wickedness. "A good tree cannot bring forth evil fruit, neither can a corrupt tree bring forth good fruit." A true prophet, a teacher sent from God, does not bring forth good fruit sometimes only, but always; not accidentally, but by a kind of necessity. In like manner, a false prophet, one whom God has not sent, does not bring forth evil fruit accidentally or sometimes only, but always, and of necessity.

"Every tree that brings not forth good fruit is hewn down, and cast into the fire" (Matt 7:19). Such infallibly will be the lot of those prophets who bring not forth good fruit, who do not save souls from sin, who do not bring sinners to repentance. "Wherefore," let this stand as an eternal rule, "By their fruits you shall know them" (Matt. 7:20). They who, in fact bring the proud, passionate, unmerciful, lovers of the world to be lowly, gentle, lovers of God and man— they are true prophets, they are sent from God, who therefore confirms their word. On the other hand, they whose hearers, if unrighteous before, remain unrighteous still; or, at least, void of any righteousness which "exceeds the righteousness of the scribes and Pharisees"—they are false prophets; they are not sent of God; therefore their word falls to the ground. And, without a miracle of grace, they and their hearers together will fall into the bottomless pit!

5. O "beware of these false prophets!" For though they "come in sheep's clothing, yet inwardly they are ravening wolves." They only destroy and devour the flock: they tear them in pieces, if there is none to help them. They will not, cannot, lead you in the way to heaven. How should they, when they know it not themselves? O beware they do not turn you out of the way, and cause you to "lose what you have wrought!"

Listening to False Prophets

6. But perhaps you will ask, "If there is such danger in hearing them, ought I to hear them at all?" It is a weighty question, such as deserves the deepest consideration, and ought not to be answered but upon the calmest thought, the most deliberate reflection. For many years I have been almost afraid to speak at all concerning it; being unable to determine one way or the other, or to give any judgment upon it. Many reasons there are which readily occur, and incline me to say, "Hear them not." And yet what our Lord speaks concerning the false prophets of his own times seems to imply the contrary. "Then spoke Jesus unto the multitude, and to his disciples, saying, "The scribes and the Pharisees sit in Moses' seat"—are the ordinary, stated teachers in your Church: "All, therefore, whatsoever they bid you observe, that observe and do. But do not ye after their works; for they say and do not." Now, that these were false prophets, in the highest sense, our Lord has shown during the whole course of his ministry; as indeed he does in those very words, "They say and do not."

Therefore, by their fruits his disciples could not but know them, seeing they were open to the view of all men. Accordingly, he warns them again and again, to beware of these false prophets. And yet he does not forbid them to hear even these: nay, he, in effect, commands them so to do, in those words: "All therefore, whatsoever they bid you observe, that observe and do." For unless they heard them, they could not know, much less observe, whatsoever they bade them do. Here, then, our Lord himself gives a plain direction, both to his apostles and the whole multitude, in some circumstances, to hear even false prophets, known and acknowledged so to be.

7. But perhaps it will be said, "He only directed to hear them, when they read the Scripture to the congregation." I answer, at the same time that they thus read the Scripture, they generally expounded it too. And here is no kind of intimation that they were to hear the one, and not the other also. Nay, the very terms, "All things whatsoever they bid you observe," exclude any such limitation.

8. Again: unto them, unto false prophets, undeniably such, is frequently committed (O grief to speak! for surely these things ought not so to be), the administration of the sacrament also. To direct men, therefore, not to hear them, would be, in effect, to cut them off from the ordinances of God. But this we dare not do, considering the validity of the ordinance does not depend on the goodness of him that administers, but on the faithfulness of him that ordained it; who will and does meet us in his appointed ways. Therefore, on this account, likewise, I scruple to say, "Hear not even the false prophets." Even by these who are under a curse themselves, God can and does give us his blessing. For the bread which they break, we have experimentally known to be "the communion of the body of Christ." And the cup which God blessed, even by their unhallowed lips, was to us the communion of the blood of Christ.

9. All, therefore, which I can say, is this: in any particular case, wait upon God by humble and earnest prayer, and then act according to the best light you have: act according to what you are persuaded, upon the whole, will be most for your spiritual advantage. Take great care that you do not judge rashly; that you do not lightly think any to be false prophets: and when you have full proof, see that no anger or contempt have any place in your heart. After this, in the presence and in the fear of God, determine for yourself. I can only say, if by experience you find that the hearing them hurts your soul, then hear them not; then quietly refrain, and hear those that profit you. If, on the other hand, you find it does not hurt your soul, you then may hear them still.

Only "take heed how you hear": beware of them and of their doctrine. Hear with fear and trembling, lest you should be deceived, and given up, like them, to a strong delusion. As they continually mingle truth and lies, how easily may you take in both together! Hear with fervent and continual prayer to him who alone teaches man wisdom. And see that you bring whatever you hear "to the law and to the testimony." Receive nothing untried, nothing till it is weighed in the balance of the sanctuary: believe nothing they say, unless it is clearly confirmed by passages of holy writ. Wholly reject whatsoever differs therefrom, whatever is not confirmed thereby. And, in particular, reject, with the utmost abhorrence, whatsoever is described as the way of salvation, that is either different from, or short of, the way our Lord has marked out in the foregoing discourse.

A Few Words to False Prophets

10. I cannot conclude without addressing a few plain words to those of whom we have now been speaking. O ye

false prophets! O ye dry bones! Hear ye, for once, the word of the Lord! How long will you lie in the name of God, saying, "God has spoken," and God has not spoken by you? How long will you pervert the right ways of the Lord, putting darkness for light, and light for darkness? How long will you teach the way of death, and call it the way of life? How long will you deliver to Satan the souls whom you profess to bring unto God?

11. "Woe unto you, you blind leaders of the blind! For you shut the kingdom of heaven against men. You neither go in yourselves, neither suffer you them that are entering to go in." Them that would "strive to enter in at the straight gate," you call back into the broad way. Them that have scarce gone one step in the ways of God, you devilishly caution against going too far. Them that just begin to "hunger and thirst after righteousness," you warn not to "be righteous overmuch." Thus you cause them to stumble at the very threshold; yea, to fall and rise no more. O wherefore do you this? What profit is there in their blood, when they go down to the pit? Miserable profit to you! "They shall perish in their iniquity; but their blood will God require at your hands!"

12. Where are your eyes? Where is your understanding? Have you deceived others, till you have deceived yourselves also? Who has required this at your hands, to teach a way which you never knew? Are you "given up to" so "strong a delusion," that you not only teach but "believe a lie"? And can you possibly believe that God has sent you; that you are his messengers? Nay; if the Lord had sent you, the work of the Lord would prosper in your hand. As the Lord lives, if you were messengers of God, he would "confirm the word of his messengers." But the work of the Lord does not prosper in your hand. You bring no sinners to repentance. The Lord does not confirm your word; for you save no souls from death.

13. How can you possibly evade the force of our Lord's words—so full, so strong, so express? How can you evade knowing yourselves by your fruits—evil fruits of evil trees? And how should it be otherwise? "Do men gather grapes of thorns, or figs of thistles?" Take this to yourselves, you to whom it belongs! O you barren trees, why cumber ye the ground? "Every good tree brings forth good fruit." See ye not that here is no exception? Take knowledge, then, you are not good trees; for you do not bring forth good fruit. "But a corrupt tree brings forth evil fruit;" and so have you done from the beginning. Your speaking, as from God, has only confirmed them that heard you in the tempers, if not works, of the devil. O take warning of him in whose name you speak, before the sentence he has pronounced take place: "Every tree which brings not forth good fruit is hewn down and cast into the fire."

14. My dear brethren, harden not your hearts! You have too long shut your eyes against the light. Open them now before it is too late; before you are cast into outer darkness! Let not any temporal consideration weigh with you; for eternity is at stake. You have run before you were sent. O go no farther! Do not persist to damn yourselves and them that hear you! You have no fruit of your labors. And why is this? Even because the Lord is not with you. But can you go this warfare at your own cost? It cannot be.

Then humble yourselves before him. Cry unto him out of the dust, that he may first quicken your soul; give you the faith that worketh by love; that is lowly and meek, pure and merciful, zealous of good works, rejoicing in tribulation, in reproach, in distress, in persecution for righteousness' sake! So shall "the Spirit of glory and of Christ rest upon you," and it shall appear that God has sent you. So shall you indeed "do the work of an evangelist, and make full proof of your ministry." So shall the word of God in your mouth be "a hammer that breaks the rocks in pieces!" It shall then be known by your fruits that you are a prophet of the Lord, even by the children whom God has given you. And having "turned many to righteousness," you shall "shine as the stars for ever and ever!"

BUILD YOUR HOUSE
ON A ROCK

Not everyone that saith unto me, Lord, Lord, shall enter into the kingdom of heaven; but he that doeth the will of my Father which is in heaven. Many will say to me in that day, Lord, Lord, have we not prophesied in thy name and in thy name have cast out devils and in thy name done many wonderful works? And then will I profess unto them, I never knew you: depart from me, ye that work iniquity.

Therefore whosoever heareth these sayings of mine, and doeth them, I will liken him unto a wise man, which built his house upon a rock. And the rain descended, and the floods came, and the winds blew, and beat upon that house; and it fell not: for it was founded upon a rock. And every one that heareth these sayings of mine, and doeth them not, shall be likened unto a foolish man, which built his house upon the sand. And the rain descended, and the floods came, and the winds blew, and beat upon that house; and it fell: and great was the fall of it.

—Matthew 7:21–27

Introduction

1. Our Divine Teacher, having declared the whole counsel of God with regard to the way of salvation, and observed the chief hindrances of those who desire to walk therein, now closes the whole with these weighty words; thereby, as it were, setting his seal to his prophecy, and impressing his whole authority on what he had delivered, that it might stand firm to all generations.

2. For thus says the Lord, that none may ever conceive there is any other way than this, "Not everyone that says unto me, Lord, Lord, shall enter into the kingdom of heaven; but he that does the will of my Father which is in heaven. Many will say to me in that day, Lord, Lord, have we not prophesied in thy name and in thy name have cast out devils and in thy name done many wonderful works? And then will I profess unto them, I never knew you: depart from me, you that work iniquity. Therefore, everyone that hears these sayings of mine, and does them not, shall be likened unto a foolish man, which built his house upon the sand. And the rain descended, and the floods came, and the winds blew, and beat upon that house; and it fell: and great was the fall of it."

3. I design, in the following discourse, first, to consider the case of him who thus builds his house upon the sand; secondly, to show the wisdom of him who builds upon a rock; and, thirdly, to conclude with a practical application.

I. A House upon the Sand

1. And, first, I am to consider the case of him who builds his house upon the sand. It is concerning him our Lord says, "Not everyone that saith unto me, Lord, Lord, shall enter into

the kingdom of heaven." And this is a decree which cannot pass; which stands fast for ever and ever. It therefore imports us, in the highest degree, thoroughly to understand the force of these words. Now what are we to understand by that expression, "That saith unto me, Lord, Lord"? It undoubtedly means, that thinks of going to heaven by any other way than that which I have now described.

"Lord, Lord" Implies All Verbal Religion

It therefore implies (to begin at the lowest point) all good words, all verbal religion. It includes whatever creeds we may rehearse, whatever professions of faith we make, whatever number of prayers we may repeat, whatever thanksgivings we read or say to God. We may speak good of his name, and declare his lovingkindness to the children of men. We may be talking of all his mighty acts, and telling of his salvation from day to day. By comparing spiritual things with spiritual we may show the meaning of the oracles of God. We may explain the mysteries of his kingdom, which have been hid from the beginning of the world. We may speak with the tongue of angels, rather than men, concerning the deep things of God. We may proclaim to sinners, "Behold the Lamb of God, who taketh away the sin of the world!" Yea, we may do this with such a measure of the power of God, and such demonstration of his Spirit, as to save many souls from death, and hide a multitude of sins. And yet it is very possible, all this may be no more than saying, "Lord, Lord." After I have thus successfully preached to others, still I myself may be a castaway. I may, in the hand of God, snatch many souls from hell, and yet drop into it when I have done. I may bring many others to the kingdom of heaven, and yet myself never enter there. Reader, if God hath ever blessed my word to your soul, pray that he may be merciful to me a sinner!

"Lord, Lord" Implies Refraining from Harm

2. The saying, "Lord, Lord," may, secondly, imply the doing no harm. We may abstain from every presumptuous sin, from every kind of outward wickedness. We may refrain from all those ways of acting or speaking which are forbidden in holy writ. We may be able to say to all those among whom we live, "Which of you convinceth me of sin?" We may have a conscience void of any external offence, towards God and towards man. We may be clear of all uncleanness, ungodliness, and unrighteousness, as to the outward act; or (as the apostle testifies concerning himself), "touching the righteousness of the law," that is, outward righteousness, "blameless." But yet we are not hereby justified. Still this is no more than saying, "Lord, Lord"; and if we go no farther than this, we shall never "enter into the kingdom of heaven."

"Lord, Lord" Implies Good Works

3. The saying, "Lord, Lord," may imply, thirdly, many of what are usually styled good works. A man may attend the supper of the Lord, may hear abundance of excellent sermons, and omit no opportunity of partaking all the other ordinances of God. I may do good to my neighbor, deal my bread to the hungry, and cover the naked with a garment. I may be so zealous of good works as even to "give all my goods to feed the poor." Yea, and I may do all this with a desire to please God, and a real belief that I do please him thereby (which is undeniably the case of those our Lord introduces, saying unto him, "Lord, Lord"); and still I may have no part in the glory which shall be revealed.

4. If any man marvels at this, let him acknowledge he is a stranger to the whole religion of Jesus Christ; and, in particular, to that perfect portraiture thereof which he has set before us

in this discourse. For how far short is all this of that righteousness and true holiness which he has described therein! How widely distant from that inward kingdom of heaven which is now opened in the believing soul, which is first sown in the heart as a grain of mustard-seed, but afterwards puts forth great branches, on which grow all the fruits of righteousness, every good temper, and word, and work.

Many Will Say, "Lord, Lord"

5. Yet as clearly as he had declared this, as frequently as he had repeated, that none who have not this kingdom of God within them shall enter into the kingdom of heaven; our Lord well knew that many would not receive this saying, and therefore confirms it yet again. "Many," saith he (not one; not a few only; it is not a rare or an uncommon case), "shall say unto me in that day," not only: We have said many prayers; We have spoken your praise; We have refrained from evil; We have exercised ourselves in doing good—but, what is abundantly more than this, "We have prophesied in thy name; in thy name have we cast out devils; in thy name done many wonderful works."

"We have prophesied"—we have declared your will to mankind; we have showed sinners the way to peace and glory. And we have done this "in thy name"; according to the truth of your gospel; yea, and by your authority, who did confirm the word with the Holy Ghost sent down from heaven. For in or by your name, by the power of your word and of your Spirit, "have we cast out devils"; out of the souls which they had long claimed as their own, and whereof they had full and quiet possession. "And in thy name," by thy power, not our own, "have we done many wonderful works"; insomuch that "even the dead heard the voice of the Son of God" speaking by us, and lived.

To Them Christ Will Say, "I Never Knew You"

"And then will I profess" even "unto them, I never knew you"; no, not then, when you were "casting out devils in my name." Even then I did not know you as my own; for your heart was not right toward God. You were not yourselves meek and lowly; you were not lovers of God, and of all mankind; you were not renewed in the image of God; you were not holy as I am holy. "Depart from me, you" who, notwithstanding all this, are ἀνομία, *workers of iniquity*—you are transgressors of my law, my law of holy and perfect love.

6. It is to put this beyond all possibility of contradiction, that our Lord confirms it by that apposite comparison: "Every one," saith he, "who heareth these sayings of mine, and doeth them not, shall be likened unto a foolish man, which built his house upon the sand. And the rain descended, and the floods came, and the winds blew, and beat upon that house"—as they will surely do, sooner or later, upon every soul of man; even the floods of outward affliction, or inward temptation; the storms of pride, anger, fear, or desire—"and it fell: and great was the fall of it"; so that it perished for ever and ever. Such must be the portion of all who rest in anything short of that religion which is above described. And the greater will their fall be, because they "heard those sayings, and" yet "did them not."

II. A House upon the Rock

He Is Wise and Poor in Spirit

1. I am, secondly, to show the wisdom of him that does them, that builds his house upon a rock. He indeed is wise, "who doeth the will of my Father which is in heaven." He is truly wise, whose "righteousness exceeds the righteousness of the scribes and Pharisees." He is poor in spirit; knowing

himself even as also he is known. He sees and feels all his sin, and all his guilt, till it is washed away by the atoning blood. He is conscious of his lost estate, of the wrath of God abiding on him, and of his utter inability to help himself, till he is filled with peace and joy in the Holy Ghost. He is meek and gentle, patient toward all men, never "returning evil for evil, or railing for railing, but contrariwise blessing," till he overcomes evil with good. His soul is athirst for nothing on earth, but only for God, the living God. He has a heart of love for all mankind, and is ready to lay down his life for his enemies. He loves the Lord his God with all his heart, and with all his mind, and soul, and strength. He alone shall enter into the kingdom of heaven, who, in this spirit, does good unto all men; and who, being for this cause despised and rejected of men, being hated, reproached, and persecuted, rejoices and is "exceeding glad," knowing in whom he has believed, and being assured these light, momentary afflictions will "work out for him an eternal weight of glory."

He Knows Himself, the World, and God

2. How truly wise is this man! He knows himself; an everlasting spirit, which came forth from God, and was sent down into an house of clay, not to do his own will, but the will of Him that sent him. He knows the world; the place in which he is to pass a few days or years, not as an inhabitant, but as a stranger and sojourner, in his way to the everlasting habitations; and accordingly he uses the world as not abusing it, and as knowing the fashion of it passes away. He knows God; his Father and his Friend, the parent of all good, the center of the spirits of all flesh, the sole happiness of all intelligent beings. He sees, clearer than the light of the noon-day sun, that this is the end of man, to glorify Him who made him for himself, and to love and enjoy him for ever. And with equal clearness he sees

the means to that end, to the enjoyment of God in glory; even now to know, to love, to imitate God, and to believe in Jesus Christ whom he hath sent.

He Builds on the Everlasting Rock

3. He is a wise man, even in God's account; for "he buildeth his house upon a rock," upon the Rock of Ages, the everlasting Rock, the Lord Jesus Christ. Fitly is he so called; for he changeth not: he is "the same yesterday, and today, and for ever." To him both the man of God of old, and the apostle citing his words, bear witness: "Thou, Lord, in the beginning hast laid the foundation of the earth; and the heavens are the works of thine hands: they shall perish; but thou remainest. And they all shall wax old as does a garment; and as a vesture shalt thou fold them up, and they shall be changed. But thou art the same, and thy years shall not fail" (Heb. 1:10–12).

Wise, therefore, is the man who builds on Him; who lays Him for his only foundation; who builds only upon his blood and righteousness, upon what he has done and suffered for us. On this cornerstone he fixes his faith, and rests the whole weight of his soul upon it. He is taught of God to say, "Lord, I have sinned; I deserve the nethermost hell; but I am justified freely by thy grace, through the redemption that is in Jesus Christ; and the life I now live, I live by faith in Him, who loved me, and gave himself for me. The life I now live; namely, a divine, heavenly life; a life which is hid with Christ in God. I now live, even in the flesh, a life of love; of pure love both to God and man; a life of holiness and happiness; praising God, and doing all things to his glory."

His House Will Stand in the Storm

4. Yet, let not such an one think that he shall not see war any more; that he is now out of the reach of temptation. It still

remains for God to prove the grace he has given: he shall be tried as gold in the fire. He shall be tempted not less than they who know not God: perhaps abundantly more; for Satan will not fail to try to the uttermost those whom he is not able to destroy. Accordingly, "the rain" will impetuously descend; only at such times and in such a manner as seems good, not to the prince of the power of the air, but to Him "whose kingdom ruleth over all." "The floods," or torrents, will come; they will lift up their waves and rage horribly. But to them also, the Lord that sitteth above the water-floods, that remaineth a King for ever, will say, "Hitherto shall ye come, and no farther: Here shall your proud waves be stayed." "The winds will blow, and beat upon that house," as though they would tear it up from the foundation. But they cannot prevail: it falleth not; for it is founded upon a rock. He buildeth on Christ by faith and love; therefore, he shall not be cast down. He "shall not fear though the earth be moved, and though the hills be carried into the midst of the sea." "Though the waters thereof rage and swell, and the mountains shake at the tempest of the same," still he "dwelleth under the defense of the Most High, and is safe under the shadow of the Almighty."

III. Practical Application

1. How nearly then does it concern every child of man, practically to apply these things to himself; diligently to examine on what foundation he builds, whether on a rock or on the sand! How deeply are you concerned to inquire, "What is the foundation of my hope? Whereon do I build my expectation of entering into the kingdom of heaven? Is it not built on the sand upon my orthodoxy, or right opinions, which, by a gross abuse of words, I have called faith upon my having a set of notions, suppose more rational or scriptural than others

have?" Alas! what madness is this! Surely this is building on the sand, or, rather, on the froth of the sea! Say, "I am convinced of this: Am I not again building my hope on what is equally unable to support it? Perhaps on my belonging to 'so excellent a church; reformed after the true Scripture model; blessed with the purest doctrine, the most primitive liturgy, the most apostolical form of government!" These are, doubtless, so many reasons for praising God, as they may be so many helps to holiness; but they are not holiness itself. And if they are separate from it, they will profit me nothing; nay, they will leave me the more without excuse, and exposed to the greater damnation. Therefore, if I build my hope upon this foundation, I am still building upon the sand.

2. You cannot, you dare not, rest here. Upon what next will you build your hope of salvation—upon your innocence? Upon your doing no harm? Your not wronging or hurting anyone? Well; allow this plea to be true. You are just in all your dealings; you are a downright honest man; you pay every man his own; you neither cheat nor extort; you act fairly with all mankind; and you have a conscience towards God; you do not live in any known sin. Thus far is well: but still it is not the thing. You may go thus far, and yet never come to heaven. When all this harmlessness flows from a right principle, it is the least part of the religion of Christ. But in you it does not flow from a right principle, and therefore is no part at all of religion. So that in grounding your hope of salvation on this, you are still building upon the sand.

3. Do you go farther yet? Do you add to the doing no harm, the attending all the ordinances of God? Do you, at all opportunities, partake of the Lord's supper? Use public and private prayer? Fast often? Hear and search the Scriptures, and meditate thereon? These things, likewise, ought you to have done, from the time you first set your face towards heaven. Yet

these things also are nothing, being alone. They are nothing without "the weightier matters of the law." And those you have forgotten: at least, you experience them not—faith, mercy, and love of God; holiness of heart; heaven opened in the soul. Still, therefore, you build upon the sand.

4. Over and above all this, are you zealous of good works? Do you, as you have time, do good to all men? Do you feed the hungry, and clothe the naked, and visit the fatherless and widow in their affliction? Do you visit those that are sick? Relieve them that are in prison? Is any a stranger, and you take him in? Friend, come up higher! Do you "prophesy" in the "name" of Christ? Do you preach the truth as it is in Jesus? And does the influence of his Spirit attend your word, and make it the power of God unto salvation? Does he enable you to bring sinners from darkness to light, from the power of Satan unto God? Then go and learn what you have so often taught, "By grace you are saved through faith"; "not by works of righteousness which we have done, but of his own mercy he saveth us." Learn to hang naked upon the cross of Christ, counting all you have done but dung and dross. Apply to him just in the spirit of the dying thief, of the harlot with her seven devils, else you are still on the sand; and, after saving others, you will lose your own soul.

5. Lord, increase my faith, if I now believe! Else, give me faith, though but as a grain of mustard-seed! But "what does it profit, if a man says he has faith, and has not works? Can" that "faith save him?" O no! That faith which has not works, which does not produce both inward and outward holiness, which does not stamp the whole image of God on the heart, and purify us as he is pure; that faith which does not produce the whole of the religion described in the foregoing chapters, is not the faith of the gospel, not the Christian faith, not the faith which leads to glory. O beware of this, above all other snares of

the devil—of resting on unholy, unsaving faith! If you lay stress on this, you are lost for ever: you still build your house upon the sand. When "the rain descends, and the floods come, it will surely fall, and great will be the fall of it."

6. Now, therefore, build thou upon a rock. By the grace of God, know thyself. Know and feel that you were shaped in wickedness, and in sin did your mother conceive you; and that you yourself have been heaping sin upon sin, ever since you could discern good from evil. Own yourself guilty of eternal death; and renounce all hope of ever being able to save yourself. Be it all your hope, to be washed in his blood, and purified by his Spirit, "who himself bore" all "your sins in his own body upon the tree." And if you know he has taken away your sins, so much the more abase yourself before him, in a continual sense of your total dependence on him for every good thought, and word, and work, and of your utter inability to all good unless he "water thee every moment."

7. Now weep for your sins, and mourn after God, till he turns your heaviness into joy. And even then weep with them that weep; and for them that weep not for themselves. Mourn for the sins and miseries of mankind; and see, but just before your eyes, the immense ocean of eternity, without a bottom or a shore, which has already swallowed up millions of millions of men, and is gaping to devour them that yet remain! See here, the house of God eternal in the heavens! there, hell and destruction without a covering!—and thence learn the importance of every moment, which just appears, and is gone for ever!

8. Now add to your seriousness, meekness of wisdom. Hold an even scale as to all your passions, but in particular, as to anger, sorrow, and fear. Calmly acquiesce in whatsoever is the will of God. Learn in every state wherein you are, therewith to be content. Be mild to the good; be gentle toward all men; but especially toward the evil and the unthankful. Beware, not only

of outward expressions of anger, such as calling thy brother, Raca, or thou fool; but of every inward emotion contrary to love, though it go no farther than the heart. Be angry at sin, as an affront offered to the Majesty of heaven; but love the sinner still; like our Lord, who "looked round about upon the Pharisees with anger, being grieved for the hardness of their hearts." He was grieved at the sinners, angry at sin. Thus be thou "angry, and sin not!"

9. Now do thou hunger and thirst, not for "the meat that perisheth, but for that which endureth unto everlasting life." Trample underfoot the world, and the things of the world; all these riches, honors, pleasures. What is the world to thee? Let the dead bury their dead; but follow after the image of God. And beware of quenching that blessed thirst, if it is already excited in your soul, by what is vulgarly called religion; a poor, dull farce, a religion of form, of outside show, which leaves the heart still cleaving to the dust, as earthly and sensual as ever. Let nothing satisfy you but the power of godliness, but a religion that is spirit and life; the dwelling in God and God in you; the being an inhabitant of eternity; the entering in by the blood of sprinkling "within the veil," and "sitting in heavenly places with Christ Jesus!"

10. Now, seeing you can do all things through Christ strengthening you, be merciful as thy Father in heaven is merciful! Love your neighbour as yourself! Love friends and enemies as your own soul! And let your love be longsuffering and patient towards all men. Let it be kind, soft, benign; inspiring you with the most amiable sweetness, and the most fervent and tender affection. Let it rejoice in the truth, where-soever it is found; the truth that is after godliness. Enjoy whatsoever brings glory to God, and promotes peace and goodwill among men. In love, cover all things, of the dead and the absent speaking nothing but good; believe all things which

may any way tend to clear your neighbor's character; hope all things in his favor; and endure all things, triumphing over all opposition. For true love never fails, in time or in eternity.

11. Now be thou pure in heart; purified through faith from every unholy affection; "cleansing yourself from all filthiness of flesh and spirit, and perfecting holiness in the fear of God." Being, through the power of his grace, purified from pride, by deep poverty of spirit; from anger, from every unkind or turbulent passion, by meekness and mercifulness; from every desire but to please and enjoy God, by hunger and thirst after righteousness; now love the Lord thy God with all thy heart, and with all thy strength!"

12. In a word: let thy religion be the religion of the heart. Let it lie deep in your inmost soul. Be thou little, and base, and mean, and vile (beyond what words can express) in thy own eyes; amazed and humbled to the dust by the love of God which is in Christ Jesus. Be serious. Let the whole stream of your thoughts, words, and actions flow from the deepest conviction that you stand on the edge of the great gulf, you and all the children of men, just ready to drop in, either into everlasting glory or everlasting burnings! Let your soul be filled with mildness, gentleness, patience, long-suffering towards all men; at the same time that all which is in you is athirst for God, the living God; longing to awake up after his likeness, and to be satisfied with it! Be thou a lover of God and of all mankind! In this spirit do and suffer all things! Thus show your faith by your works; thus "do the will of thy Father which is in heaven!" And, as sure as you now walk with God on earth, you shall also reign with him in glory!